What These Otaku
Anime and

"Anime is easily the most complex and interesting animation genre. The only rival to watching anime is thinking about it, and Steiff and Tamplin have assembled a smorgasbord of thought. Combining scholarly erudition with fan-boy passion, this collection is as rich, deep, and fun as anime itself. It sure beats talking to yourself."

> —ANDREW HUEBNER, Animation Producer

"A brilliant combination of pop culture investigation and philosophical thinking, *Anime and Philosophy* is a startlingly impressive collection of chapters by writers who use their great love for, and knowledge of, anime for serious probing and accessible philosophical questioning."

> —MATTHEW PATEMAN, Director of Film and Media, University of Hull

"As befits a genre that came of age in the wake of the Hiroshima bombing and the humiliating surrender of Japan to the Allies in 1945, anime asks difficult questions about war and violence, the limits of human life and the self, and the frontiers of experience (space travel, apocalyptic scenarios, cyborgs and androids). This timely volume shows us scholarly dissections—don't fret, Shaorin— of anime from the wildly popular to the bizarre and obscure. The result is stimulating and enlightening in equal measure."

> —CAROLE M. CUSACK, editor, *Journal of Religious History*

"In the unique cultural sub-verse worlds of anime, manga, animanga, and on and on, anything is possible. Our imagination determines the boundaries, and we approach each new world with a slightly different philosophical slant. *Anime and Philosophy* is an enlightening read and a brilliant addition to any anime lover's bookshelf. It's also an atlas of the anime universe, a welcome guide for anyone intrigued by anime but unsure of just where to start their journey."

> —DEL HARVEY, publisher, *FilmMonthly.com*

"Perhaps the only thing more fascinating than great anime is what goes on inside the heads of those who really get it. Here at last is a fascinating explanation of an art form that is re-defining pop culture all over the globe, told by those who have dipped deep into the psyche behind Japanese animation."

—DOUG RICE, Emmy Award-winning Animation Artist

"This book is a launching point for fans who recognize that anime don't only make us laugh and cheer and cry but also think. *Anime and Philosophy* surveys the anime that have made the biggest splash among Western audiences, helping fans connect their best-loved shows with the deeper questions behind them, bringing out the larger philosophical themes that make anime so powerful for Western viewers."

—ADA PALMER, founder, *TezukaInEnglish.com*

"Anime makes your average American or British Saturday morning cartoon look slow and shallow. Why does anime— a medium primarily but not exclusively aimed towards young children in its native country—tackle "deep" themes such as identity and the self, sacrifice and self-awareness, while Sponge Bob scratches around looking for another shrimp? This book helps us understand that there's a lot more to anime than just pretty girls with big eyes and giant robots smashing up Neo-Tokyo—again! To truly appreciate films like *Akira*, *Ghost In The Shell* and even *My Neighbor Totoro*, you just have to read this book."

—JEROME MAZANDARANI, Acquisitions and Marketing Manager, Manga Entertainment Ltd

"Thought-provoking and mind-blowing! Anime fans will gain new insight into their film favorites through readable commentary and analysis of animation classics."

—JOHANNA DRAPER CARLSON, founder, *MangaWorthReading.com*

Anime
and
Philosophy

Popular Culture and Philosophy®
Series Editor: George A. Reisch

For full details of all Popular Culture and Philosophy® books, visit www.opencourtbooks.com.

POPULAR CULTURE AND PHILOSOPHY®

ANIME
AND PHILOSOPHY

Edited by
Josef Steiff
and
Tristan D. Tamplin

WIDE
EYED
WONDER

OPEN COURT
CHICAGO AND LA SALLE, ILLINOIS

Volume 47 in the series, Popular Culture and Philosophy®, edited by George A. Reisch

To order books from Open Court, call toll-free 1-800-815-2280, or visit our website at www.opencourtbooks.com.

Open Court Publishing Company is a division of Carus Publishing Company.

Library of Congress Cataloging-in-Publication Data

Anime and philosophy : wide eyed wonder / Josef Steiff and Tristan Tamplin [editors].
     p. cm.—(Popular culture and philosophy ; v. 47)
     Includes bibliographical references and index.
     ISBN 978-0-8126-9670-7 (trade paper : alk. paper)
     1. Animated films—Japan—History and criticism. 2. Animated television programs—Japan—History and criticism. 3. Steiff, Josef.
II. Tamplin, Tristan D. III. Title.
     NC1766.J3A53 2010
     791.43'34—dc22

                                     2009050134

Main Menu

Special Features

Previews and Coming Attractions

Believe It!

Ghosts in the machine. Atomic-powered heroes. Pubescent girls programmed to kill. Children who disobey their parents. Brothers trying to protect their little sisters.

Anime has become a worldwide phenomenon, painting its stories across a variety of genres, eras, and landscapes, as well as influencing live action filmmakers like the Wachowski Brothers and Quentin Tarantino.

> If life has no purpose, then you're already dead.
>
> —Kiba, *Wolf's Rain*

In the following pages, we will examine some of the most loved, best-known, and intriguing anime in order to find what lies at their core, underneath the typical but by no means ubiquitous visual elements of big eyes, big hair and bright colors. *Akira, Armitage the Third, Astro Boy, Chrno Crusade, Dragon Ball Z, Fooly Cooly, Fullmetal Alchemist, Ghost in the Shell, Grave of the Fireflies, Gunslinger Girl, Highlander, La Blue Girl, Magnetic Rose, Mobile Suit Gundam, My Neighbor Totoro, Nausicaa of the Valley of The Wind, Neon Genesis Evangelion*, and *Spirited Away* are just a few of the films you'll find here. Some you may have heard of, others may be completely new to you.

But don't be fooled, these are not children's stories. These are stories about monsters, witches, robots, children, and spirits who grapple with questions of societal violence, ethics, morality, justice, heroism, identity, and the soul, whether in the midst of World War

II or long after World War III, whether in a magical valley or on a malevolent space station.

If you've been wondering why so many people love anime or even if you're already a true otaku, we hope this book will give you a deeper appreciation for not just the art but also the storytelling of Japan's animated films, TV series, and OVA.

> May those who accept their fate be granted happiness; to those who defy it, glory.
>
> —EDEL, *Princess TuTu*

This book wouldn't be possible without our contributors, including the work of three artists: Shane, whose cover design links with our companion volume, *Manga and Philosophy*; Amada, who created our title page and "special features" divider for the appendixes, and Neko, who drew inspiration from the chapters to create a unique divider for each of the book's seven main sections. In addition, we would like to thank Margo Coughlin Zimmerman, Manga Entertainment, and Jackie Smith at FUNimation Entertainment for their support and enthusiasm. A big thanks goes to Series Editor George Reisch, Editorial Director David Ramsay Steele, Victor Cotic, Andrew Dowd, and the herd of Mount Pleasant Caribou (Steven, Laura, Joe, Jori, Jeni, Kari, Jen, Cassie, Stephanie, Megan and Dillon) who kept the caffeine coming.

> Chrno, the map is upside-down.
>
> —AZMARIA, *Chrno Crusade*

For Western audiences, *anime* refers only to those animated films, television series, and direct-to-DVD releases that originated in Japan. But in Japan, *anime* is a more generic term that means any type of animation, regardless of whether it was produced in Japan or another country. This book will address animation that originates in Japan.

If you are new to anime, you may not know that the traditional Japanese sequence of one's name is to have the family name or surname first, followed by the given name. In other words, in Japanese culture, your editors' names would be written Steiff Josef and Tamplin Tristan. However, most anime that is marketed outside of Japan has the filmmakers' names sequenced in the Western tradition, putting the given name first. Granted, this is less authentic to Japanese culture, but for Western readers, this approach can be less confusing. Likewise, this book is being marketed mainly outside of Japan as well, so we will be following the Western tradition of name sequence.

Accidental Anime

MARGO COUGHLIN ZIMMERMAN

If you're reading this book, it's because you're a fan of anime or want to know more about it. Be it a result of the films' complexity, the beauty of their images, stories based in mythology and philosophy, cultural artistic inspiration, the range of tastes from *Astro Boy* to *Urotskidoji*, or your appreciation for Japanese culture, anime has captivated you, and you may not understand why others don't recognize its value as you do.

When I first began working for Manga Entertainment, a well-respected pioneer in anime distribution, I was not familiar with anime. I imagine that I'd seen reference to it in passing; the big eyes, bright colors, and sometimes sexy female characters. I do remember being aware of the fanciful outfits some women in Tokyo had been wearing, carrying around stuffed animals, their hair in pig tails and faces in bright make-up, some even more overtly dressed as "the sexy schoolgirl." I had heard stories of their high platform shoes, which had almost become a competition among the Harajuku girls, causing them ankle breaks. But those references did nothing to scratch the surface or prepare me for true anime. At Manga Entertainment, a fantastical world was opened up to me.

I was in film school at the time and looking to get my foot in the door somewhere in the entertainment world. Though I started at the bottom, answering phones, sending packages, and doing other general office work, over the next several years I was able to work my way up to post production and international distribution.

Homework!?!?!?

I remember being sent home that first day with a stack of DVDs to watch. This was my "homework," and I was so excited to discover this new (to me, at least) type of film. My boss suggested I begin with *Ninja Scroll*. He thought it would be the easiest to understand and relate to, from a Western perspective.

I loved it!

I may have been surprised and confused by the adult themes contained in the framework of animation, but I was thoroughly entertained with Jubei's quest to find the Shogun of the Dark, battling the eight Devils of Kimon, each more fearful and superhuman than the last. Jubei is an attractive, unflappable hero, who saves the damsel in distress. Each "devil" is a creative and powerful foe in unexpected ways, from an indestructible rock man to a snake lady with deadly venom. For an anime virgin, this tale has everything you could want in a movie: beautiful animation, good performances and writing, action, sex, romance and monstrous villains.

With my new vigor and excitement for this world I had been lucky enough to join, I'm pretty sure I irritated the rest of the Manga staff. I expected to be involved in every meeting and give my opinion on any undertaking to help the group. I may have stepped on some toes with my unquenchable thirst to learn and do more. Thankfully, the head of marketing took pity on me and began to include me in some of the editing sessions for trailers. Being one of the only Manga staff with any film background, it seemed to me a natural choice.

We worked into the night and on weekends to perfect the trailer that would support the theatrical release for *Perfect Blue*. I will never forget working on the copy and bones of the trailer and then finding the right clips and the best combination with music and voiceover to create this compelling piece. This was one of my favorite memories, and I learned so much working with our editor, whose day job was also as one of the Oprah show's editors.

Art Is Still a Business

Perfect Blue is the story of Mima, a young, pretty pop star, who quits her girl group to star in a sexually-charged TV show. One fan in particular does not agree with her choice and begins stalking her. As a result, Mima sinks into a state of paranoia, where she is lost between reality and delusion. This compelling thriller sucked me in immediately.

The company set up a private screening in a local theater in Chicago, my first "private screening." I felt transported into the inner sanctum of the entertainment world. I was amazed and energized. The film was so cool; I just couldn't imagine everyone not loving it. I was proud to be a part of bringing it to the public.

Perfect Blue was definitely considered an "Art House" picture and so only a few prints would be made, traveling slowly around the country. Our goal was to create awareness of the film and a buzz to hopefully spur DVD sales. And then we got a call from Madonna's "people." They wanted permission to show clips of *Perfect Blue* as background during the song, "What It Feels Like for a Girl," for her tour. She had a huge screen on stage and had a few clips of different anime films, including the hentai [AKA anime pornography], film *Urotskidoji*. I remember thinking, "This is going to be huge. People are going to clamor to buy the *Perfect Blue* DVD." But I was wrong. It had only modest sales by Hollywood standards, though the box office was respectable for the anime genre.

Coming out of film school, you have these ideas that you'll make films that will be artistic and intelligent, and somehow they'll make blockbuster money. It took awhile to sink in that just because I considered this genre exciting and appealing, that doesn't mean mainstream audiences will get it. The reality is that outside of Japan, anime is considered a small niche market. One of our goals was to find and develop a wider audience. I began to realize that it was one of our greatest challenges as well.

For audiences in the West, anime refers to any animation project produced in Japan. However, the term "anime" is the word for animation in Japanese, so there it could refer to any type of animation, produced in any country. The term itself and our understanding of how and what it references, is an example of the difficulties in translating and adapting an anime project for non-Japanese audiences.

Otaku

Our small team of less then ten people, in the US office, worked hard on distribution. First we created the marketing materials, designed the poster, edited a trailer and determined how the film will be presented to buyers. Our theatrical distribution guru would work feverishly to get screenings for the film. With so much competition and the theater bookers having little knowledge of Japanese animation at the time, this proved difficult.

When we would begin to translate a new project, there would often be many different ways to translate the same word, so we would choose what makes sense in context. This "true translation" is what would then be used for the subtitled version. For the dubbed version, we would start with this translated script and then work to create a new script, which would closely match the lip flaps and intonations of the character onscreen, attempting to stay as close to the translation as possible. However, in the early days of dubbing anime, it was often thought the practice should be to adapt the script to audiences not familiar with Japanese history, mythology, and sense of humor. Some jokes would be changed or references watered down to try and appeal to an unfamiliar audience.

But as viewers became more sophisticated, the glimpse into another culture became an important reason that diehard fans watched. These otaku made their preferences known: authenticity over all else. This didn't always work how you would imagine. For instance, in *Perfect Blue* there's a scene where Mima is talking to her mother on the phone. Her mother is from the country and therefore speaks a different dialect than a person from Tokyo. To illustrate this, the voiceover actor was directed to put on an American "southern" accent to give the viewer the idea that her mother was from a different area and not the city. But many fans didn't approve, and we did our best to keep adaptation changes to a minimum going forward.

This is the harmony between business and art. It is necessary to keep the fans happy, but it's not always possible. This was our challenge as a business: creating the balance to get projects distributed quickly, before they could be pirated, and to try to sell as many DVDs as we could to keep growing as a company. If we didn't sell, then we couldn't continue to bring new and exciting anime to the expanding audience outside of Japan.

Who's Running This Show?!?!?!

Anime is such a niche market that otaku have felt a certain amount of ownership of the industry. Creating their own websites and blogging about the upcoming releases has steered the distribution and presentation of the films. Many fans are so excited about an upcoming release, they will buy it from Japan and produce their own "fan-sub," which they'll then either post to a website for free download or make copies and sell at the anime and manga conventions. In the interim, negotiations between the producers and potential distributors haven't been completed, let alone delivery of everything needed to release the film in other territories.

I don't recall any project more contentious then *Neon Genesis Evangelion*. *Evangelion* is an apocalyptic series wherein a paramilitary organization, Nerv, fights monstrous beings called Angels, primarily using giant mecha called Evangelions which are piloted by select teenagers. We initially released the original conclusion to the twenty-four-episode series called *Death and Rebirth*, which included a recap of the first twenty-four episodes and an unfinished version of the conclusion. The fans were left confused, Director Hikeaki Anno felt unsatisfied, and the subsequent release, *End of Evangelion*, concludes the series more satisfactorily.

Even then, there was criticism of the last line, which could have been translated several ways. "Kimochi warui" was translated for the Manga release as "How disgusting," but could also be "I feel sick," "I feel bad," or even "I feel unwell." The latter translation had been circulated prior to the Manga release, so there is a debate about Anno's intentions for this line and how it effects the story. It's also said that he had changed his mind several times, which complicates the intention. Others took issue with an addition of a line, where there was no corresponding Japanese line and the addition of some profanity, which hadn't been used in other releases.

Inspiration

Art in its many forms will continue to struggle with this dilemma of being true, yet appealing to the masses so that you can profit and continue to create. How well you strike that equilibrium is often a matter of opinion.

As other distributors decided that there might be some profit to be made with anime distribution, the market has become very crowded. Companies and individuals buy up anything they can from Japan, sometimes even producing their own anime-style projects to cash in. This extends from otaku showing up uninvited at our office to pitch their projects, all the way to Hollywood making films like *The Matrix*, with its obvious inspiration from *Ghost in the Shell*.

Being a part of the anime world is a time I will never forget. Though I found anime accidentally, my perspectives on animation and storytelling in general have been blasted open. These are not "cartoons" in the American sense; these are commentaries on mythology, philosophy, post-apocalyptic survival, monsters, sex, nuclear power, and humanity as a whole. These are stories more easily told with animation, filled with images that could not be obtained without the limitless universe of animation.

I have to think that anime has had an influence, not just on western film aesthetics but also on western storytelling, which holds the possibility of improving all visual, moving image and artistic media. I look forward to more complex storytelling in our films, animation, and television, as filmmakers challenge the audience more and refuse to "dumb down" in order to appeal to a mass market.

My history with anime is filled with memories of great stories and challenges, some I had long forgotten. *Blood: The Last Vampire* is a project I saw through from script to screen, even working on the trailer, and I am so excited to see the live-action version after all this time of talking about and working on it. I miss my job, but I have taken time off to raise our two beautiful daughters, watching the latest *Astro Boy* film with them and introducing them to anime. I sincerely hope that people continue to embrace intelligent, fun storytelling, and like you, I look forward to keeping up with the cutting edge of animation. The future looks amazing!

1

Take a Ride on the Catbus

SHANA HEINRICY

I'm in love with Totoro. Since the first time I saw Hayao Miyazaki's *My Neighbor Totoro*, I've dreamed of handing Totoro my umbrella to replace the giant leaf on his head while we wait together in the rain for the Catbus. We both laugh together as he stomps on the ground to make the water droplets from the trees fall on the newly discovered umbrella. When I have a bad day, I think about giving Totoro a big hug and grabbing onto his coarse fur while we fly above the forest. When I heard that Pixar had the Catbus in their lobby, I thought about taking a trip to go see it, but alas, I know it won't really be the Catbus, not the one in my head. Other people, especially Miyazaki fans, like Totoro, but few understand why he comforts me so much. Totoro sparked my interest in the posthuman. You see, Totoro is a monster, as is the Catbus. I really love these monsters, but they are monsters nonetheless. The Catbus is a weird, contorted, hollowed out Cat-body that people can ride inside of. Creepy. Totoro is a big, bloated, furry thing inhabiting some sort of world outside of human or animal. Their bodies morph, change, and are much less stable than human bodies. What I like about Totoro and the Catbus are the possibilities that they offer, possibilities of what bodies may become and possibilities for rethinking bodies.

Becoming Bodies

Most people, especially in the West, fear changing bodies. Think of all the films that focus on zombies and vampires (bodies changing from human to something else) and cyborgs (human bodies intersecting with technology to become something else). How many times have Terminators tried to destroy life on Earth? How many zombie outbreaks have threatened existence? Scholars even have a term for this: "the grotesque." The grotesque is bodies exceeding their boundaries. We like to pretend that bodies are a clear separation between the self and world and clearly bounded. In reality, things come in and out of our bodies all the time, food, waste, sweat, even lotions. When we see a body exceeding its boundaries, such as vomiting or bones sticking out in places they shouldn't, that's considered grotesque, and we recoil from it because it breaks the fantasy of a bounded body. This continues into more extreme or fantastical breaks in the boundaries of the body, such as cyborgs which are part machine and part organic or zombies which are part dead and part alive (zombies prefer the politically correct term: "undead").

Despite the fear of these changes evident in Western culture, anime tends to embrace bodies in states of "becoming." Think about Haku in *Spirited Away* changing from human form to a dragon. This was not portrayed as something to fear, but instead something magical. Our bodies are always changing, always "becoming" something new. We shed and regrow our skin constantly. Our bones remake themselves. We grow. We age. I am literally not the same person I was when I was twelve, but I take comfort in the *myth* that somehow "I" am a stable entity since I was born, that there is a continuity between the "I" I was and the "I" I am. Somehow, anime does not fear changing bodies the way the West does; instead they see possibilities. Why?

In her book *Anime from Akira to Princess Mononoke*, Susan Napier argues that Japanese culture sees possibilities rather than fear in technologies, changing bodies, and the combination of the two due to the collective experience of nuclear bombing. This may seem counterintuitive at first. Wouldn't the bombing of Hiroshima and Nagasaki make people more fearful of technology and of the harm that technology can do to bodies? But after World War II, Japan was not allowed to develop its military. Money that may go towards military technologies and spending in other countries was used towards developing consumer technologies. This helped to make Japan a technological hub of the world, and technology was seen as a way to protect the body from threats, a way to effectively armor the soft, vulnerable human flesh. Technology could then protect bodies from future disasters such as radiation and bombing.

There is a second aspect of Japanese culture that contributes to this: a rich history of storytelling about changing bodies. Magical figures change shape often, such as those seen in most of Miyazaki's films, like Prince Turnip changing from a jumping scarecrow to a Prince in *Howl's Moving Castle*. This mythology of changing bodies along with the technological development of Japan has created a cultural site for anime to show morphing creatures and cyborgs as possibilities, rather than monsters.

The Posthuman

POST-human? So we're currently *after* the human? If this is after the human, what am I? Posthumanists argue that technology is so pervasive and invasive in culture that what it means to be human is now something new. What it meant to inhabit a human body in 1200 B.C.E. was very different than what it means now. They are no longer the same bodies due to the ways that our bodies have been altered by technology. Firstly, bodies are constantly encased in technology, from the plastic designed shoes to the chair I am sitting in to the paint on my walls. Secondly, bodies are altered due to technology, from carpal tunnel syndrome to fatness. *WALL-E* depicted the ultimate result of that Western fear of technology taking over human lives, bodies that were not even able to walk any longer. Thirdly, bodies become technology, making everyone cyborgs. Posthumanists do not say this is yet to come, in the future. No, they argue it has already happened. Clearly this applies to people with artificial hearts and limbs, but what about everyone else?

"Cyborg Studies" is a large area of posthumanist scholarship, starting with Donna Haraway's famous "Cyborg Manifesto" (from her book *Simians, Cyborgs, and Women*), which argued that we are all already cyborgs. We are all cyborgs, and therefore after the human. After all, a Terminator governs the state of California. My blood is made of technologically developed antibodies from the vaccines I've received. My food is genetically manipulated and fortified with vitamins. The water I drink is chemically treated and processed. My cells have evolved with technology, and technology is part of me.

Humans like to consider themselves "exceptional," as above and beyond other species and in control of other technologies. Donna Haraway argues in *When Species Meet* that human exceptionalism has caused many people to disregard the ways that humans are altered and how that changes our culture in favor of the myth that we are all stable and singular beings. Anime helps to break that thin veneer of the pretense of human exceptionalism in favor of imaging the magic of what bodies may be.

Cyborg Studies and Posthumanism rarely focus on popular culture representations of the combination of humans and technology. Instead, scholars are interested in issues such as who and what counts as a citizen in an age of artificial intelligence, cybernetics, virtual worlds, and medical procedures which combine organic and machine, for example Chris Hables Gray's *Cyborg Citizen*. Our definition and understanding of who is considered alive and how citizenship rights are awarded will surely have to change with our technology. Another issue addressed by posthumanists is how technology is used to better write gender upon the body, such as in the case of plastic surgery (as Anne Balsamo discusses in *Technologies of the Gendered Body*). For example, women's bodies are technologically altered in order to give them large breasts, which helps those bodies to better fulfill the societal standards of gender. However, these standards are not "natural," as large breasts on thin women rarely occurs without technological intervention.

A few scholars of posthumanism, including myself, focus on popular culture representations of posthuman bodies. For example, in *Cyborgs and Barbie Dolls*, Kim Toffoletti examines popular culture artifacts such as Barbie dolls and Marilyn Manson for the ways that they help us to imagine what the body can be. She calls Barbie a "posthuman prototype" due to the ways its hard plastic torso, rubbery limbs, and unachievable proportions serve as a cultural manifestation of what posthuman bodies may be. Popular culture representations say something about the culture the representations developed out of. Representations on television and film show what people in a particular culture fear or love. Sometimes, as in anime, these representations are fantastical: what people would like to exist or what they fear may come to exist. This is why popular culture is an important area of study for the posthuman, as it shows cultural attitudes towards technology and bodies in an age of dramatic advances in genetics, cloning, robotics, and nanotechnology. In popular culture, people tell stories about these advances and their potential to transform humanity, which reveal something about the cultures these stories emerge from.

Anime is a particularly rich medium for exploring cultural attitudes towards the posthuman, as the representations of the posthuman are extremely abundant in anime, perhaps more abundant than in any other medium. In *Mechademia 3: Limits of the Human*, scholars from a variety of areas came together to explore the posthuman in anime. The posthuman is such a common theme in anime that the editors of the series felt an entire volume in the Mechademia series was warranted.

The Ghost in the Machine

There are two valences of the posthuman that are clearly presented in anime. The first I term the "Ghost in the Machine" perspective, which is personified in the anime film *Ghost in the Shell* as well as the entire mecha genre. The Ghost in the Machine perspective on posthumanism sees advantages in leaving the human body altogether. The idea is that perhaps human consciousness could be transferred to a machine, thus negating the necessity of the human body and all the frailties that go with it. This myth is seen in cultures throughout the world, as well as in cybernetic research.

In *Ghost in the Shell*, the cyborg cop Motoko Kusanagi links herself to information networks in order to catch a hacker called the Puppet Master. Motoko is still part human herself and is somewhat limited by her human body. In the end, she discovers that the Puppet Master is actually a computer program that has become conscious. This bit of consciousness moves throughout the information network as a Ghost in the Machine. Finally, Motoko herself merges her consciousness with the information network, experiencing a freedom unlike any she had experienced while she was still tethered to her body. This film embraces the possibilities that exist through completely merging with technology to exist only as a consciousness.

While not specifically addressing *Ghost in the Shell*, N. Katherine Hayles critiques this common view of cyberneticists on the grounds that human consciousness is dependent on embodiment (*How We Became Posthuman*). Her critique is considered a pillar of posthuman thought. She argues that when the body is taken away, or another body is put in its place, the consciousness itself dramatically changes. In other words, mind and body are not separate but are a unified whole. My body creates my moods, my pain, my energy. Bodies are not something to be liberated from. Instead, they create identity and existence. Consciousness *is* embodied. I see many cultural reasons to long to be without a body. Imagine what it would be like to no longer feel pain or to be limited by a frail, feeble body. However, it is not possible to know who we would be without our bodies, as our consciousness would surely change. While I could be freed from pain, I'd also be liberated from my senses, including wonderful sights, smells, tastes, and touches. Posthumanists don't want to escape bodies, but instead want to know how body and consciousness change with various configurations of body and technology.

The mecha genre of anime embraces human bodies encased in larger mechanical suits, combining human and machine to create a cyborg, such as in *Robotech* and the various *Gundam* series. *Transformers* is a US franchise which seems to similarly embrace the Ghost in Machine mythos, but is a cross between mecha and *Ghost in the Shell*. Transformers are not the metal boxes on utility poles (perhaps they evolved from them), but are large "transforming" machines that fight similarly to mecha, yet are not dependent on organic beings. And they are incognito among us as vehicles. I think Herbie may be the first transformer to come to Earth, later joined by his long lost son Bumblebee. Unlike mecha, transformers do not need organic bodies, but may allow humans the privilege of riding with them.

The mecha suits enable the human bodies to do things they otherwise couldn't do, such as defeat giant invaders. Mecha is about protection, but also about union. The technology protects bodies, and the bodies help to organize technology. The human body is like the Ghost in the Machine, but it is a different variation of this mythos. The body is not entirely eliminated, but instead drives the machines, creating and utilizing technology. This is a new configuration of human existence, living in conjunction with these huge suits. The possibilities of this configuration are what posthumanism is all about.

Morphing Bodies

Animation, all forms of animation, focuses on plasticity of bodies. As we already noted, all bodies are constantly changing. However, only in extreme cases are we able to see that change happening, such as in a bad car accident. Usually the changes in our bodies happen too slowly to see them take place or at too microscopic a level to view with the naked eye. Animation, however, is the perfect medium to portray changing bodies. Animated bodies can be—

and often are—pulled, tugged, torn, and even blown up. They are able to change shape and then return to their original shape if needed. These changes are often extreme and comical because they are so unrealistic. In animation, bodies need not be subjected to the laws of space and time. Think of Wile E. Coyote pedaling his feet as he is frozen in mid-air until he realizes his situation. Think of characters aging instantly on the screen as some form of comic relief.

Animated bodies can also be altered for additional effect, for example, to show different aspects of the character. In the Disney film *Mulan*, Mulan's body changes depending on whether she is a boy or a girl. As a boy, her neck is widened and her jaw is squared. This is very different than an actress merely putting on different clothes to portray a boy or girl. Instead, Mulan's body changes for the character, rather than just being dressed differently. Similarly, because size can be greatly exaggerated in animation, bodies can change to show mood, such as making a character physically much smaller when she or he is afraid or much larger when he or she is angry. Bodies are also changed to draw the viewer's focus. For example, bodies may at first look relatively normal, with an image of the character's regular body. A close-up then shows gruesome aspects of the body, such as hair sticking out in inappropriate places or festering sores. These items were not drawn on the original body, but are in close-up drawings, making it appear similar to a film zooming in. However, in a live-action film when a camera zooms, the item which it is zooming in on is also present, though perhaps smaller, in the wide shot. Animation adds characteristics to the body with these shots, morphing the body. The body is presented as pliable and changing, and these "morphing bodies" are the second valence of the posthuman readily found in anime.

Altering bodies is just as popular in anime as it is in US animation. In *Pokemon*, the Pokemons' bodies change dramatically from their peaceful, complacent form to their fighting form. In their peaceful form, Pokemon are adorable. They are drawn with neotony, meaning characteristics of infants such as large, round eyes. When they turn into their fighting form, the lines become much straighter and harsher, making their bodies fierce rather than cuddly.

I love animated bodies because they are so ripe with the human body in a state of becoming. And I don't always know what they are becoming, which is exciting. Animation can help to alter how people think about bodies, since it challenges the discourse that bodies are stable, unchanging entities. Anime helps to excite people's imaginations, conceiving of what the human may become.

Miyazaki is better at this than any other anime director. But let's face it, I'm a fan, and so I'm a bit biased. In one of Miyazaki's most underappreciated films, *Porco Rosso*, the main character has the head of a pig. None of the other characters have pig heads. Everyone else is just a regular, boring human, but not Porco Rosso. His pig head came from a curse, but Porco Rosso is about as posthuman as they come, merging not with technology, but with an animal. Of course, we are all constantly combined with animals, millions of which live in, on, and make up our bodies at any given moment. The "I" that I am is actually a "we." I am a combination of many. Posthumanists are concerned with the potentials of human existence in combination with other species as well, exploring the entangled web of species in which we all exist. The character of Porco Rosso is oddly human for such an inhuman pig-man, flawed with jealously and lustfulness. Miyazaki appears fond of pig-people, changing Chihiro's parents in *Sprited Away* into pig-people as well, as a magical punishment for their gluttony. They transform before the viewer's eyes from human to pig, and finally back to human as the story concludes.

I love the imaginative possibilities that Miyazaki poses, such as a living fire in *Howl's Moving Castle*, or No Face in *Spirited Away* morphing from a giant gob of faceless, speechless goo into something beautiful.

Although technology is not the focus of his films, Miyazaki's characters are not outside of technology. Kiki in *Kiki's Delivery Service* lives in a city with all of the modern conveniences but also uses magic. In *My Neighbor Totoro*, they have hospitals, telephones, and buses. *Porco Rosso* is centered around airplanes and war. In *Spirited Away*, Chihiro and her parents are brought to this place in automobiles. In *Howl's Moving Castle*, a large castle contraption moves around the countryside, created through technology. Miyazaki's films do not return to an idyllic time before technology, a time when the myth of magic created things that could now be done through technology. Instead, they are about having some magic in everyday life, about magic co-existing with technology.

Wave Goodbye from the Catbus

Anime offers more insight into posthuman theory than any other medium. Posthumanism did not develop with anime in mind, but I find it hard to believe that it didn't have a large influence on the thinking of posthuman scholars. One of anime's most significant contributions to popular culture is allowing for new ways to think about the body, offering fantastical and magical possibilities about what the body may become.

The Catbus in *My Neighbor Totoro* is still the most iconic image of posthumanism, and the Catbus isn't even human at all. Instead, it is a vehicle-body that transports us to a crazy world of monsters, cyborgs, and morphing bodies in a state of becoming. This animal-technology-magic-fantasy combination drives our imaginations and helps us to see the world in a new way. Once we understand that we are all already cyborgs and that we are not singular beings, but instead multitudes of beings living under the assumption of being singular, it can be an eerie transformation of our consciousness. Once onboard the Catbus to the realm of the posthuman, the world and our bodies never quite look the same again. And there's no going back. Come on. Take a ride.

2
The Making of Killer Cuties

CHRISTIE BARBER, MIO BRYCE, and
JASON DAVIS

Since the 1960s, Japan has produced a considerable number of cyborg narratives in manga and anime, particularly in works targeting male children or adolescents. From early manga examples such as Kazumasa Hirai and Jirō Kuwata's *8 Man* and Shōtarō Ishinomori's *Cyborg 009*, and their subsequent anime versions, the protagonist is commonly cyborged without their knowledge or against their will or desires.[1] This positions them as victims, regardless of how physically powerful they are. Their sense of inferiority and vulnerability usually underpins these narratives, either subtly or explicitly.

The depiction of female cyborgs adds complexity to the positioning of cyborgs in manga and anime, especially in terms of gender. Female cyborgs may be equipped with remarkable physical strength, combined with voluptuous, eroticized bodies (for instance Major Motoko Kusanagi in Masamune Shirow's original manga and Mamoru Oshii's anime version of *Ghost in the Shell*); and these powerful female cyborgs are also frequently ascribed roles as protectors or supporters of incompetent and insecure male protagonists. Although some female cyborgs may possess characteristics that indicate a transgression of the conventional boundaries of gender, this transgression is often limited and undermined by other elements of their depiction. As Kumiko Sato points out in her essay "How Information Technology Has ªNot, Changed Feminism and

---

[1] A notable exception is the *kikai ningen* (literally, machine human) in Leiji Matsumoto's *Galaxy Express 999*. The protagonist Tetsurō desires a machine body because he believes it will secure him eternal life, hence social status and wealth.

Japanism", "female cyborgs and androids have been safely domesticated and fetishized into maternal and sexual protectors of the male hero" and thus "their function is usually reduced to either a maid or a goddess obediently serving her beloved male master, the sole reason for her militant nature."

As we shall see, though, the representation of female cyborgs in anime is complex and sometimes ambiguous. In her much-discussed "A Manifesto for Cyborgs," Donna Haraway asserts that as constructed, part-human, part-machine beings, the cyborg transgresses the boundaries of humanness; this transgression involves blurring conventional distinctions between male and female. In breaking down boundaries in this way, Haraway argues that cyborg imagery challenges conventional understandings of gender—the cyborg inhabits a "post-gender world." She sees great potential in the cyborg, for as the cyborg blurs conventional distinctions, it symbolizes liberation from the patriarchal domination that forms and reinforces those distinctions. Although this work is not new, and Haraway herself has since re-evaluated some of the ideas she presented, it still provides a relevant framework for examining the representation of gender in Japanese anime. This is because the representation of gender (or variations of it) is a conspicuous and interesting element of anime narratives, and examining these representations helps to convey their complexity. However, the fictional cyborgs in the first series of the anime *Gunslinger Girl* fall far short of realising the "post-gender" potential that Haraway envisions.

Gunslinger Girl

First published in 2002 in *Dengeki Daioh*, a monthly manga publication targeted at adolescent and young-adult males, *Gunslinger Girl* is a cyborg narrative by Japanese artist Yū Aida. The first and second volumes of the manga series were adapted into a thirteen-episode anime series that was directed by Morio Asaka in 2003. While the themes in both formats remain consistent, the anime series presents a much more explicit and thorough portrayal of the imagery and concepts that make *Gunslinger Girl* especially thought-provoking.

The storyline involves an Italian-based government-run anti-terrorist group, known as the Social Welfare Agency (Shakai fukushi kōsha), which selectively "adopts" abandoned or orphaned girls who are critically injured or severely disabled. Medical technology is used to modify the girls physiologically and psychologically, refashioning them as expert, powerful killers. They possess cybernetically enhanced senses and synthetic materials are used to replace much of their human body. They are controlled by drugs, a process termed "conditioning," and each young, cute female cyborg is paired with an older male handler. The cyborg's duty is to protect the handler and complete any assassinations requested of her. When on assignment they are efficient, ruthless and brutal; they have superhuman physical strength and reflexes, and are highly trained in hand-to-hand combat and the use of high-powered weapons.

We are frequently reminded just how lethal these cute little girls can be. They are regularly depicted with weapons of all kinds—perhaps cleaning a dismantled pistol, polishing a rifle, or innocently staring ahead with wide eyes and a blank facial expression, focusing a weapon directly at the viewer's face. The components and usage of the guns are shown in all their complexity, and this creates a striking contrast to the depiction of the girls themselves. Although each cyborg is visually depicted with unique traits, physically they all share the fundamental characteristics of cute (or more specifically, what would be termed *kawaii* in Japanese) style: large, round eyes, oversized heads, small mouths, and small slender bodies with long, straight legs. They are drawn simply and cleanly, and with a limited range of expressions.

The visual attraction of these girl cyborg images lies in the blatant incongruity of young bodies handling oversized killing weapons. And this contrived contrast between high-powered weapons and their capacity as killing instruments in the small hands of girls may seem at first glance to be a deliberately transgressive depiction.

Repressing the Self

In "A Manifesto for Cyborgs," Haraway asserts that due to the blurring of boundaries between human and machine, newer cyborgs have a degree of autonomy and subjectivity that earlier machines did not. Their unique position in this post-human landscape affords them modes of agency never before possible—the very nature of their subjectivity is unsettled and uncertain, and this opens up a range of possibilities not available to either humans or more simple machines. And this broadening of the scope of their subjectivity simultaneously expands the potential scope of their autonomy. But this potential is not realized by the cyborgs of *Gunslinger Girl*, as their ongoing victimization diminishes their capacity for self-awareness and severely limits their autonomy.

Even before the protagonists are altered by the Agency, they are already the victims of misfortune or abuse. Angelica is deliberately run over by her parents; Henrietta is the victim of a violent attack, in which her family is murdered and she is brutally raped; Rico has spent her life in hospital, unable to walk, and her disability forced her parents to abandon her. The Agency, presenting their activities to the wider community as a benevolent service for the critically ill and unfortunate, rescues them from their suffering and, at least apparently, ends their victimization. After all, the process by which the cyborgs are created essentially involves the repair and enhancement of often severely damaged bodies.

But the agency does not simply create new cyborgs; it also conditions them, a process that eliminates personal memories and apparently removes any feelings of fear, horror or guilt that might arise from their role as assassins. Conditioning ensures obedience and a heightened sensitivity to any threat against the handler; the cyborgs must protect the handler, even at the cost of their own life, because they are always replaceable. Conditioning also produces intense loyalty towards the male handlers, which can lead to feelings of romantic love. The conditioning process remains imperfect, and the adverse effects include loss of memory and concentration, inability to control movement and emotion, and a reduction in life span.

In addition to being conditioned, the cyborgs are also isolated and restrained. They are allowed outside of the Agency compound only when accompanied by their handler, usually for the completion of a mission; otherwise they have no contact with society. The cyborgs' situation is poignantly described by the promotional slogan for the first volume of the Japanese manga, which, literally translated, is, "These girls have been given a large gun and a small happiness."[2] Their lives are only possible within that "small happiness," a secret, isolated world, like an ephemeral bubble. In this confined and controlled environment, the cyborgs are not entirely

---

[2] In Japanese this is, " 少女たちに与えられたのは大きな銃と小さな幸せ ." The term "*ataerareta*" implies that the girls have no control over their situation. The phrase, "*chiisa na shiawase*" conveys that the happiness given to the girls is not total or deep happiness.

dissimilar to many Japanese youths, whose lives can be constrained in what is often an oppressive, competitive educational system with little clear prospect for independence. The cyborgs may also be a displaced reflection of the apparent target audience—boys them-selves—who are helplessly "conditioned" by the pressure of social conformity to act their required roles.

The cyborgs' method for understanding relationships with oth-ers is restricted by the limited structures they are exposed to in the *Gunslinger Girl* universe. They find it difficult to understand rela-tionships that do not subscribe to the norms that have been set for them by the dominant male figures in the narrative. For example, while on a preliminary reconnaissance operation at his workplace, Rico is befriended by a hotel porter, Emilio. Initially, she is over-whelmed by shyness, and his kind attention and the possibility that he may care for her temporarily distracts her from her mission. But Rico's hopes for a relationship with Emilio soon seem distant and unreal, for when he catches her during her assassination mission, she stares straight into his eyes and shoots him.

Perhaps unsurprisingly, the relationships the cyborgs share with their male handlers can be dysfunctional. These relationships are always unequal and defined by submission and dominance, but they may also be based on misunderstanding, fear or jealousy, and they often lack honesty and meaningful interaction. Henrietta feels overwhelming love for her handler Jose and constantly desires his approval and reassurance; she admits she would commit suicide if she lost him, and in one episode, she stands doubled over with breathlessness, brought on by the stress of the simple task of ask-ing Jose to spend Christmas with her. Triela's handler Hilshire buys her teddy bears as gifts, assuming that stuffed toys are what she wants; what she really wants is for him to treat her like she means something to him. Rico's handler Jean physically abuses her: in one episode she returns from training with a bloodied mouth, after Jean has hit her, but a smiling Rico seems emotionally unaffected by this treatment.

The conditioning seems to prevent self-reflective questioning, and inhibits the cyborgs' ability to distinguish between genuine emotions and those they are forced to feel by the drugs. As a con-sequence, their self-awareness is limited. Triela and Claes do try to understand who they are and why they exist, but for cyborgs like Henrietta and Elsa, their existence is made meaningful solely through their relationship with their male handler. For Rico, her cyborg existence, where she has a strong body that moves freely, and where she can be outside and enjoy the friendship of the other cyborgs, is far preferable to her former life of solitude and disability.

The cyborgs don't usually seem to consciously acknowledge or display any internal conflict as a result of their incongruent behaviors and mental states as simultaneously cute, caring girls and ruthless killers. Henrietta does show concern about her position, but her concern is that as a cyborg, she will not be able to be the "normal" girl that her handler Jose wants her to be. The lack of such turmoil seems starkly unnatural, given their situation, and indicates that their integrity as individuals has been severely fractured by the technology and control that the Agency uses to dominate them. That the cyborgs accept such an existence indicates not ignorance or denial, but an acute recognition of their "reality"—the impossibility of their life outside the Agency and/or away from their handler. They are imprisoned in their submissive role, and only two possible choices exist: death, or acceptance of their carefully crafted "small happiness."

The narrative does attempt to present some kind of counterbalance to the portrayal of the cyborgs as powerless and dominated. The project of developing these girl cyborg assassins is regarded as questionable by some of those in the government who are aware of its existence. After Elsa murders her handler and commits suicide, the activities of the cyborg program are investigated and criticized by another section of the Agency. Also, some of the handlers show concern and compassion towards the cyborgs; a recurring motif of the series is the conflict the handlers feel over their role as superiors and their relationship with the cyborgs, their loyal and obedient protectors. For example, despite the official policy of the Agency being that the cyborgs are tools that will eventually be replaced, there is constant debate between some of the handlers on the appropriate level of conditioning. Some handlers (such as Henrietta's handler Jose, and Triela's handler Hilshire) maintain the conditioning drugs at lower levels with the aim of limiting the adverse side effects and providing the cyborg with a "normal" existence. Claes' handler Raballo leaves the Agency because he cannot accept the Agency's treatment of the cyborgs (he is however killed soon after), and when constant repairs and conditioning cause severe deterioration in Angelica, her handler Marco is so affected that he wants to abandon her and the Agency. This positioning of the handlers resembles many conscientious teachers in the regulated, restrictive Japanese school system, who suffer in their inability to help those students in difficulty. They too are helplessly trapped between the victimized children and the system, which tends to ignore the suffering of the individual.

However, although the series may be self-conscious and sympathetic, to some extent, in its portrayal of the abuse of the cyborgs, this is constantly undermined by the overt focus on such elements as the submissive position of the cyborgs in their relationship with their male superior, and the cuteness—or physical appeal—of the female characters. The prevailing impression is that the cyborgs of *Gunslinger Girl* fall desperately short of the ideals of autonomy and self-development envisaged by Haraway in her Manifesto.

Fearful Technologies

"A Manifesto for Cyborgs" argues that although cyborg technology confuses or deconstructs the distinctions between human and machine, this confusion and deconstruction should not be feared; instead, Haraway sees a model for the breaking down of other boundaries in society, such as gender boundaries.

However, in *Gunslinger Girl*, although cyborg technology is used to repair the damaged or disabled bodies and minds of the protagonists, and create the cyborgs' superhuman physical power and abilities, this same technology is also often the exact cause of the cyborgs' physical and psychological weakness and suffering. It is this deliberate victimization of the female cyborgs that makes the narrative especially unsettling.

Significantly, despite their importance in the narrative, the technologies in *Gunslinger Girl* are almost invisible; there is only limited and simplistic verbal and visual exposition of the cybernetic enhancement and conditioning processes in this apparently advanced society. This indicates that the narrative is not attempting to inform or entertain the viewer with visions of progressive technologies. This is in stark contrast to *Ghost in the Shell*, which depicts Motoko Kusanagi's superb connectedness and intelligence through cyberspace as her unique value and identity, and her abilities enable her to question her own corporeality and presence as an individual.

The victimization of the girl cyborgs is acutely visualized by the cyborg Claes, who becomes the Agency's test subject after she is deemed unusable in field operations. She is unfit for service because of severe psychological trauma brought on by the death of her handler Raballo (her memories of whom have been all but erased by the Agency). Claes is bookish, thoughtful, and more mature than some of the other cyborgs, and her sincere efforts to find meaning in her existence, despite her demotion from assassin to test subject, stand in harsh contrast to the actions of the Agency. During relentless strength testing, Claes's shoulder is violently dislocated. In pain, she is left attached to monitors inside a sealed room as a voice over an intercom calmly explains to her that pain medication will be administered soon, and then orders that she be sent for repairs.

Despite being aware that their handler is responsible for their conditioning, the cyborgs are not always capable of controlling their overwhelming emotions of loyalty towards them and are scolded by their handlers when these feelings lead to errors in judgment. If a cyborg makes a mistake in an operation or drill, their reaction is one of shame and fear; when they are injured they feel inadequate and try to understate or deflect attention from their suffering, desiring only to return to their duties and regain their handler's favour. In fact, the narrative often focuses on one cyborg or another making a mistake during an operation or training exercise, usually the result of an impulsive and excessive reaction to a perceived threat to a handler, or triggered by feelings of jealously or competitiveness. For example, soon after she has entered the Agency, Henrietta accompanies Jose in an operation to capture a man who has witnessed terrorist activity. A member of the terrorist group physically and verbally threatens Jose, and Henrietta's response is uncontrolled and disproportionate: she bombards the terrorists and their hideout with a stream of bullets, leaving none of them alive. Her actions almost cause the mission to fail, and she is wounded in the exchange; Jose admonishes her, and her greatest concern is that she has failed him. In another episode, Triela has captured a man her handler, Hilshire, wants to question; when her captive reaches into his pocket, Triela shoots him, perceiving a threat to Hilshire. And although the conditioning is supposed to prevent the cyborgs from murdering their handlers, Elsa does exactly this and then commits suicide by shooting herself in the eye. Like Henrietta, Elsa is utterly devoted to and protective of her handler, Lauro. She is intensely jealous of Henrietta and Jose's warm relationship, and Lauro's cruel criticism of her when she fails to perform during an operation is the catalyst for her actions. She is driven to murder Lauro and commit suicide from despair, caused by her obsessive and unrequited love for him – emotions the Agency's conditioning had a role in generating.

Thus with their ability to cope with their experiences disabled, the narrative persistently emphasises the vulnerability and suffering of the cyborgs. Ultimately the cyborgs are not liberated by their status as hybrids, they are disempowered.

Reinforcing Boundaries

In "A Manifesto for Cyborgs" Haraway asserts that the cyborg is a fluid, ironic hybrid: a "creature in a post-gender world." It does not fit within the boundaries set by conventional gender roles, and as such presents new possibilities for understanding who we are and our relationships with others. Haraway also argues that although in western patriarchal society technology has been used to control, dominate, and exploit others, reinterpretation of the cyborg shows its potential to blur and reconstruct the boundaries between established positions and identities. Patriarchal domination is undermined by the cyborg, which exists outside gender.

Haraway also asserts that unlike humans, who are the product of heterosexual reproduction, cyborgs are "uncoupled from organic reproduction." She connects them to regeneration, not reproduction. From a feminist perspective she envisions great possibilities in this regeneration because not only is heterosexual reproduction unnecessary, cyborg conception involves creation of new, fluid, progressive existences that transgress dualistic boundaries. Haraway's vision is a "monstrous world without gender" (p. 39).

If we relate Haraway's ideas to the cyborgs of *Gunslinger Girl*, they fail to destabilize conventional ideas about gender. Their characterization sits firmly within, and thus reinforces, traditional ideas about femininity.

The cyborgs of *Gunslinger Girl* are unable to reproduce, as most of their internal organs are removed and replaced by cybernetic implants. A new cyborg is created when the Agency requires one. Taking this into account, we might argue that the cyborgs are outside the human concern of reproduction. However, removing the ability to reproduce is not liberating for these girl cyborgs. In one episode, Triela endures severe menstrual cramps, but given that her body is largely synthetic and unable to bear a child, it is both unnecessary and implausible for her to suffer such pain. The possibility of Triela's future pregnancy is doubly denied, in that the cyborg implants drastically shorten her life expectancy. That Triela is placed in this position of suffering indicates that these characters are not examples of progressive female cyborgs, and their technological advancement does not liberate them from a subordinate position.

The female characters are persistently depicted as dependent and vulnerable, their bodies and minds altered and manipulated by the often harmful or faulty technology employed by the Agency. The narrative's central aim sometimes seems to be to highlight the abuse of the cyborgs and evoke pity from the viewer: we frequently see their devoted submission to the harsh demands of their male superiors, and the suffering they experience as a result. In their relationship with their handler, they are loyal and obedient, constantly seeking approval and requiring direction (although Triela, on occasion, is willing to disagree with or disobey a male superior). Neither motherly figures nor external peers are seen to neutralize male dominance. Although the girls do not usually see themselves as dominated or exploited, we the viewers see them as such. In portraying the cyborgs in this fashion, *Gunslinger Girl* intensifies traditional notions about inequality between genders, wherein women submit to male domination.

One element of their characterization that intensifies their positioning in a submissive role is their youth. The explanation given in the narrative for making the cyborgs female children is that the cybernetic modifications and conditioning are more effective on younger (but not necessarily female) bodies. As children, the cyborgs not only appear physically weaker (although this is obviously a deceptive appearance), they are also distanced from the maturity or independence that might generally be associated with an older female. The girl cyborgs might be interpreted as an exaggerated expression of the fantasy object and the protective mother figure, bundled into an emotionally stilted, partly artificial young female body. That is, the male can possess and dominate the attractive helpless object; but this object can also protect, be relied upon, and trusted. The female has been reduced to a manageable, nonthreatening form.

As we've mentioned, the cyborgs are depicted with typically *kawaii* features, such as disproportionately large eyes and heads, and thin bodies. Each girl is dressed by her handler in keeping with a particular style. For example, Triela often wears a masculine pants suit with a tie and visible gun holsters, her long, flowing, fair hair tied in pigtails with ribbons. Henrietta alternates between various school uniform styles, including sailor suits, or short pleated skirts, ribbon bow ties and over-the-knee socks. Their cuteness is further enhanced by their belongings (for example, Triela's collection of teddy bears), and their behavior when off-duty—they share tea and cake, read books, cook, or play musical instruments.

Kawaii encompasses a multiplicity of meaning. As Sharon Kinsella's "Cuties in Japan" suggests, in *kawaii* we can find sweetness, gentleness, and innocence; *kawaii* also embodies vulnerability and immaturity, both in appearance and behaviour. The cyborgs exhibit an impossible yet cunning combination of sweetness and vulnerability with physical strength and brutality. When they're not engaged in combat or murder, the *Gunslinger Girl* cyborgs are adorable and seem utterly innocent, gentle and childlike. When such a pretty child shoots a defenceless, innocent boy without remorse—as Rico does to the hotel porter Emilio—there is a resounding visual and psychological clash. This combination subverts the generally accepted symbolism of cute as good or kind or natural.

Essentially, the Agency engineers a cyborg that has an attractive feminine appearance, because this makes them useful and powerful as assassins—their cuteness serves as a disguise during operations. However, the Agency discards or alters their interior, both physical and mental. Cybernetic implants make them strong, fast and lethal, and conditioning makes them loyal and obedient, but their technological alterations also render them incapable of reproduction and eventually cause mental and physical deterioration. These female cyborgs are depicted as an object of the male gaze, and as a result, *Gunslinger Girl* perpetuates physical attractiveness and youth as ideals. Further, disguising their superhuman capabilities with excessive immaturity and adorable appearances highlights their position as psychologically and (externally) physically inferior to their male superiors, again reinforcing a conventional gender role.

The cyborgs' vulnerability is stressed by the lack of comicalness in their cuteness. Many manga and anime series rely heavily on the "gag" value of an often-awkward relationship between a female cyborg and her male owner or companion, as exemplified by CLAMP's *Chobits*. Like the girls in *Gunslinger Girl*, the protagonist of *Chobits*, Chi, exemplifies cuteness. She is socially inept and rather vacuous at the beginning; she is also affectionate and adorable. Her fumbling, sexually-charged owner is a suitable counterpart to the innocent but provocative Chi, and her interaction with her owner is in typical manga/anime romantic comedy style. However, Chi's comical cuteness is significantly different to the cuteness in *Gunslinger Girl*: Chi is ostensibly non-human yet possesses her own desire and initiative; she is not manipulated by those closest to her, and the narrative ultimately recognises her unique value to society.

Cuteness is thus a key element in establishing the vulnerability of the girl cyborgs, and again contributes to this narrative's departure from the image of strong female cyborgs. This concept of cuteness—created, developed, and participated in by so many females in Japanese society—has been used to serve the purpose of a narrative that undermines the concept itself. Such representations of cyborgs diminish any progress made by the independent hybridized female heroines common in many manga and anime (such as Motoko Kusanagi in *Ghost in the Shell* and Alita in *Battle Angel Alita*), who may have eroticized bodies, but also have physical and psychological strength and are able to maintain their autonomy. The cyborg has regressed here; she is fixed in a conventional gender role.

Looking Inwards

The fictional cyborgs in *Gunslinger Girl* do not represent the new possibilities that Donna Haraway envisioned in "A Manifesto for Cyborgs"; these cyborgs do not serve as models for either potential boundary confusion or reconstruction. Instead, the portrayal of these fictional cyborgs has a dual function: to position the female in a conventional gender role, and uphold traditional ideals of femininity; but also to reflect the condition of individuals in contemporary (Japanese) society, who may feel trapped or victimized under the pressure of social conformity and hierarchy. Assuming that the target audience of this work is probably male, the possibility of male viewers aligning themselves with the experiences of the victimized cyborgs is real. Such an interpretation might highlight that when gender roles are reinforced, or reconfigured, (even to the limited extent that they are in *Gunslinger Girl*, where the cyborgs exhibit apparently "masculine" strength and "feminine" appearances) masculinity, too, is involved, and changed.

Sue Short writes in *Cyborg Cinema and Contemporary Subjectivity* that fictional cyborgs, in having to contend with being subject to the authority of others while desiring subjective agency, reflect the experiences of all viewers to some extent. They "not only encapsulate the metaphysical fact of our limited existence, but question our relative freedom also" (p. 195). Although the representation of female identity in *Gunslinger Girl* may be problematic, the series allows us to consider some valuable questions about the nature of our existence and our relationships with others.[3]

---

[3] This chapter is a revised version of a conference presentation given by the authors at the CERI International Conference, "Le Manga, 60 Ans Après . . ." [Manga, Sixty Years On . . .], Maison de la Culture du Japon, Paris, (15th March, 2008).

3

Just a Ghost in a Shell?

ANGUS McBLANE

How can humans interact with machines? This question is at the heart of modern stories that focus on technology. Central to this question is the idea of cyborgs or more specifically, cyborg enhancements. Mamoru Oshii's cyberpunk masterpiece *Ghost in the Shell* explores not only the possibility of these enhancements—up to and including full-fledged cyborgs—but also portrays a liminal space in humanism which is sent into crisis when these technologies deeply question the fundamental underpinnings of what it means to be "human."

Crucial to the various strands of humanism (renaissance, enlightenment, secular, among others) are notions of human perfectibility, emancipation, progress, control, and rational mastery of the world. Posthumanism not only seeks to orient the world in such a way that agency is not seen as a unique "human" characteristic but one which can be possessed by machines or machinic hybrids (and further extended into the realm of other animals), but also to work through the ideas presented within the various humanist discourses, in order to rewrite humanism into its post, not as a radical break, but as a way which allows a notion of the "human" to be removed from its central place.

These machinic hybrids or cyborgs are boundary figures that represent in cyberpunk literature and film a transitional place in the development from humanism to posthumanism. Cyborgs serve not only as transitional figures of human-machine hybridity, but also as a representative of this shift if it comes to pass. These figures embody the tensions around technological bodies and the question of embodiment in the technologically focused culture(s) of the contemporary West. The boundary line between natural and artificial in posthumanism is blurred, especially by cyborgs; this promotes a deep questioning of the limits of what is called the "human." *Ghost in the Shell* not only deals with this incredibly aptly, but through the film's paradoxical representations of embodiment, it pushes the limits to their breaking point through the consideration of new modes of being (that which is).

The cyborg protagonist of *Ghost in the Shell*, Major Motoko Kusanagi, struggles within the interstitial space between a humanist identity grounded in individual agency and consciousness as a seat of identity (her "ghost") and a posthuman distributed cognition in which "grounding" of experience becomes expanded and fluid. The "body" and by extension embodiment, are not viewed as mutually exclusive categories. The material body is extended to allow formulations in which a "material" body is not limited to an organic, biological body, but can also be a technological body (a cyborg body) or an informational body which exists in the material representations of data, or, pushing this one step further, simultaneously physiological, technological and informational, with the designator "organic" being increasingly removed. A data "body" is still a body. It is not a purely "immaterial" construct; it is rooted in the informational structures, which underlie the system(s) it inhabits. The film's cyborg protagonist, Major Motoko Kusanagi, reveals these tensions as they are developed through her struggle with identity, her subjectivity, and her ultimate fusion with the Puppet Master, which solidifies a previously unconsidered mode of being: the informational. The film highlights the tensions between humanism and posthumanism via paradoxical representations of embodiment and subjectivity, which are both equally limited within a humanist framework, by pointing the viewer to different modes of being, or more narrowly being-in-the-world (the as is, as it is in the world), through the different types of embodied beings: the human, the cyborg, and the informational.

Meet Motoko

The paradoxical nature in the way Oshii's *Ghost in the Shell* presents embodiment alerts the viewer to the critical nature of the tensions caused by interactions between human and machine and the overarching competing frameworks of humanism and posthumanism. *Ghost in the Shell* depicts a world that can be characterized as posthuman. In the year 2029, Major Motoko Kusanagi is a cyborg working for a secret policing organization known as Section Nine. Motoko's journey through the film highlights many important characteristics of what has been termed posthuman and provides a paradoxical representation of one of the central themes of posthuman thought: embodiment. Embodiment is seen as one of the quintessential questions pertaining to the development of technoscience and is played out in science fiction and cyberpunk movies and literature. Oshii's *Ghost in the Shell* provides a paradoxical view of embodiment through the tensions presented as Motoko struggles for identity in a posthuman world.

On the one hand, the film uses humanist notions of a search for an essential feature that can be labeled as "human." Motoko is a full replacement cyborg in that her mindbody[1] is nearly one hundred percent technological; the only organic components that remain are the brainstem and certain parts of her brain. Can the "body" then be viewed as the grounding for identity (the body as "shell" which houses the "mind"—consciousness, soul, Motoko's "ghost")? What kind of body provides this grounding? Is it only organic or can mechanical or even completely digital "bodies" provide a form of grounding? Or is it the "Ghost" (soul or consciousness), which provides this grounding?

On the other hand, the film develops posthuman tendencies as Motoko struggles with her identity through the titular "ghost" in her bodily "shell." As the film progresses she encounters an entity known as the Puppet Master, who potentially provides the answers she seeks. The film never gives a clear answer, but rather provides a paradoxical representation of embodiment, contrasting humanist notions of a Cartesian split between mind and body and consciousness (the "ghost") as the seat of identity with a posthuman unification of the mindbody via distributed cognition (consciousness as rooted throughout the mindbody - you have as much consciousness in your finger as you do in your brain, and they are distinctly linked together). To pinpoint this paradox, there is a fluidity and flexibility in "embodiment" which can no longer be limited merely to that which is viewed as "natural" or "organic," but rather can be extended into the "artificial" or "technological."

---

[1] This term is used in order to identify the shift between a mind-body split—following Descartes—and mindbody unification.

Multiple bodies, multiple consciousnesses become the norm by the end of the film for Motoko as she evolves via a fusion with the Puppet Master; the posthuman mindbody, as information, as a mode of being, can be "anchored" in everything: material, "immaterial" or both simultaneously.

Informational Bodies and Distributed Cognition

In Robert Mitchell and Phillip Thurtle's edited collection of essays, *Data Made Flesh: Embodying Information*, the contributors are linked by viewing the body as an informational circuit. In their introduction to the collection, the editors seek to depart from what they view as a distinction between the material and the immaterial. Referencing the Human Genome Project, *Star Trek* and *The Matrix*, they conclude that:

> all of these projects and imaginings officially ground themselves on the distinction between immaterial, transcendent information and fleshy, unique bodies. Information, so this story goes, exists between elements, whereas bodies are the elements themselves. . . . Information, in short, operates through the metaphysics of absence, whereas bodies depend on the metaphysics of presence. (p 1)

Yet information is not something which is necessarily "transcendent" in sharp contrast to "fleshy, unique bodies." Information works without the boundaries delineated by Cartesian dualism and a humanist conception. Rather, they are linked together in how the body becomes viewed as a circuit containing and composed of coded information.

The body as circuit, as informational code, links into the notion of distributed cognition. Katherine Hayles ("Flesh and Metal: Reconfiguring the Mindbody in Virtual Environments," *Data Made Flesh: Embodying Information*) argues that the informational mindbody is not limited by a Cartesian split or consciousness being viewed as the "seat of identity." Rather, the informational mindbody forms a unity not only within itself as circuit, but also expands to encompasses the environment, either the material environment of physical existence or the so-called "immaterial" environment of digital space. Mitchell and Thurtle isolate this tension by stating "life in our informational mode of development involves a complicated co-constitution of information and bodies"

(*Data Made Flesh*, p 11). Addressing the key issue of embodiment, the problematic notions that arise out of a strictly humanist split between mind and body and the view of consciousness as the seat of identity are central to the film. Motoko is searching for a "real self," some form of essential core that designates her selfhood. Her "self" cannot be linked to her body because her body is presented as only a "shell," a swappable "thing," owned and maintained by Section Nine.

This co-constitution, however, is not only limited to the relationship between information and bodies, but also via the apparent separation between embodiment and the body. This separation is housed in seemingly distinct notions of the body as an "abstract concept that is always culturally constructed" and embodiment which is also "culturally constructed, but emerges from the physiological structures that have emerged from millennia of biological evolution" (Hayles, "Flesh and Metal", p 229). The abstract "body" as a culturally created, and therefore a limited, normative "body," works in conjunction with a physiological based notion of embodiment. Thus, "body" and "embodiment" can no longer be viewed as mutually exclusive categories, but rather, within a posthuman framework they become mutually inclusive, in which an abstract conception of the "body" has no normative basis, and embodiment is removed from its physiological, i.e., biological/organic, bias. *Ghost in the Shell* works with *both* a humanist split of mind and body and a posthuman unification.

Boundary Beings

A central part of posthuman thought is human-machine hybrids known as cyborgs. Cyborg bodies are inherently informational bodies as they are created via technological means. The cyborg figures presented in *Ghost in the Shell*, most notably the protagonist, Motoko Kusanagi, have to work through a maze of dualisms (see Donna Haraway's "A Cyborg Manifesto"), which are tied into humanist modes of thought. The film paradoxically highlights *both* aspects in which the cyborg becomes a boundary creature highlighting the transition from "human" to "posthuman."

---

[2] A cyborg is a hybrid of "human" (using a minimalist, biological-organic definition) and machine, whereas an android is a wholly technological being. Motoko is a cyborg, but a figure like the Terminator is an android.

There are various types of cyborgs represented in the film, ranging from "humans" with only nominal cybernetic upgrades, to full mindware replacements with an "E-Brain" which allow invisible connections to other E-Brains and direct connections to the film's version of cyberspace, or body modifications that enhance kinesthetic response and musculature. The levels of cybernetic enhancements are based on how much organic material remains in the body; these determine how much a character is considered a cyborg. Motoko's struggle stems from the marker of a "true" self which is initially an organic, "human" demarcation. She is a full-replacement cyborg because the only trace of organic material remaining is her brainstem and parts of her brain. She possesses a cyborg body and an augmented mind. However, the film is not populated solely by cyborgs; even within her unit, Togusa is only nominally connected to cybernetics, having only a neural implant in order to allow connection to the other members of the team and the databases of information. It is for this reason that Motoko specially selected him to be part of the unit. Because he does not possess an E-Brain, the threat of someone hacking into his mind or possessing his body is minimal, relieving a potential threat. Even in a posthuman world of cyborg bodies and extended minds, there is still a need for unaugmented, at least not augmented to the degree that Motoko and others are, humans. Because they are not augmented, they are not susceptible to the same problems that can plague cyborg existence. Rather than there being a hierarchical divide between posthuman cyborgs and traditional humans, they are both equally needed in order for Section Nine to work effectively.

Cyborgs have become commonplace in the world which Motoko inhabits; it appears that the figure of the cyborg marks a transitional stage into posthumanity. While these machines have made distinctions ambiguous, the film brings to the surface this ambiguity by seeking to present a posthuman world full of human-machine interaction. Yet, Motoko questions her identity, her "self" as rooted in her body/mind, inhabiting liminal space within humanism and its post. Hence, the film can be interpreted as presenting cyborgs as transitional figures, serving to demarcate the boundaries between an unambiguous humanist world and an ambiguous posthuman one. This is further expressed when Motoko decides to fuse with the Puppet Master and become an entity which transgresses all boundaries of traditional demarcation. She navigates a maze of dualisms.

The title sequence of the film introduces the genesis of Motoko as her body is assembled. This construction highlights a humanist construction but problematizes it because it "dramatizes the cyborg's concurrently organic and technological assemblage" (Dani Cavallaro, *The Cinema of Mamoru Oshii: Fantasy, Technology and Politics*, p. 197). The cyborg embodies both the organic and the technological via the circuit of information; the organic becomes technologically mediated. Her body is birthed within a technological framework that raises the issue of linking embodiment within a specifically humanist framework, one in which organic components are the markers of a "human" identity. This question of an organic marker of "human" identity guides Motoko as the narrative of her humanist crisis progresses throughout the film. She is an organic-technological hybrid, struggling to find a "root" or "core" to her identity (linked to consciousness, her "ghost") yet has a fascination with the Puppet Master as a being which has potential to liberate her from a humanist crisis.

Motoko in Crisis

The film's core lies within Motoko's identity crisis as she struggles with two main forms of embodiment. The first form of embodiment, a persistent struggle until the end of the film, is the division between a body and mind in which the body is viewed as a container for the mind. The mind is linked to the "ghost." Although the "ghost" is not defined, it is linked with the notion of "soul," however ambiguous as that idea is. Regardless, possessing a "ghost," as something that is differentiated from the body, becomes the marker of identity.

> **MOTOKO:** Maybe all full-replacement cyborgs like me start wondering this. That perhaps the real me died a long time ago and I'm a replicant made with a cyborg body and a computer brain. Or maybe there never was a real "me" to begin with.

> **BATOU:** You've got real brain matter in that titanium skull of yours. And you get treated like a real person, don't you?

The second form of embodiment is represented through the fusion of Motoko to the Puppet Master at the end of the film. Motoko's "consciousness" is merged with the Puppet Master to form a new entity of distributed cognition, enabling multiple consciousnesses and multiple bodies to simultaneously emerge, and access to Being (the abstract as is) expands from the purely "human" (or what Heidegger calls Dasein) and into the technological and informational. While this is only implied at the end of the film with the closing statement, "The net is vast," in Oshii's sequel, *Ghost in the Shell 2: Innocence*, Motoko's return heralds this simultaneity, exploring this concept more fully.

However, the cyborg bodies of Batou and Motoko both need regular maintenance. At first, this might strike the viewer as odd, as there may be a preconceived notion that a technological body should not need "human" intervention in the form of regular maintenance, yet it does. By linking their cyborg bodies to an idea of regular maintenance, it affirms that there is not an essential difference between "human" and machine. Both need regular maintenance. While a "human" will go the doctor when the body breaks down, a cyborg will go to a technodoctor when its body is in need of repair. However, the problem with this linkage is that it works within a humanist notion of the body as dysfunctional, the body as weak, the body as "meat," essentially distinct from the mind. The body becomes a "thing" in need of "repair" as opposed to a more holistic orientation of a posthuman mindbody unification.

Since the body is viewed as merely a shell for the mind, identity is then located within the brain. Yet Motoko's brain is in fact a cybernetically enhanced E-Brain, so how can she locate a fixed identity within a humanist framework? The simple answer is that she cannot. The location of the "real you," according to Batou, is found within the human brains cells which exist within Motoko's vastly expanded mind. Therefore a "real" identity, a humanist self, is not found in a unification of body, mind and environment, but is the privileged condition of the mind, so the body becomes nothing, simply a shell. While this establishes that there is a broken link between mind and body, Motoko's crisis deepens as she calls into question the existence of her "ghost."

Did she even have a "ghost" to begin with? Can she even remember a strictly organic existence? "Ghosts" can be hacked and individuals are taken over by the Puppet Master repeatedly throughout the film. In one sequence near the beginning of the film, an interpreter has had her e-brain hacked and Section Nine attempts to trace the source. They realize that she is being hacked through phone lines on a garbage route, and Togusa and Motoko investigate. The person that they find also turns out to be a hacked individual. However, while the garbage man is only nominally cybernetically enhanced, the real target of Section Nine is a cyborg. Batou lucidly sums up these hacked individuals: "There's nothing sadder than a puppet without a ghost, especially the kind with red blood running through them."

Batou in a sense represents humanism. As he attempts to sort out Motoko's crisis by edging her towards the humanist fold an entity appears, which can easily hack into these individuals' e-brains, or even hack someone's "ghost." This causes a profound crisis for Motoko, but leaves Batou relatively untouched, even though he is susceptible to the same issues which plague her. Batou is sure of his identity, while Motoko is not. Once Section Nine establishes that there is an entity, simply dubbed the Puppet Master, conducting the hacks, Motoko withdraws into her crisis of identity and throws herself into the search for it. In a posthuman world the "conscious mind can be hijacked, cut off by mutinous cells, absorbed into an artificial consciousness, or back-propagated through flawed memory" (Hayles, *How we Became Posthuman*, p 279).

After the encounter with the puppets of the Puppet Master, Motoko and Batou have a lengthy conversation on her boat. This dialogue emphasizes the transitional phase with which Motoko is struggling:

> **MOTOKO:** We do have the right to resign [from Section Nine] if we choose, provided we give the government back our cyborg shells and the memories they hold. Just as there are many parts needed to make a human a human, there's a remarkable number of things needed to make an individual what they are. A face to distinguish yourself from others. A voice you aren't aware of yourself. The hand you see when you awaken. The memories of childhood, the feelings for the future. That's not all, there's the expanse of the data net my cyber-brain can access. All of that goes into making me what I am. Giving rise to the consciousness that I call "me." And simultaneously confining "me" within set limits.

Embedded in this statement is a link to the posthuman. Motoko has realized that there are multiple components which go into creating a "self" or "consciousness." The body becomes a circuit embodying the physiological, technological, and informational. The seat of posthuman subjectivity is distributed throughout body, mind, and environment. Yet, paradoxically there is still a "consciousness" which defines her as a "me," an "I." Even with this expansive notion of identity and self there is a seed of doubt in the limitation imposed. The circuit is not complete. Her questioning of the limitations of her-self works towards something posthuman; her statements here serve as transitional ones. It is not until her ultimate encounter with the Puppet Master in a female torso that she is able to move beyond these limitations. "We can no longer simply assume that consciousness guarantees the existence of the self. In this sense, the posthuman subject is also a postconscious subject" (Hayles, *How we Became Posthuman,* p. 280).

Transcendence or Expansion

The Puppet Master questions humanist notions of subjectivity and embodiment.

> MAJOR MOTOKO KUSANAGI: You talk about redefining my identity. I want a guarantee that I can still be myself.
>
> PUPPET MASTER: There isn't one. Why would you wish to? All things change in a dynamic environment. Your effort to remain what you are is what limits you.

The Puppet Master is an entity born in a "sea of information" and does not possess a "body" as it would be strictly defined within humanist discourse: an organic biological "human" body. Rather, the "body" of the Puppet Master is the netting that it is enmeshed within: a data body of pure information. However, the face-to-face encounter, which happens between the Puppet Master and the Major, occurs after the Puppet Master has put him/her/itself into a shell. The boundary is broken because the Puppet crosses the threshold from "immaterial" information into a "material" physical body. The reactions of the various people who are present in the interrogation of the Puppet Master are rather telling. Some express disbelief at the Puppet Master's request for political asylum; it does not really "exist" according to principles inherited from humanism. The Puppet Master is attempting to move away from the initial status as "Project 2501" of Section Six, having gained sentience and able to roam the nets relatively unhindered. As the Puppet Master states, "I am not an AI. . . . I am a living, thinking entity that was created in the sea of information." Much like the titular *Neuromancer* of William Gibson's novel, the Puppet Master is attempting to break the bonds that limit its interaction with the world. The Puppet Master does not want to be limited, as even a "single virus could destroy it." However, the Puppet Master is limited, much as Motoko is, perhaps even more so, within the confines of the net and humanism. There are still boundaries, which it cannot cross. The Puppet Master explicitly seeks out Section Nine because of its affinity for Motoko and their mutual struggle with the limitations imposed upon them.

While the Puppet Master is an entity that can be seen as distinctly posthuman, it paradoxically works within a framework in which it yearns to be biological. In Motoko and the Puppet Master's final encounter, the Puppet Master discusses that although it is able to roam the vast nets, it cannot pass its "genes" like biological animals and since "a copy is just a copy," there is no genetic variance. This is the root of why it desires to merge with Motoko and become a new entity. The Puppet Master seeks to transcend the boundaries imposed on its subjectivity, yet does so within a humanist framework: the Puppet Master seeks to become biological. Motoko, on the other hand, has struggled through her humanist crisis and is already a posthuman subject. She wishes to push this further by having "subjectivity" become "subjectivities."

Yet, paradoxically, the transformation of the two is filled with angelic imagery of transcendence, a specifically Christian notion of transcendence. The Puppet Master even states, "It is time to move to a higher plane." This is an example of the problem associated with the idea of transcendence in the various forms of posthumanism. Transcendence continues to be presented as a sharp divide between body and mind, in which the mind becomes disembodied and perfected. The film falls prey to this leaning in its use of angelic imagery despite the posthuman orientation of the film, which is less about transcending the body and more about unifying and expanding the circuit of the mind-body. This is echoed in the final scene, in which despite moving "to a higher plane," the new entity created has not only a physical body, the body of a little girl, but is also connected to the net in a databody enacting an entirely new form of being, no longer limited to a purely organic physiology. Being-in-the-world becomes expanded. The film closes with the new entity stating, "The net is vast, and limitless."

The Transforming Body

While *Ghost in the Shell* does decenter the privileging of the human body as the site of the self, it does so with much difficulty due to its paradoxical presentation of embodiment and subjectivity which simultaneously affirms and denies both humanist and posthumanist conceptions. Two clear forms of embodiment and subjectivity are represented: one showing a clear distinction between body and mind with the "self" being limited to only "humans," the other presenting a unification between the two via a circuit and an expansion to posthumans. The cyborg body, and by extension embodiment, is an informational circuit of distributed cognition which extends subjectivity or "consciousness" purely from the domain of the mindbrain and into the body, the mind, and the environment (being-in-the-world). Its forms may include the physiological, technological, purely informational, or all three. The film is about the difficulty of the *transition*, clearly portrayed by Motoko.

She struggles with her humanist crisis, finding difficulty locating a "self" within her "ghost" (mind, consciousness, soul). Yet she also finds difficulty locating her "self" within a unified arrangement of mind, body, and environmental referents for identity. While this forms a posthuman understanding via Hayles notion of distributed cognition, it does not go far enough for Motoko. Motoko is only satisfied after merging with the Puppet Master and becoming an entirely new entity, one which expands to allow for multiple subjectivities. As the newly merged entity, now in the body of a little girl, states in the final sequence, "Here before you is neither the program known as the Puppet Master nor the woman that was called The Major." The paradoxical representations of embodiment thus reframe the philosophical question of Being in new and unexpected ways.

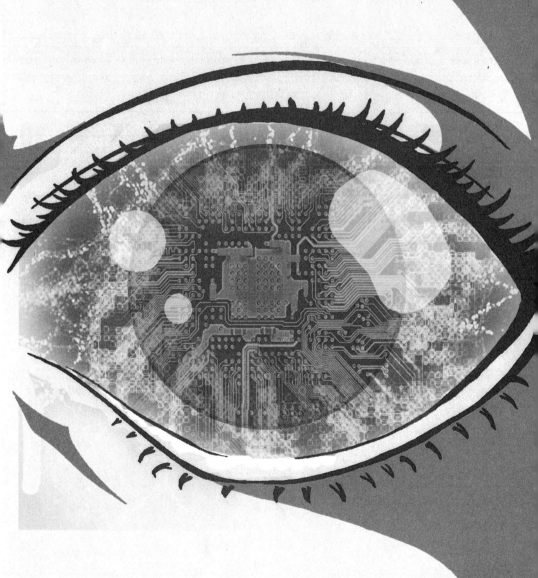

4

I Am Tetsuo

BENJAMIN STEVENS

At the very end of Katsuhiro Otomo's *Akira*, a perfectly white screen is shot through with grey concentric circles—an after-image recalling Akira's power—before resolving into the red-hued negative image of an eye, over which we hear a voice intone: "I am Tetsuo."

At first, this may not seem confusing. After all, we've just watched two hours of mind-bending anime featuring a character named Tetsuo. "I" must be that "Tetsuo" indeed, the young man whose unwitting journey into a world of closely guarded military secrets and incredible psychic powers is the movie's main drama. And the voice certainly sounds like Tetsuo's. But coming as it does at the end of a movie full of mysteries, not to mention mysterious powers including possession, ventriloquism, and voices in your head, can we take that voice at, er, face value?

Assuming we're not totally confused, at least we're right to wonder what to make of this voice proclaiming, "I am Tetsuo." The last time we saw Tetsuo, his powers had just rampaged out of control, causing a horrible expansion and distortion of his body. That gruesome transformation ended only when he was absorbed into the expanding white sphere of Akira's apocalyptic power.

In light of that climax, I think we're right to wonder—at least, I ("I"?) wonder!—three things:

1. ***Who* says "I am Tetsuo"? (who is "I"?);**

2. ***How* does he (or it?) know, or *why* does he think he knows?; and**

3. ***What* is the thing that does the thinking?**

Sure, these questions can be asked about other characters in the film, most of whom are already complicated (neo-Tokyo is no easy place to live!) and many of whom go through—or have gone through—changes, including a few as profound as Tetsuo's. They can also be asked about *us*.

Put broadly, the questions link *identity* to thinking (*cognition*) and to a thinking subject's awareness of its thinking and being (*consciousness*). Identity is thus something like a thinking subject's awareness of its own thinking and being, with emphasis on continuity. We can then ask how thinking is related to physical being: the problem of embodiment or, as it's often called, the *mind-body problem*.

As we try to understand what the film's final scene means for its thinking beings, we thus get to wonder what it might mean for *us* as embodied thinking beings, or as "rational animals," a phrase from the fourth-century B.C.E. Greek philosopher Aristotle, who used it in his *Metaphysics* to define "human beings." Raising questions about Tetsuo's identity, cognition, and consciousness, and about how they relate to his physical being, brings us to another important question that is easy to ask but much harder to answer:

4. Is Tetsuo a Human Being? And what is a "Human Being" anyway?

I think he is . . . in a way. And I think a human being is someone—maybe also something? —somehow like us. But the "somehow" matters: how is Tetsuo, or for that matter any fictional character, sufficiently like us to be, like us, a human being?

By defining "human being" to include someone or something like Tetsuo, we may be redefining ourselves: as *posthuman beings*.

Who Is "I"?

Is the voice that says "I am Tetsuo" really Tetsuo? It sounds like Tetsuo, but we're also made to wonder what's happened to him in his gruesome transformation and his absorption by Akira. Other characters wonder even earlier: on encountering Tetsuo in their favorite dive bar, his friend Yamagata asks, "Are you Tetsuo? Or somebody else?" So when "I" speaks, is it the same "I" or "Tetsuo" as before?

Who thus asks about sameness or identity. "Identity" comes from the Latin *idem*, "the same," related to *identidem*, "again and again" or "continuously," as if we are the same over time. To explore such continuity, consider two thought-experiments from ancient Greece, "Heraclitus's River" and the "Ship of Theseus."

In the sixth century B.C.E., Heraclitus (as transmitted by the fourth-century B.C.E. Plato in his *Cratylus* and by the third- and fourth-century C.E. Eusebius in his *Praeparatio Evangelica*) raises the question of identity or continuity by asking: Can we step in the same river twice? He argued that we can't: since a river is always flowing, by the time of our second step, there's a whole new river! If a river seems a long way off from the continuous identity of thinking or human beings, consider something more obviously bodily:

> Imagine a ship built of wooden planks (as first- and second-century C.E. Greco-Roman writer Plutarch did in his *Life of Theseus*). Now imagine that the planks are replaced, one at a time, until all have been replaced. There is still a ship – it might even still belong to Theseus, the mythical Athenian hero –, but with 100% plank replacement (replankment?), is it "the same" ship?

If we accept the implication of these examples, we might conclude that "I" is not the same Tetsuo, at least not the same as before, because of the substantial changes he's undergone.

But we could reach a similar conclusion about most, maybe all, of *Akira*'s characters, most of whom are shown undergoing some change over the course of the story. It wouldn't be a very dramatic story if they didn't, and it's a very dramatic story indeed, ending in nothing less than the apparent second destruction of neo-Tokyo! If everyone is changed, is it meaningful to single out Tetsuo as especially changed? If everyone is always changing—including us: we are affected by experience, and every cell in our bodies is periodically replaced—then it would seem that a thinking being can undergo even complete change and still be the same being.

Maybe it's not the degree of change (its quantity), but the kind (or quality) of change that matters. For our purposes, there are two kinds of changes to consider, divided roughly into "mental" and "bodily" . . . although the connection between the two is just as interesting as their separation. Both are made even more complicated by *Akira*'s interest in psychic powers that bridge the gap, the mind directly affecting other bodies in the world.

How Does "I" Know? Or Why Does "I" Think So?

How does the voice, or the speaking person whose voice it is, know that it is Tetsuo, or at least *why* does it think so? In addition to being a question of *epistemology* generally (the philosophical study of knowledge, from the ancient Greek *episteme* and *logos*: how do we know what we know?), this is specifically a question of *cognition*: what are the thoughts or thought-processes that led to the voice's declaration of identity? This includes asking, first, "Why does 'I' think that he is Tetsuo," or in other words, "What are his or her reasons or arguments?" This initial set of questions is about general patterns of thought, about connections logical or illogical.

A second set of questions comes from the specific fact that it's not any old "someone" who thinks that he is Tetsuo, but an "I" who thinks it about himself. That reflexivity is a link between cognition and *consciousness*: thought's awareness of thought, or the thinking being's awareness of itself as a thinking being. If we define consciousness as reflexivity in thinking, then the voice that says "I am Tetsuo" has clear consciousness so long as his speech accurately represents his thought.

In other words, we think we know that the speaker of "I am Tetsuo" is conscious because he uses a language, because language can represent thought, and because this use of language in particular, by being reflexive, represents its representation of thought. That kind of recursion—the repeated application of a function to the results of same function—has been taken as a hallmark of consciousness, at least as it's expressed in language.

But *how* do we, who seem to be thinking beings, know that the voice belongs to a thinking being of sufficient similarity to us to be a human being? *Why* do we think so?

We're close here to one of the most famous phrases from Western philosophy: the seventeenth-century French philosopher René Descartes's "I think, therefore I am": in the popular Latin, *cogito ergo sum*; in the original French "Je pense, donc je suis." *Cogito ergo sum* is a summary of Descartes's attempt to ground his philosophy in the only thing he thought he could be certain of: his awareness of his thinking. In the terms I've been using, and with just a bit of philosophical jargon, we can say that Descartes predicates his identity, even his existence, on his consciousness and therefore on his cognition.

Does Descartes's formula tell us anything about someone or something like Tetsuo, a seemingly disembodied voice from the transcendent void?

Another thought-experiment may help to clarify some of the philosophical complications involved, "The Turing Test." This particular experiment highlights areas of interest held in common by philosophy since basically forever and by cognitive science since roughly the middle of the 20th century: what is thought, who or what does the thinking, and is there a difference between cognition and computation?

In 1950 the computer scientist Alan Turing proposed an "imitation game." Imagine yourself at a computer, IMing with two strangers, one of which is human, the other of which is a computer. If you can't tell the difference between them, then, Turing argued, computation is functionally indistinguishable from—is the same as—cognition. In other words, such an "artificial" constructed intelligence would be the same as "natural" human intelligence. From this perspective, a machine that seems to be thinking actually is thinking!

Add this idea to Aristotle's definition of human beings as "rational animals," and to Descartes's only certainty ("I think, therefore I am"), and we would have to conclude, with Turing, that a seemingly-thinking machine is a human being. But our test for Tetsuo needn't be so stringent. We don't need to imagine the voice behind "I am Tetsuo" as belonging to a machine—and would of course be wrong to do so, based on what the movie shows us—to treat it the same way. It sounds like a human being so it is a human being.

But if we identify successful language use—or, more precisely, the appearance or semblance of such use—as the key to "human being," aren't we missing something essential about "human beings"? About ourselves? To better decide whether appearance or semblance is sufficient, we need to think a bit more about thinking—*cognition*—and how it relates to *computation*.

Cogito Ergo Tetsuo?

Because of questions like these, the Turing Test has inspired generations of researchers to work in the field of artificial intelligence as well as legions of science fiction writers to create characters like the cyborg Major Motoko Kusanagi of *Ghost in the Shell* or the computerized Dixie Flatline and Wintermute in William Gibson's *Neuromancer*. But does it get us any closer to defining "human being?" However convincing the computer may be—and it's worth pointing out that in official contests, no computer has ever convinced a majority of the judges (although some humans have come across as computers!)—there can be the lingering feeling that, even if the computer puts on a good performance, it's still not *really* thinking, is it?

In other words, we might feel that because a sophisticated artificial or constructed intelligence only *seems* to be natural intelligence and gives only the *appearance* of "thinking," such a semblance or appearance isn't the same as actual human existence: seeming to think isn't a sufficient definition for "human being." After all, Descartes's formula isn't "I *seem* to think, therefore I am!" Computation isn't really (or sufficient for) cognition in the sense of human understanding, much less for the somehow qualitatively distinct self-awareness or reflexive thinking we call consciousness.

This position, that the successful application of rules by a machine isn't meaningful, has been given a handy shorthand in linguistic terms: "syntax isn't sufficient for semantics." This quotation comes from the philosopher John Searle, who illustrates it with his famous Chinese Room Argument.

The Chinese Room can be thought of as the Turing Test from the inside out. Imagine a windowless room with a slot in its single door. In the room are paper and pens, a rulebook that shows how to respond to certain strings of Chinese characters using certain other strings of Chinese characters, and a person who doesn't know Chinese. Outside of the room is a Chinese speaker, who slips through the slot in the door pieces of paper with Chinese characters and sentences on them. The person in the room—Searle, in his own example!—looks up the characters and sentences in the rulebook, copies the responses given by the rulebook, and slips those responses back through the slot. The Chinese speaker outside of the room reads the responses and has no reason to doubt that someone in the room knows Chinese. But we know better (weirder?): no one in the room knows Chinese; it just *seems* like someone does.

We might then have the same feeling as before: semblance or appearance isn't enough for reality, the syntax isn't sufficient for true semantics, the mechanical application of a rulebook's rules isn't really speech (much less consciousness), and computation isn't cognition.

On the other hand, we could read the results of this thought-experiment in reverse, as showing *not* that computation isn't sufficient for cognition *but* that we need to redefine cognition, and equally consciousness, in terms of computation . . . and, more radically and maybe a little weirdly, as taking place through a combination of individual and environment. Maybe the 'mind' that knows Chinese is only and precisely a combination of Searle, room, and rulebook all together! Cognitive scientist and anthropologist Edwin Hutchins advanced this interpretation as an analogy for ship's navigators, who "know" where their ship is not as individuals but only in concert with each other and with the ship's instrumentation (*Cognition in the Wild*).

From this changed perspective, although the voice that says "I am Tetsuo" is only a voice, we're licensed to treat it as if there's a speaker behind it, since that's how we're used to treating speech. Because of that habit, and in line with Descartes's *cogito ergo sum*, we assume that someone called Tetsuo exists because he—a mind, spirit, soul—thinks of himself (is conscious) as thinking something behind the statement. So we could read "I am Tetsuo" like Descartes's famous phrase, as a way of predicating existence on consciousness of cognition: "I think, therefore I am Tetsuo" (*cogito ergo Tetsuo!*). Of course, this would mean accepting a semblance or appearance of consciousness as evidence of consciousness: updating Descartes to be, precisely, "I *seem* to think, therefore I am (a human being)."

But should Descartes's formula, even passed by Turing and updated by Hutchins, be applied to someone—or something—that isn't already recognizably a thinking being? Tetsuo may not qualify. His body has been, first, horribly transformed and, second, apparently absorbed into the timeless, bodiless inner space of Akira's power! Can he have (or be?) a mind without a normal body, or any body? And more: can he have evidently more mind than the rest of us – his immaterial thoughts affect material reality directly!—without a body? If, as Morpheus puts it in *The Matrix*, "the body cannot live without the mind," how do we feel about minds without bodies? More generally, what is the relationship between "mind" and "body," and, as that question implies, are they really two separable things?

What Is the Thing that Does the Thinking?

Descartes argued that his existence is predicated on his consciousness of cognition—his "mind"—alone, and not on its existence in his body. After him, *Cartesian dualism* argues that immaterial "mind" and material "body" are distinct (even if they're not usually separated!).

This is among the oldest, most important, and most disputed ideas in Western philosophy, treated by, among others:

- the fourth-century B.C.E. Greek philosopher Plato, whose dialogue *Phaedo* has his master Socrates arguing, just before his execution, that the soul is immortal, such that a philosopher ought not to fear death;

- the first-century B.C.E. Roman poet Lucretius, whose epic *On the Nature of Things* argues that the soul, like everything else in the world, is entirely material and thus mortal . . . with a similar recommendation for philosophical fearlessness; and

- early and medieval Christian thinkers like Augustine of Hippo and Thomas of Aquinas, both arguing, although for different reasons than Plato, that the soul is immortal, with the important caveat that only in combination with a body does it make a "person."

It continues to be a hot topic after Descartes, as authors reject or refine his dualism:

- via philosophy of mind, patching holes in the Cartesian fabric: for example, Immanuel Kant, who tried to achieve Descartes's conscious certainty without reference to an external ground (for Descartes this external ground had been God)

- via cognitive scientific research, science of brain, starting over with different material: for example Steven Pinker, who writes that he is as certain of the fact of his consciousness as he is of anything in the world (*How the Mind Works*) and Daniel Dennett, on whom just a bit more below.

If mind and body are distinct, how do they interact?

There are two rough types of answer. The first is *embodiment*. Either a mind needs a body generally, or needs the human body in particular, and there is a limit to the quantity or quality of change allowed to brain or body before the "mind" no longer exists to define "human being" (a consciously or recursively thinking being, a "rational animal"). If no changes are allowed—if there is *total* embodiment—then the mind is the body, or an inseparable part of the body, or depends on it for its existence. From this first perspective, Tetsuo is a human being only if he still has a brain in a body whose voice is the one that says, "I am Tetsuo."

This is close to the perspective of cognitive science, explained well by Steven Pinker's *How the Mind Works*. Briefly, the argument is that it's the brain that makes "mind," such that embodiment is more or less clearly (if complexly!) the answer. From a similar perspective, Daniel Dennett argues that "identity" or "self" is not a thing but a story that consciousness tells itself, a "center of narrative gravity." Fuller discussion on these lines would take us away from philosophy to the roots of cognitive science in information theory and cybernetics; see N. Katherine Hayles's *How We Became Posthuman*.

The second, opposite category is *disembodiment*. Either a mind doesn't need a body, or doesn't need a human body in particular. Even with substantial changes to brain or body—perhaps including *no* body at all—the "mind" is still sufficient to define "human being." If all changes are allowed—if there is *total* disembodiment—then the mind is less a material thing than an immaterial pattern potentially separable from the human body and, so, potentially transferable to other bodies.

This potential could take the form of the information-age image of "mind uploading"—the mind as the ghost in the shell, feared by Hans Moravec (*Robot: Mere Machine to Transcendent Mind*) and hoped for by Judith Halberstam and Ira Livingston (*Posthuman Bodies*, after Donna Haraway's "A Cyborg Manifesto")—or of bodilessness, as in the Aquarian age ideas of clairvoyance, psychic travel, or astral projection (as when Kei is possessed). From this second perspective, Tetsuo is easily a human being . . . although we may wonder whether we've defined "human being" too broadly.

So which is it? Immaterial mind and material body, separate but interacting? (And dualists would need to explain the interaction.) Or a material mind-body? (With the question asked previously: How much and what sorts of bodily change do we allow before a "mind" no longer defines "human being?")

So, Is Tetsuo Human? Are We? Is Anyone or Anything?

Tetsuo was certainly human at one point, while at the end of the movie . . . well, maybe. With careful attention to, and some slight redefinitions of, critical terms (especially identity, cognition, consciousness), we've reached a point where Descartes's *cogito ergo sum* seems to allow for *cogito ergo Tetsuo*, precisely "I am Tetsuo," even if that statement and our sense of a thinking being behind it must be modulated by other thought-experiments. At the same time, we're left wondering about how much "human being" depends on embodiment.

In this connection, a final thought-experiment to consider is Katsuhiro Otomo's own: Akira, the ghost who haunts the anime (and the manga before it) and its shell of a decimated city.

In the anime Akira says nothing audible, does nothing visible, and generally barely exists. At first he's a mystery, then he appears in memories, and when he finally enters fully into the story . . . well, instead of a body, Akira has—is?—only bits of biopsy material stored in jars, cryogenically frozen and buried beneath an Olympics construction site. At the most, his giant cryogenic pod looks a bit like a brain. Even so, though, he is able to interact with bodily things: he destroys the city (twice, it seems!). Tetsuo may have undergone grotesque transformation, but he still has a body. By contrast, Akira has no body because he's undergone dissection, and to enter at all into the picture he requires a sort of reconstitution by the combined powers of the other psychic children.

But still there's a connection. Tetsuo's body starts to change when his mental power is at its uncontrollable strongest (he cries out in fear: "My body's not doing what I tell it to!"). Akira's body barely exists as frozen pieces, and still he levels the city (uncontrollably? even unconsciously?). Add to this the three other psychic children featured in the film, all of whom are rightly child-sized but prematurely aged (evidently as a side effect of the psychotropic drugs that keep their powers under control). All five children have supernatural powers, and all five have—whether temporarily or permanently, and with diverse surface manifestations—unnatural or denaturalized bodies: they are mutated, prematurely aged, operated on, dissected. Is superhuman psychic power—the direct effect of immaterial mind on material bodies—related to changes in the human body? Does *Akira* thus argue that disembodiments are linked to, or lead to, what the Colonel calls—in reference to Akira—"transcendental awakening?"

The Posthuman Condition via the Problem of Representation

Whatever the answer, by simply raising the question, *Akira* points us to what writers like Haraway, Moravec, Halberstam, and Hayles have called the "posthuman condition." This idea redefines "human being" according to the more radical implications of the perspectives and experiments we've discussed: a decentering of identity or the self (the same river never!), a fragmentation of the thinking subject or its consciousness (where "mind" is not a thing but a story, a "center of narrative gravity!"), and taking seriously the possibility that "mind" is affected by embodiment but not entirely determined by it.

To get at this, let's step back from characters like Tetsuo and Akira to consider *Akira*, the anime, for what it is: a fiction or, maybe more precisely, a *representation*.

We've already complicated Descartes's formula, "I think therefore I am," by pointing out that it and formulas like it are really preceded by an unvoiced "I seem to myself," or, shorter but similar, "I think that . . .," such as "(I think that) I think therefore I am" or "(I think that) I am Tetsuo." In a similar way, any spoken utterance is introduced by an unvoiced voice. So "I think therefore I am" is really something like "*Descartes writes that* he thinks therefore he is," and "I am Tetsuo" is really "*A voice says that* it thinks that it is Tetsuo."

This can get even stranger and go on forever (thanks to the property of language we've called recursion). We'll do just one more. If you've seen *Akira*, then the next step is for you to say, "*I know that Akira* says that a voice says that it thinks that it is Tetsuo." If you haven't seen the film and therefore have to trust what I say, your next step is, "*The author of that chapter says that Akira* says that . . ."

These highest levels of language are examples highlighting what I mean by *representation*. We don't have direct access to Descartes's or Tetsuo's thinking or even their speech, as if they were present before us. Instead, their thinking or speech is re-presented: in Descartes's case by written language; in Tetsuo's case by audio recording.

So what does all this complication in representation have to do with whether *Akira* teaches us something about disembodiment and the posthuman condition? In a nutshell, it gives us a more precise way of wondering what sorts of representation, appearance, or semblance we should accept as standing in for presence or reality; whether "human beings" are ever more than merely represented to us or are ever actually present before us. In other words, are we human beings ever actually present, or always only re-presented?

Let's go back a couple of thought-experiments. Searle's Chinese Room may have merely seemed like a mind, but an animated movie like *Akira* doesn't even seem like Searle's Chinese Room. A movie will never pass the Turing Test, unless we trivialize the test by asking only one question—"What have you got to say for yourself?"—only once, just before the opening credits, and then listen patiently to a two-hour "answer." So we would be wrong to think of a movie as having a mind, even as we find ourselves responding to it as if it were real. We can wonder something similar about Tetsuo, Akira, and the other characters, since without exception they're fictional, only representations of human beings.

But this seems a lot like—in a rough order from "most real" to "least real"—videoconferencing, IMing, watching a live telecast, watching a live-action but recorded movie, listening to recorded music, looking at photographs or other images, or reading about characters in a book. In each case we think of ourselves as responding to or even interacting with people, and we're usually not bothered by the discrepancy between representation and presence. Often we don't even notice it . . . unless we've made it our professional philosophical business or have been reading a chapter by someone who has (*coughs*).

We know that representations aren't—or don't have—minds of their own, but we respond to them as if they did because we know (or think?) that there are human beings represented by them. But we treat fictional characters similarly. We know they're not people, we know they don't really have minds, in part because they don't have human bodies. We might catch ourselves feeling for them; a famous example of this in philosophy is from Augustine, who in his *Confessions* reprimands himself for shedding tears at the represented death of a fictional character called Dido in the Roman poet Virgil's epic *Aeneid*.

Maybe we should agree with Augustine: even if fictional characters bring us to tears, we recognize that they're not people because, in his terms, they don't have souls or, in our terms, minds. Right? Because, first of all and despite Descartes's insistence on the mind as proving existence, they don't have human bodies . . . and have never had them?

Is Everybody Disembodied? (or, Have We Always Been Posthuman Beings?)

On the other hand, since we're questioning everything in order to figure out how cognition gets human beings, and as a result whether Tetsuo is a human being, we might note that no one seems to wonder whether a voice at a distance (telephony, video-conferencing, IM) is "human."

Instead, we seem to assume that aspects of human being are perfectly abstractable from embodiment, or at least able to be reproduced or represented at a distance. The cases I've mentioned are mostly distance in space (and we could add something theoretical, matter teleportation, a power Tetsuo displays), but others involve distance in time, like books written long ago ... or even this book: I assume you've assumed that "I" am (is?) human, just as I've assumed it of you (which takes us back to our first question!).

In other words, we routinely think of representations as coming from people even though their bodies aren't present or, in some cases, any longer in existence. We normally treat a represented human being as just as human as a present human being . . . and we should, because we expect representations of ourselves to be treated the same way by other people. Granted, this may get us too close for Augustine's comfort to being unable to distinguish compelling fictional characters or stories from real people and stories that deserve our attention.

But it also lets us pose a more precise—or at least more particular—version of the simple but impossible fourth question from earlier: is Tetsuo a "human being," and what is a "human being" anyway? Think of it as Question 5 (and think about it!):

5. Have we always been posthuman beings?

We normally and unproblematically respond to decentered identity and fragmented consciousness as continuous and coherent: the river may flow but we know it's "the same;" the ship is replanked but it, too, is "the same."

We regularly respond to the semblance of thinking as evidence of actual thinking, of thinking beings, of minds, of human beings.

We let many things pass the Turing Test, and—unless we're cognitive scientists—don't usually wonder what goes on in Searle's Chinese Room.

We normally treat representations as re-presentations: as pointing to an original presence. And we expect representations of ourselves to be treated in the same way. Despite our own decentered, fragmented, and re-presented disembodiments, we expect other thinking beings to treat us as fellow thinking beings, even though it seems that only an "I" can know its consciousness for sure.

As a result of all this, instead of wondering whether Tetsuo is sufficiently like us to be a "human being," we may find ourselves wondering instead whether we are—and always have been—decentered, fragmented, discontinous, and re-presented posthuman beings, not so different from Akira and Tetsuo afterall.[1]

•

---

[1] I have several people—I think they're people!—to thank for helping with this chapter: Joel Wright (Bard College '06) for drawing my attention to Open Court's Popular Culture and Philosophy series; Robyn Bianconi (Bard '07) for drawing Joel's attention to me; and especially Leah Faye Norris (Bard '11), who gave an early draft of this chapter her full mental attention even though she was embodied on spring break.

5
The CPU Has Its Reasons

JOHN HARTUNG

Driving to the secret lab where she was assembled, Armitage asks Ross, "Why are you helping me?" Angry at her impetuousness in asking this over and over again, Ross barks, "Stop that! You sound like a little child! Why? Why? *There is no reason.*"

Imagine former police detective Ross Syllabus's situation. He came from Earth to get away from the memories of his former partner Jennifer who was killed by an android. He transferred to the Mars Police Department with a strong prejudice against robots, especially ones meant to simulate humans. On Mars, a series of such models, called the Seconds (as in Android 2.0), have assumed many jobs in the service sector of the Martian economy. This prevented many ordinary humans from finding employment and created social unrest. However, a new advanced series has been uncovered. These Third models closely resemble human beings. They seem to be self-directed in their behavior, work in creative professions, and have gone unnoticed by others, even those who have formed close relations with them. But their existence has been made known because several of them have been victims of a "killing" spree conducted by a self-appointed android "assassin" who is trying to make Mars aware of these cryptic robots.

To top it off, Ross has discovered that his partner and close friend, detective Naomi Armitage, is one of these Thirds. Before he can decide exactly what she is—I mean, she is clearly not human, as a biological category, but perhaps she is still a *person* in the same sense as Ross, a rational and free agent who is entitled to basic rights—the police department discovers that Armitage is a Third and sees her as a piece of runaway illegal technology to be rounded up and destroyed. Ross has decided to throw away his career and help Armitage protect herself from the assassins and the police, and find her "father." Accused of terrorism against the Martian government, Ross teams up with Armitage and goes on the run to her father's lab.

It's not surprising that Armitage asks Ross the question, since she herself is troubled by the idea that she is "only a monstrous doll." By adding this little domestic scene in the midst of heavy artillery mayhem and hot pants *moe*, the screenwriters have provided a means for the audience to stop and reflect on the central question raised in Hiroyuki Ochi's *Armitage the Third: Poly-Matrix*, namely whether robots can have moral standing, and for me the more interesting related question of whether Ross (and we) can be justified in thinking that a robot does have moral standing.

Consider why the question, "Why are you helping me?" makes Ross so upset. I suspect that he mistakes what the question is asking. He thinks that Armitage wants a reason in the sense of evidence, as if she had asked why Ross is convinced that Armitage is a person and not just a machine. Ross has just made enormous sacrifices based on the proposition that Armitage is a person of moral standing, even though a robot. But no evidence is available that proves this important claim and this lack has upset Ross, inclining him to act out. Ross has been confronting this difficulty since the briefing he received on the termination of the first Third, Kelly McCannon, the last country singer in the solar system, who arrived on Mars on the same shuttle with him. Ross at the time reported that he could not tell her from a human being.

However, Armitage did not necessarily ask for evidence for Ross's belief in her personhood. Rather it is a request for a reason for why Ross made a decision, a practical matter rather than a theoretical matter. In theoretical reasoning, we try to argue for the truth of some hypothesis. In practical reasoning, we try to deliberate about which purposes to pursue and the best course of action to obtain them. Instead of evidence for believing that she is worth helping, Armitage could be asking for a reason why Ross *chose* to help her as someone worth helping. This assumes that Ross had the option to believe or not believe and act accordingly. This distinction between evidence and prudence suggests the possibility that even if someone does not have sufficient evidence for believing something is true, it does not follow that the person has no sort of reason at all for believing that thing is true. Ross could have practical reasons for believing in Armitage's standing.

Or could he? Ross no doubt understands what it means to have evidence to believe a theory, what it means to have good practical reasons for choosing one option rather than another, and the difference between the two. But can practical considerations support the adoption of a hypothesis? Is Ross entitled to choose to believe in that for which he has no evidence?

Let's accept as true—at least in the world of Armitage—that there are Thirds, and that these Thirds are impossible to tell apart from humans, at least in terms of behavior and demeanor. However, we can easily tell them apart from humans if we examine their internal workings. And as a result, skepticism about their moral status is possible.

But I'm particularly interested in the idea that it is *reasonable* for Ross to believe that Armitage is a person and not a mere machine because of the peculiar features of the *choice* to believe in her case. In his classic essay "The Will to Believe," American philosopher William James argues that in certain cases it is not only permitted but even obligatory that one allow one's passions to decide whether or not to believe in something.

The Genuine Article

According to William James, any claim that Ross might consider whether or not to believe is a *hypothesis*. Any such hypothesis, like a wire, may be said to be either *live* or *dead*. A hypothesis is live to Ross if and only if it is a hypothesis that seems plausible to Ross personally. If a hypothesis seems implausible to Ross personally, then it is a dead hypothesis to Ross. Which hypotheses are live or dead to Ross depends only on the peculiar character of Ross and not on the hypotheses themselves. A particular hypothesis, such as that the Martian government is behind the termination of the Thirds, might be a dead hypothesis to Ross but a live one to Armitage. To James, the measure of how live a hypothesis is to Ross would be how willing Ross is to act on the hypothesis. To act without hesitation on a hypothesis is, for all practical intents and purposes, to believe that hypothesis. So if Detective Eddie bet a Martian year's salary that Mars would never give up seeking complete independence from Earth, there is a sense in which he believes this is true. This is the sense of belief that James has in mind.

A decision between believing in one of two or more hypotheses is a belief option. Belief options, according to James, can be of several kinds:

- **Living or dead.**
- **Forced or avoidable.**
- **Momentous or trivial.**

Ross faces a living belief option if he chooses between hypotheses which are all live hypotheses. A belief option for him in which one of the two hypotheses he may choose is to believe that Mars is full of chocolate custard or that Detective Eddie is a brilliant wit would not be a live belief option, those being quite dead hypotheses to him.

A forced option is one where you must decide between the hypotheses. Often enough, we may find that we may simply suspend judgment and choose not to believe any of the hypotheses. But according to James this is not always the case. For example, in the assassin attack on Armitage, Ross, and Julian Moore in the sewer systems below the city of Saint Lowell, Ross is left behind to be picked up by the police because he needs emergency surgery to receive new cybernetics. What if it turned out that his condition was even more severe than it was? What if the only option to avoid a quick and inevitable death was to try an experimental cybernetic surgery that only was understood in theory, but only Armitage had the power of attorney to approve the procedure? Here Armitage must decide to believe that the surgery will be successful and permit it or believe that the surgery won't make a difference and not permit it. To suspend judgment in this case and thus to not act at all would lead to the same result as acting on the belief that the surgery won't make a difference. In that sense, deciding whether to believe in the surgery or not to believe in it is a forced option for Armitage.

Finally, a belief option is momentous if there is a lot at stake if you do believe, if believing is a unique opportunity, and if you don't have the liberty to back out of it once you have committed yourself to it. In the second feature film, *Armitage the Third: Dual-Matrix* (directed by Katsuhito Akiyama, Makoto Bessho and Tekuya Nonaka), Ross is offered a one-time-only chance to represent Mars in an Earth conference on robot rights, which if passed would clear his and Armitage's name and allow them back into regular society.

These conditions make a momentous belief option for Ross. Typically, belief options in scientific inquiry are not momentous in this sense. We can often make mid-course corrections if our hypotheses fail to be confirmed by the search for evidence.

Keeping these distinctions in mind, James names cases where the choice between beliefs is a belief option that is live, forced, and momentous as *genuine belief options*. The idea of a genuine belief option allows James to state his answer to the question of whether or not it is legitimate to believe in a hypothesis when we do not have enough evidence to show that it is true or most likely to be true. It is, says James, but only if believing the hypothesis is a case of a genuine belief option. If so, then one may let passion decide which option to believe and act on. By "passion," James means something broad that not only includes emotions and affections but also values and concerns. For the sake of his point, James sees no reason to account for these. He simply takes it that the concerns of a Ross or an Armitage are peculiar to them. And so to let passion decide is to choose according to what is most important to you. Borrowing a phrase from Pascal, James calls the passions the reasons of the heart (or in Armitage's case, reasons of the CPU, I guess) of which reason knows nothing.

Martians Believing Badly

James admits his answer is controversial. It seems that it would not be legitimate under any circumstance to believe in a hypothesis without enough evidence upon which to base that belief. For example, Ross came to Mars by space shuttle. Suppose the company that maintained the shuttle believed that the shuttle was overdue for a major inspection from routine wear and tear on the ship. If the company thought that since the shuttle still made successful interplanetary trips and worked fine, they might let the ship fly anyway without the inspection. If then the shuttle had blown up because of jet flames coming through an old and brittle seal, we would certainly blame the company for neglecting the inspection. But even if the shuttle made it to Mars, we would still think that the company would be just as guilty. The crime would be that the company let the shuttle fly without sufficient evidence that the flight would be safe. So it seems that one morally ought not to believe something unless there is sufficient evidence for it. One only ought to believe what one can see, whether it is a genuine belief option or not.

Certainly, this standard makes sense if applied to a very important practice of belief forming, namely science. At Conception, a
Martian robotics corporation, Dr. René D'anclaude and Dr. Asakura
are scientists with passions for the development and use of artificial intelligence and cybernetic technology, for military purposes or
for terra forming respectively. Yet their passion for achieving breakthrough developments is balanced as scientists against the desire to
avoid error. According to James, this is reasonable because science
deals with the physical world and its uniform properties about
which we can only observe and record. (He wrote before the
advent of quantum mechanics, but his point remains germane to
it.) In science there is no special concern to rush matters and we
have the luxury of waiting for all the facts to be discovered, and so
there is no motivation to take risks by believing hypotheses in
advance of all the evidence. So in science, the idea of not believing anything without sufficient evidence makes sense. Given the
great achievements of science—interplanetary travel, terra forming,
artificial intelligence, and what not—Ross's feeling that he should
not accept beliefs without evidence is understandable.

Still, is it always right to wait until all the evidence is in before
accepting a belief? One problem: what about believing that we
should only believe a hypothesis that has sufficient evidence for it?
Do we—could we—have sufficient evidence for that as a hypothesis? If not, then it fails its own standard, and we could not apply
it consistently. But in particular, aren't there cases of genuine belief
options where judgment cannot be suspended and where momentous possibilities are at stake and where we cannot expect that
inquiry will present the needed evidence in time to make the right
decision? Consider the previous case where Armitage has to decide
whether to permit surgery for Ross or not. If she follows the prescription not to believe without sufficient evidence, then she
should suspend judgment about whether to permit surgery and
thus not permit it. But if she did this, then Ross will die. Suppose
that Lt. Randolph, on behalf of the late Ross, asked Armitage for the
reason why she did not permit surgery. If she answered that it is
wrong to believe anything without sufficient evidence, we would
expect moral disapproval from the Lieutenant rather than approval.

In cases of android research, Dr. Asakura may choose between
accepting a hypothesis, say that artificial life forms can be based on
silicon, denying that hypothesis, or suspending judgment between
the two until he has more evidence. If he opts to either accept or

reject the hypothesis before the evidence is all in, the worst case is that he would simply be wrong and is perhaps on a snipe hunt and wasting time and resources, but if he suspends judgment, he is at least not at the risk of being wrong. In Asakura's case, the value of not being wrong is greater than risking that he might be right since he would have to go on testing and researching either way.

But in Armitage's case, she does not have the option of suspending judgment, since that would have the same effect as not believing in the surgery. Her belief options are forced. Yet the possibility of success is theoretically sound even though not confirmed, making the option of permitting surgery a live option for her. But the value of not being wrong does not seem so valuable compared to the possibility that Ross might be saved. And unlike Asakura, Armitage would not be able to go back on her commitment once it is underway. The option is momentous. In short, it is the fact that Asakura's case is not a genuine belief option and Armitage's is, that makes sense of why suspending judgment makes sense for Asakura but not for Armitage. The value of avoiding error has been trumped by the value of not missing out on an even more important truth, in Armitage's case.

In the case of Ross's shuttle trip mentioned earlier, not only would the shuttle owners have risked believing falsely that the shuttle was safe, but they would also have risked the lives of their passengers, including the last country singer in the universe. If they had been right it would have been a normal trip. But the shuttle owners also had the option of suspending judgment. In this case, avoiding being wrong and avoiding people getting killed is even more worthwhile than risking being right about the shuttle's safety, which is the morally valuable consideration here. This is not a genuine belief option then because it lacks one of the essential conditions. It is not a forced option. So James's account seems to make sense of why we think about Armitage's surgery case differently than the case of Asakura's silicon hypothesis or the shuttle case. In Armitage's situation, being wrong is worth the risk, and this is the case because her situation is a genuine belief option and the other two are not.

You Bet Your Life

Another way to state this is to say that according to James, what makes it appropriate to believe, without enough evidence in a situation where we must choose whether or not to act on that belief, is that the risk of believing and being right is more worthwhile than the security of not being wrong, even to the extent of being oblig- atory rather than merely permitted. James's view is similar to Blaise Pascal's famous "Wager" argument for deciding in favor of belief in God. According to Pascal, even if arguments for and against God fail to show us whether God exists or not, it would still be rational to believe in God and not just suspend judgment, since if I believe in God and I'm wrong then I lose the handful of pleasures I give up to be religious, but if I don't believe in God and I'm wrong then I lose the infinite good of God. "Believing in God" means gambling that God exists and living your life according to this belief rather than doing as you please.

Suspending judgment by being agnostic, according to Pascal, would be the same as choosing not to believe in God, since I would still lose the good of God. So I cannot refrain from choos- ing; to maximize the good I can expect, it is reasonable for me to believe in God more than not. Pascal's wager, assuming it is apt, is a candidate for being a genuine option according to James because if God is so infinitely different from us, belief in God cannot be set- tled by evidence one way or the other. But choosing to believe in God is an option that is live for some people, momentous because an infinite lot is at stake and because we must commit our lives to our belief since we cannot really know the truth before we die, and forced because we cannot avoid committing ourselves one way or another. Certainly, James thought that religion provided one of the most important cases of a genuine belief option and his idea of genuine belief options helps us see Pascal's wager as an instance of type of belief adoption that applies to more than just religion.

If this is right, then not only does James's account of genuine belief options speak to beliefs about the moral standing of Armitage and the Thirds, it also addresses other decisions about adopting a moral point of view or even a religious point of view. In the original four part OVA version of the Armitage story, when the assassin is chasing Ross into one of the many abandoned church buildings in Saint Lowell, the assassin asserts that there is no God on Mars. In a previous scene in which Ross and Armitage walk through the pleasure district where male customers satisfy their desires by utilizing Seconds, one lecherous patron with a Second designed to look like a mermaid seems envious of Ross over Armitage. The focus on these settings suggests that the secularity and hedonism are part and parcel of the ethical climate of Martian society, a society that tends also to view the Thirds as "obviously just machines." It seems as if the ethical culture of Mars would find James's account of genuine belief options unacceptable. This would be an explanation for the empty churches, boy toy Seconds, and dead Thirds. Ross's commitment to Armitage makes him a fugitive not only from the law but also from the general public. If Martians changed their minds and proactively endorsed something like James's "will to believe," we would expect not only Ross's situation to be much different but also the other aspects of daily life in Saint Lowell.

Mars Needs Women

In deciding to apply William James account of genuine belief options to Ross and Armitage, there are several things to keep in mind. One is that it only comes into play in cases where there really is insufficient evidence. If there is sufficient evidence to decide whether to believe a claim or not, then that settles it no matter what else may be said. An option being momentous and forced does not undermine sufficient evidence when we have it, rather having sufficient evidence rules such a case out as a live option. Further, when there is no sufficient evidence, one still has to satisfy jointly the qualifications James gives for being a genuine belief option. For example, if an option to believe is a live one and momentous but not forced, like the case of the space shuttle company, then according to James it isn't a time when your passions can play a role in choosing what to believe. In such cases, one ought to suspend judgment rather than believe.

Let's now see if this will help Ross with the question faced by him, the Martian police force, and the larger political society; whether or not the Thirds have moral standing, including having rights. To review, unregulated robot technology is illegal on Mars and the surplus of robots has led to rioting and unrest from loss of jobs. Because of violent attacks by the assassinroid D'anclaude (named after his inventor), Mars discovers Thirds, an even more sophisticated and illegal type of android that has been living amongst the Martians in secret. If they are mere machines, then terminating them is not so morally problematic since shooting up a Third would be no different than crushing a car. However, they seem to act like free agents. They form judgments and make decisions. They are typically professional creators: novelists, singers, dancers, and so on. And they form relationships with the humans in various degrees of intimacy. There is no discernable way to tell them apart without cutting them open. They cannot be biologically like humans, but they may still be persons.

When Ross arrived on Mars, he was teamed up with Armitage to investigate the murder or termination of the Thirds. He takes for granted that Armitage is another human like himself. Armitage is a lively and independent woman who treats Ross with respect but works often on her own by her own lights. Yet they become good partners, and Armitage starts to fill the void left by the loss of Ross's previous partner on Earth. When Ross discovers that Armitage is not human but a Third, he must decide whether to maintain his loyalty to the police (and keep his job) or do what he can to help her. This decision depends on whether he decides that being a robot means that she is just a tool or if she is a person with moral standing. The evidence indicates that she has a robotic frame and a sophisticated AI unit and that she behaves like persons do, but there is no evidence and no prospect of evidence in the future that will tell if she is a fake person or a real person.

Does James's account of genuine options shed any light on this? Sure it does. To help Armitage, Ross must quit being a good cop and become a terrorist by blowing up Shinora State Hospital and abducting Dr. Rene D'anclaude. Ross is convinced that as a result of Armitage's being declared illegal robot tech, the police cannot help them and no one else has the means or will. Unless Ross takes matters into his own hands, there is no one else who can protect Armitage, help find her "father," and find out whom she is. Time is running out before the government, the police, or another D'anclaude assassin catches up to them. This decision is certainly forced. If the police capture Armitage, she is most likely to be scrapped. Suspending judgment by not acting would lead to the same result as deciding that she is just another android.

It's a living option for Ross because Armitage plausibly behaves like an independent deliberative and feeling person, maybe even more so than bona fide humans. Time and again, Ross admits in situations where he must be telling his true view that Armitage is more human than human. In leaving his first meeting with his department head after the truth about Armitage has been discovered, Ross can only think "Armitage is not just a good cop. She's a great one." Later, when they are camping together at Asakura's secret laboratory, he tells her, "Hey. I know a human, and he isn't even asking the questions you're asking." In spite of being aware that she is a machine, Ross still cannot fail to be impressed with how much more character and depth Armitage displays than many humans.

It's also a living option for him because Ross knows that even as a machine, Armitage's design indicates that she is much more sophisticated than a standard model machine and that even Asakura was on the border of reproducing artificial life when he made her, so it may be that she's not a standard machine in the same sense that we are not standard machines.

Last, Ross himself through successive injuries and repairs is progressively finding his fleshly parts being replaced by cybernetic parts so that the distinction between himself and Armitage is getting vaguer. The impact on Ross of these states of affairs makes the belief that Armitage is a person a living option for him.

Finally, it's a momentous choice since if Armitage is a moral person, scrapping her would be taking an innocent life. On top of that, we learn that the reason why the Thirds like Armitage were all (except Julian Moore) made female was to be mothers and give birth in order to make the Martian population stronger without having to depend on Earth immigration. As Asakura saw it, this required more than just reproduction; it required true maternal affection which had to be as authentic as possible. With her being able to bear children, and with Ross's sadness over the death and loss of Jennifer back on Earth, it may be possible for Ross to marry Armitage and flourish together as a family. At least, Ross cannot fail to respond to the feelings of affection growing for Armitage as she confesses her feelings for him. Also, he knows there would be no turning back once he did help her. He would be considered a terrorist and spend the rest of his life as a fugitive if he decides to help her. So saving Armitage is a momentous decision for him.

Therefore Ross's situation includes all the necessary features— live, momentous, and forced—of a genuine belief option according to William James. With respect to the moral standing of the Thirds and to Armitage as a Third, Ross seems not merely permitted but even obliged to believe in their moral standing as persons, since in this case it is better to err on the side of being mistaken about that than to risk the possibility of a person being killed or enslaved. Beyond that, Ross is a least permitted to believe personally in Armitage's standing as a genuine person in order to commit himself to her as husband to wife. In *Armitage the Third: Poly-Matrix*, after the last battle, Ross carries Armitage, already pregnant, across the desert back to Saint Lowell. His final soliloquy on what he expects his future home will be like makes clear that the question has been put completely behind him.

Questioning the Question

Coming back to Ross's frustration in the car, we can understand it more clearly as based on a narrow interpretation of Armitage's question. But when people ask for a reason, they may not be asking for evidence. It could be that they are asking for prudential grounds that guide decision-making and action. Ross was thinking about reason as a fact or proof of Armitage's moral standing. In this case, no conclusive evidence was forthcoming, but action required making a decision about Armitage anyway. William James's account, allowing for exceptions to the general rule of believing only on sufficient evidence in cases of genuine options, provides Ross with a response to Armitage's request for a reason. Ross could answer her question by explaining how her situation counts as a genuine belief option to him by being momentous, live, and forced, thus allowing him to decide based on what really matters to him. Or he could simply say what she no doubt really wanted to hear: "Because I love you."

Still, accepting William James's account of genuine belief options granting the right to believe according to passion would not and should not take away the desire to really get to the bottom of things and form beliefs based on evidence. Even if we recommend James's form of reasoning to Ross, we still identify with the ache in Ross to know the truth. James does not ask us to pretend that believing something is true will always make it true, and what we really want is to know what is true. But the conditions of living often put us in the need for guidance even when we cannot know the ultimate truth, and James's help is worth considering. Wondering is long, but life is short. As Armitage said, "It's like an expiration date."[1]

---

[1] Thanks and praise to Hiroyuki Ochi, Chiaki Konaka, and their company for the Armitage franchise. If you by chance read this, please regard this as a much belated tribute from an American fan. \(^o^)/

EYE AM

by
Josef Steiff

Chapter 6
Josef Steiff
Columbia College
Chicago, Illinois
ocbook@gmail.com

The following analysis of the anime *Magnetic Rose* AKA *Memories* is written as a sequel to both Katsuhiro Otomo's original manga and in particular the film version written by Satoshi Kon and directed by Kōji Morimoto.

"EYE AM"

INT. KOPERNIKREV OBSERVATION DECK

An eye opens, flecks of gold sprinkled amid a circle
of hazel green. The pupil dilates, and shiny points
of reflected light slowly appear.

These steady pinpoints of ancient light fill in more
and more of the blackness, a field of stars as far
as the eye can see.

NADINE BECKNER, 30s with a tomboy's lanky body and
shortly cropped hair, stares out into space.

Her own reflection takes form before her, and the
large observation window, bulkheads, and laced beams
of the spaceship almost seem to coalesce around her.

A chirp interrupts her solitude, and she sits up to
answer the intercom.

                    NADINE
          Beckner.

                    ZEH
          We're at the edge, Nadine.

EXT. KOPERNIKREV

The spaceship slows to a stop against a backdrop of
stars and a nearby planetary system. Bold letters
spell out "Kopernikrev" across the sleek hull, followed by an emblem encircled by the words, "search
and rescue."

INT. KOPERNIKREV BRIDGE

Nadine stands behind *Kopernikrev*'s commander, ZEH, a
tough-looking man of indeterminate age and mixed
ancestry.

ESCHER, small and prematurely grey with a bushy
mustache, studies the monitors, listening through
headphones as he tweaks several dials.

One of the screens contains a stellar map, a
large portion of which is shaded green and overlaid
with a series of coordinates that include "RZ 3005."

The main monitor reveals the empty space before
them.

                    NADINE
          So this is the Sargasso?

Zeh nods.

                    ZEH
          Bayes is prepping the Remote.
          We've located the ship's
          Recorder beacon. Here.

Zeh points to a corner of the screen.

                    NADINE
          The Recorder? Does that mean —

                    ZEH
          It means the ship is not intact.

Nadine catches her breath and looks away.

                    ESCHER
          Sir. I'm getting another
          signal through all the magnetic
          distortion. It seems to be ...

Escher glances at Nadine, then Zeh.

                    ESCHER (CONT'D)
          ... using the *Corona*'s wavelength.

                    NADINE
          Where?

Escher points towards the middle of the main monitor
and flips a switch, allowing the signal to fill the
bridge: lots of static and what might be a wisp of
music.

Zeh listens as he scans the main monitor for some
sign.

                        ZEH
          Magnify.

The screen's perspective shifts, and the monitor
now reveals a massive debris field, a random
arrangement of tiny particles that become larger
and more dense in the distance, as if orbiting
around some central point.

                        NADINE
          We've got to go in.

Zeh indicates the static coming from the speakers.

                        ZEH
          On account of that? That's no signal to
          my ears. Just a jumble of magnetic
          interference. Let's see what the
          Recorder tells us before we go getting
          ourselves into trouble.

As Nadine and Zeh argue in the background, Escher
rubs his eyes and looks at the monitor more
closely, because it seems as if the debris is
starting to move, forming a shape near the center
of the field that resembles a giant metallic rose.

The static becomes worse, and Zeh turns it down.

                        ESCHER
          Hey. Do you see that?

                        ZEH
          What?

                        ESCHER
          The debris. Coming together.

Zeh studies the screen, and for a moment he can
almost see the rose as well.

                        NADINE
          It's just random movement.
          There's nothing there.

When Escher looks back at the screen, the rose is
gone, and the debris is just debris.

INT. KOPERNIKREV LAUNCH BAY

A lethal combination of British youth and good
looks, BAYES preps the automated Remote
Retrieval Unit for reconnaissance. The RRU is a
lop-sided oblong box that would be big enough to
hold two men if it weren't filled with an
engine, fuel, computer, storage space and
retractable arms folded along its sides, each
terminating in some tool or measuring device.

The low gravity field of the *Kopernikrev* allows
Bayes to easily swing the RRU into the launch
tube and seal the door.

EXT. KOPERNIKREV

The RRU glides away from the ship. Once clear,
the RRU re-orients and fires boosters that pro-
pel it into the Sargasso.

INT. KOPERNIKREV OBSERVATION DECK

Nadine watches the RRU set course.

EXT. SARGASSO SPACE

As the RRU nears the edge of the debris field,
it passes a large panel etched with the name,
"Disposer."

INT. KOPERNIKREV BRIDGE

Zeh and Escher watch the constant stream of data
and video images the RRU sends as part of its
mission.

INT. REMOTE RETRIEVAL UNIT

From the inner workings of the RRU, sensors zero
in on a faint pulse of light that is accompanied
by a slight pinging sound and a small burst of
radiation.

EXT. SARGASSO SPACE

The RRU unfolds and extends a clawed arm to scoop up the Recorder, a small black box etched with several number sequences and its ship's name: "Corona." A second arm helps tuck the Recorder inside a storage compartment before the RRU turns back towards the *Kopernikrev*.

INT. KOPERNIKREV LAB

Nadine, Zeh and Escher watch as Bayes plugs the Recorder into a computer console. The surrounding monitors burst to life with a bombardment of jumbled images, static, and opera music.

Nadine's attention is suddenly drawn to one of the screens, a static-filled black and white video image.

VIDEO:

HEINTZ BECKNER, late 30s, blond, square-jawed, and muscular, holds his ID up to the camera.

> HEINTZ
> "... acting on a mayday signal ... 05
> ... about to ...rescue ..."

In the wallet with Heintz's ID card is a photograph, only a part of which shows in the monitor, but enough to see that the picture is of Heintz, a little girl (Emily), and Nadine.

BACK TO THE LAB

Nadine gasps, and Zeh puts his hand on her shoulder.

The opera music becomes more insistent. Bayes turns down the sound.

> BAYES
> This is going to take awhile for me to
> sort out. Why don't you guys find
> someplace else to haunt.

INT. KOPERNIKREV BRIDGE

Zeh's eyes are closed, but from the way he leans in
his chair, it's difficult to know whether he is awake
or asleep.

Nadine sits at Escher's console, headphones on,
listening to the signal coming from the center of the
debris field as she watches a monitor of Bayes and
Escher working in the Lab.

INT. KOPERNIKREV LAB

Escher and Bayes pore over *Corona*'s mission logs,
studying a particular segment of the Recorder's
video.

VIDEO:

Heintz, weapon drawn, moves in front of an open
hatch, about to enter ... what? For a split second,
everything fades to white, no detail of the
environment he's about to step into.

BACK TO THE LAB

Bayes hits "pause."

                    BAYES
          There. In another few frames, he'll
          enter the Great Hall. But at this
          point on the video, it's almost as
          if there's nothing there, like the
          ship's interior comes into existence
          when Heintz is perfectly positioned
          to be able to see through the open
          hatch. He's not so much stepping
          into the Great Hall, but rather the
          room forms where he's about to step.

                    ESCHER
          Maybe the chandelier was so
          bright it took a moment for
          the Recorder to compensate.

Bayes presses "play," and the video continues in the
background, Heintz's comrade, MIGUEL, following him
into the Great Hall.

> BAYES
> That could be, but think about it.
> The Maid Robot telling Madam that
> luncheon is served doesn't appear
> until after Miguel sees the hologram
> of Eva on the hillside. And the
> hologram of Eva doesn't appear until
> after Heintz and Miguel see her por-
> trait in the Great Hall.

> ESCHER
> You're implying a traditional cause
> and effect arrangement, like they're
> somehow influencing what's happening
> on the ship.

> BAYES
> The ship certainly seems to be
> responding to them. That doll that
> Heintz finds? It looks just like
> his daughter Emily. And it even
> falls from the table.

> ESCHER
> So?

INT. KOPERNIKREV BRIDGE

Nadine stares back at her face in the monitor. She is
beginning to show signs of strain. She presses "record"
on the console and watches her lips barely move as she
whispers:

> NADINE
> I'm here, my love.

She rests her finger on the "transmit" button before
applying the required pressure. A dialogue box appears
on the monitor screen: "sent."

Nadine listens, but the incoming signal remains
unchanged. She takes off the headphones and stretches.

                    ZEH
          You're going to drive yourself
          crazy.

Zeh's eyes are still closed. Nadine looks for some
evidence that this sprawling body just spoke.

                    NADINE
          I know he's out there. And I won't
          leave without him.

Just as she thinks she imagined his voice, Zeh
responds:

                    ZEH
          It may not be your choice.

INT. KOPERNIKREV LAB

Bayes and Escher watch the video of Heintz exploring
the Rose, encountering hints that its lush ornateness
belies its true condition.

                    ESCHER
          Maybe the entire ship is a hologram.

                    BAYES
          But the problem with the hologram
          idea is that the Great Hall is real
          in a way that the hillside Miguel
          first sees through the windows is
          not. That hillside and his first
          glimpse of Eva is definitely a holo-
          gram. We can even see the field
          disruption when Miguel steps in too
          far. The other parts of the ship
          seem solid, and they are breathing
          air, so not everything can be holo-
          graphic.

                    ESCHER
          What if it operates less like a holo-
          gram and more like a work of art?

                    BAYES
          Huh?

                    ESCHER
There are art theorists who have argued
that the observer completes
or finalizes the work of art, in effect
coauthoring the text.

                    BAYES
Yeah, I've read Bakhtin and Hall, too.
But they don't mean literally. They
mean that the act of taking in and
interpreting the artwork is the final
step of the artistic process. It's not
as if the words on a page rearrange
themselves in response to the reader.

                    ESCHER
You and I could read the exact same
paragraph and remember it differently.

                    BAYES
Which is an act of interpretation, not
different words on the page.

                    ESCHER
But how would you know? If your
reading of the book affects the book
itself, how would you know? Because
you can only be aware of the book as
you perceive it.

                    BAYES
You're making my head hurt. And you
can't mean that my copy of *The Dialogic
Imagination* is different than your
copy.

An unexpected voice suddenly interrupts:

                    ZEH
What did I tell you? These two are
always at it. That's why I make them
work down here. If I wanted all this
philosophy theory stuff, I'd read a
book.

Escher and Bayes turn, surprised to see Zeh and Nadine
standing in the doorway.

Nadine smiles at the two men and glances at the monitor.

Zeh grunts and continues on down the corridor. Nadine makes as if to follow.

Escher and Bayes turn back to the monitors.

                    BAYES
          You're just winding me up.

Escher shrugs "maybe so" and smiles.

                    ESCHER
          Reception theory could help explain
          why Miguel and Heintz experience
          the roses in Eva's dressing room
          differently.

                    BAYES
          Let me guess, something about
          Bakhtin's conceptual horizon,
          right?

                    ESCHER
          Surely the physicist in you can
          appreciate the idea that two people
          can never see exactly the same
          thing, because they cannot occupy
          the exact same space at the same
          time. Their perspective and
          therefore their perceptions
          are different, literally and
          figuratively. For Miguel, the
          roses are alive — tangible and
          real. Heintz still sees the ship
          as an abandoned wreck. When he
          picks up the roses, he sees what he
          expects to see: they turn to dust.

                    BAYES
          Yeah, yeah, yeah. They experience
          the ship like a work of art.

                    ESCHER
          And each has his own interpretation
          of the artwork.

                    BAYES
          Which I guess does help explain how
          a hologram, which is a computer
          simulation that should be consistent
          and the same for both, can somehow be
          a shared experience and yet different
          for each of them. Miguel begins to
          experience Eva and the ship as alive
          before Heintz does, because they're
          interpreting differently what they see.

Both men glance up at the monitor and see that the video
log has now reached the point where:

VIDEO:

Heintz stands on the sidewalk leading to his home. EVA
is coaxing him to come into the house, to join her and
EMILY, a ten-year-old girl with pigtails, who stands in
the threshold. But another Emily falls from the roof,
and Heintz is unable to catch her in his outstretched
arms. She passes right through him like a ghost and
lies dying at his feet. He begins sobbing, trying to
pick her up.

BACK TO LAB

Unbeknownst to Escher and Bayes, Nadine has continued to
observe them from the doorway. A tear in her eye, she
turns away, no longer able to watch.

INT. KOPERNIKREV CREW QUARTERS

Nadine wakes with a start.

The crackle of radio static comes from the intercom.
A few notes of melody weave in and out with a familiar
voice.

                    HEINTZ
                (off screen)
          This is Heintz Beckner of the salvage
          freighter *Corona*, please come in. This
          is Heintz Beckner of the *Corona*, please
          come in.

Nadine jumps up.

INT. KOPERNIKREV BRIDGE

Everyone is trying to speak at once, crowded around
the communications console, Heintz's smiling face
filling the monitor as he patiently tries to answer
their questions. Nadine presses her hand to the
monitor as if to touch his face.

                    HEINTZ
               None of the Pods or ships are
               working. So I guess you'll just
               have to come and get me.

Bayes pulls Zeh aside as Nadine talks with Heintz.

                    BAYES
               I'm not sure going over there is
               such a good idea. You should
               take a look at the video logs.
               That ...

Bayes glances at Heintz's face in the monitor and
lowers his voice:

                    BAYES (CONT'D)
               ... ship is not what it seems.

                    ZEH
               Which is why I'm going to lead
               the rescue. And Nadine will sec-
               ond.

                    BAYES
               Nadine?

                    ZEH
               You think she's going to wait
               here?

EXT. KOPERNIKREV

The Launch Bay doors open, and two white ball-shaped
Life Pods exit to make their way into the Sargasso.

                        ZEH
                   (off screen)
          What about the rest of the crew?

                      HEINTZ
                   (off screen)
            I'm afraid they didn't make it.

EXT. THE ROSE

The Life Pods dock with the Rose, a space station
nearly the size of an asteroid and comprised of
hundreds of derelict spaceships.

INT. THE ROSE LANDING BAY

Massive doors close above the Pods as air begins to
be pumped into the landing bay.

The circular hatch of each Pod opens. Nadine steps
out of one, and Zeh steps out of the other.

INT. KOPERNIKREV LAB

Bayes and Escher stare at the monitor screen, replaying
the one short segment of the *Corona*'s logs they were
watching earlier:

VIDEO:

Heintz kneels on the sidewalk, sobbing, trying over
and over in an endless loop to scoop up Emily and cra-
dle her, but his hands pass right through her as if she
were unreal.

BACK TO LAB

Bayes pushes himself back from the console and turns to
face Escher.

                      BAYES
           What if it's not a hologram they're
           influencing, but reality itself.

ESCHER
You can't wrap your head around the
idea that the viewer can change a
work of art, but now you're proposing
that an observer can change reality?

BAYES
Quantum physics would not find that
so strange. Besides, art is not
separate from reality, it is a part
of reality.

ESCHER
But the idea of observer-affected
reality has only been demonstrated on
the subatomic level, not in the every
day world. Next you're going to go
on about Decay/Dead cats and
NoDecay/NotDead cats.

BAYES
Schrödinger's thought experiment is
simply a way of demonstrating the
paradoxes inherent in our current
understanding of probability. But
there's little dispute that at the
subatomic level, the act of observing
changes the reality one observes.
It's kind of like ...

Bayes presses the play button, allowing the video to
break its loop and play forward, as Bayes narrates the
images on the monitor.

BAYES (CONT'D)
At first, Heintz is unable to pick up
the dead Emily because she is just
one of two possibilities. But watch
what happens. Eventually, his
insistence makes her real, tangible
enough that he can pick her up and
hold her. But when she becomes real,
the other possibility, the Emily
standing in the doorway of the house
collapses and disintegrates. She can
no longer exist.

                    ESCHER
          The cat is either alive. Or dead.

INT. ROSE LANDING BAY

Nadine and Zeh shed their helmets and lock them in
the Pods. Zeh's comm unit bursts with static and a
distorted voice.

                    BAYES
                 (off screen)
          ... Zeh ... you need ... get out ...
          not ... Heintz ... real ...

Zeh stops, trying to concentrate on Bayes' voice, to
decipher the words.

Undeterred, Nadine heads towards the main hatch. The
door slides open to reveal the Great Hall. But rather
than the grand Victorian decor seen in the *Corona*'s
logs, the decor is now more modern and minimal.

                    ZEH
          Nadine. Wait.

Nadine steps into the cavernous empty space.

Zeh runs after her but the door seals shut before he
can reach it.

INT. THE ROSE GREAT HALL

Nadine tries to open the door, but no luck. She
presses her ear against the door and calls out Zeh's
name, but there is no response. She tries her comm
unit, but all she gets is static.

Nadine steps back and looks around the huge hall.

                    NADINE
          Heintz? Heintz?

                    HEINTZ
          Right here.

Nadine spins around to find Heintz standing right
behind her. She rushes to him and hugs him.

                    NADINE
          Help me get this door open.

INT. THE ROSE LANDING BAY

Zeh pounds on the door to no avail. He tries the
comm but no response. The bay is eerily quite, until
Zeh hears the ominous sound of air leaking out into
the vacuum.

INT. THE ROSE GREAT HALL

Nadine pulls back from Heintz.

                    NADINE
          What's wrong?

                    HEINTZ
          Nothing, now that you're here. I've
          been lonely. And your love is so
          powerful. Like mine.

                    NADINE
          Are you okay? I've never known you
          to ...

Suddenly a small hand tugs on Nadine's leg, and she
looks down into the eyes of her daughter, Emily.

                    EMILY
          Mommy? Oh, mommy.

                    NADINE
          This is not real. It can't be.

Nadine looks at Heintz with dawning awareness.

INT. THE ROSE LANDING BAY

Zeh struggles to get to his Pod, but the force of
venting atmosphere yanks him up and out into space.

INT. THE ROSE GREAT HALL

Nadine takes a step back from Heintz, ignoring
Emily's pleas.

> NADINE
> You're not Heintz.

Heintz's form flickers and then shifts to Eva's
visage.

> EVA
> I can be whatever you want me to be.

> NADINE
> Who are you really?

> EVA
> I am Eva Friedel.

> NADINE
> I don't think so.

> EVA
> I am Eva Friedel.

> NADINE
> Show me where you live.

> EVA
> I live here.

> NADINE
> No, where you sleep.

INT. KOPERNIKREV BRIDGE

Alarms clang as the magnetic field strengthens and
begins to pull the *Kopernikrev* towards the Sargasso.

Escher and Bayes scramble in their efforts to turn
the ship away from the edge of the Sargasso.

INT. THE ROSE BEDROOM

Skeletal remains occupy the small bed.

> NADINE
> Who is that?

> EVA
> She is in cold sleep.

> NADINE
> But who is she?

Eva does not answer.

> NADINE (CONT'D)
> You are not Eva. She is. Or was.

> EVA
> I am Eva.

> NADINE
> No. Eva was the artist. You're
> just her creation. Like a song.

> EVA
> I am Eva.

> NADINE
> You are just an expression of her
> memories through the circuits and
> hard drives of a computer. You are
> simply the product of science.

> EVA
> Art and science are not as distinct
> from each other as you might like to
> think. Ancient Greeks saw both as
> equally valid ways to understand the
> world around them.

> NADINE
> You are a machine. That's the
> reality here.

Eva flickers, and for a moment, Heintz appears in
her place, but the image glitches and is Eva again.
Nadine points at the skeleton.

>   NADINE (CONT'D)
>   That is Eva. Or what is left of
>   her.

>   EVA
>   I am. I. I am. Eva. I am ...

Eva's voice changes, deepens.

>   EVA (CONT'D)
>   Luncheon is served, Madam. Serve.

>   NADINE
>   You are the ship's AI. What did Eva
>   call you? You are not Eva. And she
>   is not in cold sleep. What did she
>   call you? What name did Eva know you
>   by?

>   EVA
>   I am ... SAM.

With this admission, the air pressure and centrifugal
force begins to erode. As the Rose breaks apart,
Nadine's increasing weightlessness allows her to
push herself off bulkheads as they shift and
collapse, propelling herself much faster than she
could run.

INT. THE ROSE LANDING BAY

Nadine is fully weightless as she propels herself
towards her Pod.

EXT. SARGASSO SPACE

The Pod struggles to reach escape velocity as the
magnetic field fluctuates, pulling debris from all
directions in an attempt to drag the Pod back towards
the disintegrating Rose.

INT. LIFE POD

Within sight of the *Kopernikrev*, the Pod has clearly
lost its battle and begins slipping back towards the
magnetic center of the debris field.

Now helmeted, Nadine vents the Pod's atmosphere and
opens the door into space. She grabs a tether gun and
steps out into the void.

Nadine uses her legs to give herself one strong push
towards the *Kopernikrev*.

INT. KOPERNIKREV BRIDGE

Bayes and Escher see Nadine's attempt to reach the ship
and reduce the *Kopernikrev*'s thrusters, allowing it to
drift back towards her.

EXT. SARGASSO SPACE

Nadine aims her tether gun and fires. A long string
shoots across the gap between her and the ship, it's
flat end finding and sticking to the *Kopernikrev*'s
hull.

As she follows the tether towards safety, she sees a
spacesuit floating at the edge of her peripheral
vision.

EXT. SARGASSO SPACE

Nadine pulls the floating astronaut towards her and
spins him around so that she can see the nameplate.
"Beckner."

                    NADINE
          Heintz. I'm here.

She struggles to pull the floating form upright, but as
they align helmet-to-helmet, instead of Heintz's face,
Nadine can only see hers reflected in his faceplate.
His sun shield is activated, preventing her from seeing
inside the helmet.

INT. KOPERNIKREV AIRLOCK

Nadine drags the suited figure into the airlock,
closing and sealing the hatch behind her.

The whooshing of incoming air signals the lock's
re-pressurization, and Nadine takes off her helmet.

She cradles Heintz for a moment before gently laying
him on the deck. She tries to deactivate the visor's
sun shield, but its reflective opaqueness remains,
hiding Heintz's face from her eyes.

Nadine takes a deep breath. Her fingers reach to
unlock the seals that join the helmet to Heintz's
space suit.

For a moment, the flecks of gold in the iris of
Nadine's eyes resemble a constellation of stars, like
a universe that holds its breath, waiting to see which
wave will collapse, which probability will become
real.

© 2010. Josef Steiff. "Eye Am." *Anime and
Philosophy: Wide Eyed Wonder.*

Spirit

7

Nothing that Happens Is Ever Forgotten

CARI CALLIS

Hell bent on getting to their new house in the suburbs before the movers arrive, the Ogino family—in their Audi A4, surrounded by shopping bags and junk food wrappers—take a "wrong" turn and end up in the Shinto inspired world of the *kami*. Unfortunately for the parents, their greed and ignorance get them turned into pigs and the only hope they have of rescue is going to have to come from their ten year old daughter Chihiro. And she didn't want to move in the first place. The farewell flowers her friends gave her are already wilting, just like their memory of her. And now she's got to start all over in a new school, in a new house, and make new friends and well let's face it, it doesn't get much worse than that.

The notion that it could actually get worse karate chops her upside the head, and she's got to work in a bathhouse and survive in a new reality, where all the rules have changed. She's The Littlest Prince, Alice in Wonderland, and a little bit of Edward Scissorhands all rolled into one big ball of existential angst. Like a larger version of the little soot balls she has to contend with when she gets her first task in the boiler room of the bathhouse. We fall in love with her the minute she rescues one of those little soot-sprites, even though it causes a bit of chaos in the delivery of the fuel for the bathhouse, when the "slaves" stage a rebellion and all pretend they're unable to work because they're overburdened by the soot they have to carry. But the little dirt balls decide they like her for helping one of their own, and she takes her first step in thinking of others before herself.

As Chihiro grows to understand the world around her she also begins to understand the value of her name and how to serve others. And maybe one of the reasons Hayao Miyazaki's *Sen to Chihiro no Kamikakushi*, or *Spirited Away* as it was called when it was dubbed into English and released by Disney, has such a universal appeal is because it is about a child teaching those around her how to *remember* that the most important thing we can do is to love.

Fiction and Contradiction

Do we really need to be reminded that greed and materialism defeat us, that taking our environment for granted and abusing it harms our relationships to each other and to our quality of life? That our connectedness—to family, community, the ancestors, nature and all of the *kami* spirits who reside where they are not visible—are important to who we are as individuals and in defining our cultural identity? That hard work, ritual and purification can create a causal reaction in the physical body and initiate profound changes in healing, mental balance and emotional stability? That our capacity and ability to love is the most important thing we can do? That all of us are separate and yet interconnected to the earth, and with each other through our relationships?

Hayao Miyazaki thinks we do. And he speaks directly to Japanese young people. His films, TV series, and manga are conceived by, for, and about Japanese culture. As he's made clear in interviews, he appreciates that other cultures find meaning in his stories, but his audience is mainly children, specifically Japanese (with the noted exception of *Porco Rosso* which was conceived for adults). What did he think of *Spirited Away*, the American dubbed version of his modern folktale? He has no idea; he had nothing to do with it and hasn't seen it. In fact, the only time he watches one of his completed films is when he sits down with the staff, and they screen it together. And why would he, having hand drawn of all of the storyboards himself with only a team of hand picked and trained animators to complete the story production? He isn't much interested in what CGI can do either; he's a pencil guy by nature, working without a script, flying by the seat of his pants. So what are we to make of someone who constructs a film using Shinto iconography, values, and ritual in his work and yet insists that his use of it is meant to make us *feel* Shinto rather than inspiring any militaristic or political unification ideals? When asked point blank about its use in *Spirited Away* he says:

My understanding of the history of Shinto is that many centuries ago the originators of Japan used Shinto to unify the country, and that it then ended up inspiring many wars of aggression against our neighbors. So, there is still a great deal of ambiguity and contradiction within Japan about our relationship to Shinto, many wish to deny it, reject it. My feeling is that I have a very warm appreciation for the various, very humble rural Shinto rituals that continue to this day throughout rural Japan. Especially one ritual that takes place on the solstice when the villagers call forth all of the local Gods and invite them to bathe in their baths. (2002 Press Conference for the premier of *Spirited Away*)

So are we to believe that Mr. Miyazaki, born in 1941 to a father who was the director of Miyazaki Airplanes—active in the war effort, creating parts for Zero warplanes during World War II—wants his audience to *remember* that Shinto was used to support the war based on the belief in the superiority of the Japanese culture? Or that the government used Shinto to promote loyalty to an emperor who claimed to be a divine descendant of the *kami* and rallied his nation to follow him into a devastating world war? Shouldn't he want his own people and the world to *forget* those kamikaze (god of the winds) suicide bomber efforts that were employed in the name of the emperor, who claimed to be directly descended from the original *kami* Sun God, to defeat allied forces? (Until the allied forces made one of the conditions of surrender that the emperor had to issue a statement saying that he *wasn't* divine.) The Shinto references in *Spirited Away* suggest Miyazaki thinks we should do both.

As Thomas Kasulis so elegantly proposes in his book, *Shinto, The Way Home*, the complexity of the evolution of Shinto is not easily understood by those familiar with the philosophy let alone by those who are not. And that includes Japanese people who live on islands with an estimated one hundred thousand Shinto shrines in operation today. It's likely that there would be substantial differences even among a Japanese audience in their understanding of the Shinto references in this film. The reason can be somewhat disentangled by using Kasulis's distinction between *existential* Shinto and *essentialist* Shinto, which he describes as follows:

When people say they are "Shinto," are they giving a conventional name for how they happen to think, feel, and act? Or are they designating an essential part of themselves that *leads them* to think, feel, act in certain ways? If the former (the existential identification with Shinto), the connection with the religion is ad hoc and flexible. Their Shinto spiritual identity would then be a conventional name applying to some of their typical ideas, values, and practices. To change such an existential identity would be akin to a change in preference, taste or habit. If, by contrast, the identification with Shinto spirituality is of the essentialist form, the situation is more prescriptive than descriptive. Insofar as the essentialist identity is based on people's true nature, they *must* (or should) behave in certain specified ways. The essentialist Shinto spirituality determines and prescribes, rather than simply describes, their thoughts, values, and actions. (p. 6)

To put it simply, you don't have to be Shinto to feel Shinto. Existential Shinto means that you are open to the *kami* energy and the wondrous sense of mystery and awe that it inspires. You don't have to be an official member of a National Shrine or believe in the Imperial divinity to recognize divine energy and celebrate it. Kasulis suggests all of us have felt Shinto at some point in our lives and that those experiences hold meaning for us in our human existence. He says that when we spiritually encounter mystery, something that is inexplicable, whether it's new or something we've witnessed a hundred times, that feeling of awe and wonder evokes an emotional response and we are "*struck*" by it. He goes on to say that it's more than "dumbfounded recognition and appreciation of an inexplicable power or presence," but something that resonates within and awakens our awareness that what we are seeing is beyond ordinary experience. I have felt Shinto when I came face to face with a manta ray that hovered in front of me for several moments and then glided away like a dark angel. Or when I watched lightning strike the Caribbean Sea or luminescent waves rolling upon a beach at night. But these experiences aren't limited to the natural world, they could be a piece of music that moves you profoundly or even something that evokes both fear and amazement.

Kasulis reminds us that the tension between existential Shinto and essential Shinto has always existed and at varying times in history one or the other has dominated the culture. The Japanese indigenous people had no written history and passed down the rituals and divine origin story of their existence from generation to generation. Inherent in the tradition came the honoring of not only the natural phenomena that inspired awe around them, the rocks, trees, and mountains which contained *kami* spirits but also in those who came before them in a belief that ancestors are sacred and could eventually become *kami* themselves. Miyazaki tells us he *feels* Shinto, as nine of out ten Japanese do, but that he also acknowledges the danger that any spiritual tradition undergoes when it is organized, prescribed, indoctrinated, and manipulated by social and political powers that use it to promote aggression. And in *Spirited Away* he shows us how those ideals which make Shinto uniquely Japanese have relevance and meaning to others. He references both the *existential* and the *essentialist* aspects of Shinto and enables the audience to come to the conclusion that both have value. He reminds the Japanese people to honor their cultural traditions but never to forget their past.

If You Don't Know Where You're Going, Any Road Will Get You There

The road that Chihiro and her parents take is fraught with the same dangers that we all face in a consumer-driven society. For those of us not familiar with Shinto, its difficult to come to terms with a spiritual belief system that is not quite a religion and not quite simply folklore, but a way of life that maintains a set of values that are almost inseparable from the identity of the Japanese people themselves. Whether we comprehend the complex aspects of Shinto and its many evolutions—from its earliest origins to its synthesis with Buddhism and Confucius influences and the separation from those into Shrine Shinto and then another transition from 1801–1945 into a more essentialist prescription known as State Shinto—*remembering* rather than rejecting, denying or even romanticizing Shinto traditions and values can connect our present to our past. And why is this important? The Oginos are about to find out. They have no idea where they're going as they race into their future and no idea that Miyazaki is going to take them directly into a collision with their past. But we should all fasten our seat belts; it's going to be a bumpy ride.

Once the Oginos head down that dirt path into the woods Miyazaki provides us with a *visual* history of Shinto in a matter of moments. Wisely, he keeps us in Chihiro's point of view, and we learn that her understanding of Shinto is as murky as our own. She first sees a cluster of small stone shrines at the base of an ancient tree, clearly designated as being *kami*-filled by the offerings left in the little houses and the wood *torii*, two columns with a horizontal rail connecting them, which leans against the tree. The patina of moss and age recall the "humble" origins of "rural Shinto ritual" that Miyazaki references in his interview, and when they pause like tourists gazing at them through the car window, Chihiro doesn't know what they are. Her mother has to tell her they're little shrines that people pray to. The first thing we learn about ancient existential Shinto, what is commonly called "Folk Shinto," is that the youth in Japan don't even know what it is. Chihiro isn't sensitive or responsive to the *kami* presence so she isn't prepared for the changes they're going to bring to her life.

Traveling deeper into the woods they pass an ancient statue almost hidden by the leaves, which catches Chihiro's attention. Having statues mark the entrance of Shinto temples as guardians began when Buddhism started to assimilate into Shinto traditions, and it too is separated from the other half of its pair in the same way Shinto was later separated from Buddhism and Confucianism to "preserve" the cultural purity of the tradition. A visual reference to what came to be known as "Shrine Shinto." Soon they're halted by the missing half of the guardian pair, who now serves as a bollard, one of those things that are placed in rows to obstruct traffic when you can go no further. The statue is an ancient symbol of Shinto placed into a modern context, and it directly blocks their way.

Next, confronted by a long tunnel, the parents forge ahead leaving Chihiro behind. But faced with being left behind or staying with them, she follows, hanging onto her mother and everything she's ever known for dear life. The tunnel echoes eerily and emptily and when they emerge into the abandoned train station there's no doubt that it's a memory straight out of Miyazaki's own childhood. It's a painstaking re-creation of a nostalgic 1940s era, from the light fixtures to the wooden benches, and one that clearly harkens back to the time when Shinto was used to unite the Japanese and ready them for war: a clear visual reference to "State Shinto." We're reminded of the essentialist era of Shinto—lest we forget. Kasulis makes the argument, just as Miyazaki does, that it's important to do both: ". . . because of the distinctive tensions between its existential and essentialist forms, Shinto presents us with the two faces of nostalgia. There is the kind of nostalgia nurtured to lend authority to state control. And there is the kind of nostalgia that beckons us back to a form of connectedness that has been all but erased by the rise of scientific thinking, dependence on technology, and consumerism." (Kasulis, *Shinto: The Way Home*, p. 170).

Discussing his own use of nostalgia in the film, Miyazaki says:

I believe nostalgia has many appearances and that it's not just the privilege of adults. An adult can feel nostalgia for a specific time in their lives, but I think children too can have nostalgia. It's one of mankind's most shared emotions. It's one of the things that make us human and because of that it's difficult to define. It was when I saw the film Nostalghia by Tarkovsky that I realized that nostalgia is universal. Even though we use it in Japan, the word 'nostalgia' is not a Japanese word. The fact that I can understand that film even though I don't speak a foreign language means that nostalgia is something we all share. When you live, you lose things. It's a fact of life. So it's natural for everyone to have nostalgia. (*Midnight Eye* Interview with Tom Mes, 2002)

Perhaps Miyazaki is not so strictly focused on a Japanese audience after all. That dripping water fountain invites the Oginos to resuscitate and renew their existential Shinto spirituality, but the sound of the train in the distance will remind them of the things they've lost as they emerge from the train station into a green field with more ancient statues half buried and nearly forgotten. The juxtaposition of the *sound* of the train followed by another *visual* reminder of folk Shinto evokes the every day connectedness of the spiritual world to the modern one. The train is always present in the film, even after Chihiro has crossed into the world of the *kami* she watches it passing from her room in the bath house. This haunting reminder of *essentialist* Shinto is a reoccurring image and becomes one of the strongest images that Miyazaki uses to return both Chihiro and his audience to what he hopes we understand is the existential *feeling* of Shinto.

As the Oginos ascend the field and cross a dry riverbed with only a small trickle of water, there is yet another allusion to existential Shinto with an old building constructed of stone that can only be one last historical reference to their ancient past. Last chance Ogino family to turn back! But father forges ahead and says it must be an old theme park abandoned after the bubble burst on the Japanese economy. (Miyazaki has degrees in economics and political science and references that time in Japanese history from 1986 to 1990 when real estate and stock prices became hugely inflated and then collapsed. The down turn lasted for more than a decade and prices bottomed out in 2003 until they went even lower in the global crisis that began in 2008.)

Once the parents climb the stairs and pass under the torii, they have entered the mythical representation of present day Shinto as it exists in Japan today. Here we see ancient buildings side by side with electric lights and neon signs. There's a blend of primeval and modern architecture that co-exists in harmony with Nature. But it's deserted. No humans are here, and in this place, the existential and the essential merge. As her parents race away to find the source of the delicious food they smell, Chihiro hesitates to enter this strange new world. The fat frog statue is the last thing she sees before she passes beneath the torii. The Japanese word for frog is *kaeru*, a homonym for a word meaning "to return home." Her entry into the land of *kami* is marked by the torii, a reminder for people lost in the details of every day life and disconnected to the spiritual that the way home is here.

In the first minutes of *Spirited Away* we've traveled with the Ogino family through the existential and essential aspects of Shinto from the dawn of time to the present day. Miyazaki has provided visual references to both the existential primordial beginnings of Shinto to the dark period in history when Shinto was used by the government to strengthen national solidarity through patriotic observance at shrines. It's clear that he believes the time has come for his country to reconnect to their ancient spiritual beliefs, but by having the train always in the background, that he doesn't want them to forget what that era in time evokes, and the tragic losses that occurred because of it.

It Is Only with the Heart that One Can See Rightly; What Is Essential Is Invisible to the Eye

Because Miyazaki doesn't begin a film with a clear storyline or script in place, he allows his imagination to create the story without logic by drawing storyboards. He's joked that anyone can tell a story that is logical, but that the trick is making a film which is not. He must trust that his intuition will guide him in his process and that the plot will reveal itself by digging deep into his subconscious. This is exactly how Chihiro must learn to survive as well. She can't survive on her own, she must make new friends, sacrifice to help them, and in return accept their help as well. In the beginning of the story, Chihiro is a sullen fearful girl, who is mourning the loss of her old life. In the opening scene in the car, her father calls her name, and she doesn't respond, until he calls to her again.

She doesn't value her identity or what it represents until she loses it. By the end of the film, Chihiro has remembered her name that was stolen by the witch Yu-baaba, when she finds the card from her friends that is in the pocket of her old clothes. In these two pivotal scenes Miyazaki demonstrates what aspects of Shinto must be reconciled for the Japanese people as well. To lose your name is to have your identity erased, and the ancient connections to Shinto have been nearly lost for the people of Japan. They too have lost their cultural identity and their connection to their past. Miyazaki uses Shinto to evoke the memories of his culture and asks the Japanese people to remember the old traditions and customs and to find meaning in them in the present.

Chihiro must first become purified, and she accomplishes this by the physical labor of working in the bathhouse and cleansing the Stink Spirit, who turns out to be a River God filled with trash. She later remembers an encounter that she had as a child with Haku, and this helps him to remember his name. She has become receptive to the *kami* and responsive to it and with her sacrifice in helping No-Face, Haku, the soot sprites, and even Yu-baaba's Baby, she has demonstrated her purity of heart and mind which the Japanese call, *makoto no kokoro*. As Kasulis tells us,

> As a human being in the land of the *kami* one is a portion of the sacred; one is an intrinsic part of the *kami* filled, *tama*-charged world in such a way that, if the person is pure, he or she mysteriously mirrors that whole. To be genuinely receptive to the presence of *kami* and responsive to it, to make full use of the holographic entry point of the torii, people must first be *makoto*. Only then can they recognize how kami is a part of what they themselves are. They will reflect *kami* and not merely reflect on *kami*. The second part of the term,"*kokoro*"—the "heart and mind" that is to be genuine or true—requires special attention. (*Shinto: The Way Home*, p. 24)

In the Palm of Your Hand

There are really *three* resolutions to this film, though they all say that it's important to remember where we come from so that we don't lose our way. In the Japanese version *Sen to Chihiro no Kamikakushi*, Zeniba, the twin sister of Yu-baaba, gives Chihiro a hair band woven by her friends to keep her safe and protected. She doesn't *remember* what happened to her in the bathhouse or her experiences in the land of the *kami*, but the dust on the car and the hair band from her friends recall for us that as Zeniba told her, *"Nothing that happens is ever forgotten."* The experiences that she had were real, they weren't a dream and the changes they effected will be carried into her future. She will remember that it takes more than just the efforts of a single individual to overcome adversity; it takes the accumulated knowledge of her cultural history to renew spiritual awareness.

And in the Disney version of *Spirited Away*, Zeniba tells her something quite different. *"Once you've met someone you never really forget them, it just takes a while for your memories to return."* America isn't a culture that originated from a single spiritual tradition, it was founded on principles that honor and protect our *individual* right to blend our cultural identities with others to create something completely new. What Zeniba says in the English-language film becomes something very different from the original Japanese version, and in the final scene Chihiro *does* remember what has happened in the *kami* world. When her Dad tells her starting school will be a little scary, she says bravely, "I think I can handle it." An American audience wants the fantasy world to recede, but not be forgotten. The Japanese instinctively know that it is always there.

And the third ending of the film is the place that Miyazaki has said is where the film ends for him:

> . . . what for me constitutes the end of the film, is the scene in which Chihiro takes the train all by herself. That's where the film ends for me. I remember the first time I took the train alone and what my feelings were at the time. To bring those feelings across in the scene, it was important to not have a view through the window of the train, like mountains or a forest. (*Midnight Eye* Interview with Tom Mes, 2002)

If we aren't distracted by what is happening outside of the train window, we must then focus on what is inside the train with Chihiro and her friends. And the train is filled with ghosts, dressed from a time that clearly references the essentialist Shinto past again. They have no features or faces; they're drawn as if they've already become a part of our collective memory. If we equate the train with that time in Shinto history when people were forced to abandon their spirituality, then we can more fully understand why the film is complete for Miyazaki here. This is when Chihiro has already learned everything about herself that she needs to know to grow into maturity. She already knows that nothing that happens is ever forgotten because she carries the spark of the *kami* within her as do all Japanese people. The nostalgia of riding the ghostly train, with the haunting music, evokes the memories of the Japanese culture for a tradition and way of returning home that can only be a connection between the existential aspects of Shinto and the essential aspects which recall the *kami* way.

Neither *Spirited Away,* the Disney version, nor *Sen to Chihiro no Kamikakushi,* the original Japanese version, requires an audience to have an in-depth understanding of Shinto to appreciate the Ogino family's situation. The parents have no memory of being pigs or how close they came to being turned into bacon. They remain blissfully unaware of the *kami* world or how their offspring has grown through her experience with the *kami*, having forgotten everything that occurred. And maybe it isn't important that they have knowledge of their change or recognize the spiritual traditions that have preceded them. Children are after all, as Miyazaki says, only a mirror of their parents. But she provides hope for any audience that she will carry the traditions of Shinto, The Way of the *Kami*, into the future. The Vietnamese Buddhist monk Thich Nhat Hanh recalls for us, "If you look deeply into the palm of your hand, you will see your parents and all generations of your ancestors. All of them are alive in this moment. Each is present in your body. You are the continuation of each of these people." Chihiro carries the Shinto tradition in her palm; in her DNA, she holds an essence of the divine original spark of *kami* energy. As do we all.

8

Did Santa Die on the Cross?

ADAM BARKMAN

Legend has it that back in 1945, shortly after American troops occupied Japan during the Second World War, a famous Japanese department store—no doubt eager to capitalize on western traditions during the holiday season—set up a display of a life-size Santa Claus hanging from a cross. Whether this event actually happened or not we don't know, but for those who have spent any time in the Land of the Rising Sun this legend certainly has a ring of truth about it. While all cultures practice to some degree what is known as "encoding" (putting their values into its cultural products), the modern Japanese are also especially famous for embracing anything and everything foreign—not excluding elements of foreign religion—and transforming them into something . . . well, unique, to say the least.

One of the most interesting platforms where the Japanese engage in this type of cultural value transformation and encoding is in anime and manga. Japan's unique pluralism shapes how Japanese manga and anime artists portray Christianity—a portrayal that doesn't generally give an accurate picture of Christian teaching.

Do Angels Practice Voodoo?

Although the Japanese celebrate Christmas, it's not a day to mark Jesus's birth, as it is in the West; rather, Christmas is a time for lovers—a time for first sexual encounters and engagement rings. Consequently, in Japanese anime, such as *Always My Santa*, *Stellvia*, *The Big O*, and *Suzumiya Haruhi*, the fact that Christmas is Jesus's birthday is often shown to be interesting trivia, much as

Buddha's birthday, common knowledge in Asia, would be to western audiences.

Yet Christmas is not the only Christian tradition that the Japanese have appropriated: most couples celebrate Valentine's Day and many also opt for so-called Christian weddings—weddings in Christian churches—when they get married; hence the expression that the Japanese "are born Shintō, marry Christian, and die Buddhist."

And this leads to a question central to this discussion and the philosophy of religion as a whole: How should we understand religious diversity? There are three basic answers to this question.

The first answer comes from the pluralist, who, in the manner of Immanuel Kant and John Hick, thinks that there is a fundamental distinction between Ultimate Reality as it exists (the Noumena) and Ultimate Reality as it is humanly and culturally perceived (the Phenomena) (as in John Hick's *An Interpretation of Religion*, p. 80). Because of this distinction, the pluralist typically maintains that we can't *univocally* describe Ultimate Reality (where "univocity" means that the words applied to Ultimate Reality mean the same things that they do when applied to us). The best we can do is *equivocally* describe Ultimate Reality (where "equivocity" means that the words applied to Ultimate Reality mean something different than when applied to us). Thus, the important thing for the pluralist is not propositional truths or doctrines about Ultimate Reality; rather, the important thing is the way in which personal salvation or transformation is perceived. Accordingly, the pluralist typically regards as intolerant those who assert the truth of a particular religious doctrine.

The second answer comes from the exclusivist, who thinks a particular religion, such as Christianity, is propositionally truer than all other religions. In order for salvation even to be possible, one must accept both the ontological truth (the objective conditions for salvation or enlightenment must really be in place, such as Christ really dying and rising again) and the epistemological necessity (those seeking salvation or enlightenment must know about the conditions, for instance, they must hear about Christ's death and resurrection) of that religion.

The third answer comes from the inclusivist, who agrees with the exclusivist, and disagrees with the pluralist, that one religion is propositionally truer than all other religions. However, while this one religion—again, take Christianity—is truer because it's where the ontologically necessary salvific event occurred, it's not, as the exclusivist claims, epistemologically necessary for all people to know of this salvific event (for instance, while Christ's death is the *only* way for people to be saved, not all people have to *hear* of Christ's death in order to be saved).

Although we'll delve deeper into the religious history of Japan in the next section, for our purposes here we can say that modern Japanese are generally pluralistic in regard to religion. This pluralism is not merely the result of skepticism about attaining any knowledge of Ultimate Reality (the Daoist element in Japanese thought), but also involves the outright denial that there is an Ultimate Reality at all (the Shintō and Buddhist elements in Japanese thought).

Given this skepticism about, let alone outright denial of, Ultimate Reality, it shouldn't surprise us that most Japanese anime artists feel no qualms about encoding their religious anime, particularly their anime pertaining to Christianity, in a generally pluralistic way. Thus, particular doctrines are seen as largely unimportant, whereas a general spiritual mood—a mood often created by blending many different religions together—is all-important. For instance, in *Saint Tail*, the Catholic heroine, Meimi Haneoka, goes to a fortune-teller for advice about her love-life, even though in the Bible, God condemns such people (Deuteronomy 18:10–11, Galatians 5:19); in *Pita-Ten*, Misha, an angel-in-training, washes a voodoo doll of the hero, Kotarou Higuchi, in order to "cleanse the soul" of the real Kotarou; in *Maria-sama ga Miteru (The Virgin Mary Is Watching)*, Shimako Tōdō, the daughter of a Buddhist priest and a student at Lilian Catholic School, feels she has to hide her Buddhism from her classmates but later is shown to be fully accepted by all her Christian friends, who seem to think that doctrinal matters are peripheral to pluralistic tolerance; in *Demon Lord Dante*, Beelzebub, a demon mentioned in the Bible (Luke 11:15), is reincarnated (a doctrine that is Hindu-Platonic-Buddhist and incompatible with orthodox Christian teaching about the nature of the soul and bodily resurrection); and in *Devil May Cry*, *Chrno Crusade*, *Trinity Blood*, *Hellsing* and *Devilman*, good devils are the leading figures (a concept which directly contradicts the orthodox Christian teaching stating that a devil, by definition, is a *fallen* or *evil* angel).

Moreover, as is typical of pluralists, Japanese anime artists tend to view exclusivists and inclusivists—Christian or otherwise—as intolerant fanatics. Hence, the Shimabara Christians in *Ninja Resurrection* and the "Crusaders" in *Chrno Crusade* are drawn in a rather unflattering light, and in *Big Wars*, an alien race called "the gods" (who are linked to the Christian God via the destruction of Sodom) use brainwashing techniques to "subvert" humans into following them, apparently implying that those who follow a particular religion are irrational and dangerous.

However, according to orthodox Christianity (that which encompasses the core doctrines of the faith), exclusivism or inclusivism are the rational, tolerant choices and pluralism is the irrational, intolerant one. Why? Two things.

First, pluralism confuses epistemological and ethical considerations. It's a mistake to affirm both that being judgmental about truth-claims necessitates maltreating people of different beliefs, and that being tolerant implies merely accepting diverse truth-claims (as they all equivocally describe Ultimate Reality) rather than rationally assessing them.

Second, although not identical to relativism, which denies Ultimate Reality altogether, pluralism ends in agnosticism, one of the results of which is that all talk about tolerance being grounded in the nature of Ultimate Reality is subsequently futile. The reason for this is simple. In order to "know" Ultimate Reality, we must be able to describe it univocally and metaphorically (wherein metaphors entail some basic univocal concepts, such as "life-sustaining" or "powerful" when we say "God is like the Sun"). But if we can't speak about Ultimate Reality in this way (as the pluralist asserts), then we can't know what Ultimate Reality is like. It follows that the pluralist's criticism that exclusivism and inclusivism entail an *unfair* or *unloving* God is itself a groundless accusation since the pluralist seems (contradictorily) to think that he *knows* that God or Ultimate Reality is *fair* and *loving*.

As a result, while the pluralism found in most Japanese anime is aesthetically rich, it is, from an orthodox Christian perspective, rationally poor since it fails to appreciate proper, rational distinctions about God. Moreover, its apparent tolerance is itself intolerant of anything but a pluralistic view of religion.

Angel Invasion

Although the Japanese have been eager to accept and assimilate anything foreign over the past hundred and fifty years, this eagerness was not always characteristic of the Japanese. The first Japanese brought with them many of the same cultural and religious values shared by other Asian nations; indeed, Japan's own version of shamanism, called Shintō, is remarkably similar to the shamanism found in nations as close as Korea and as far away as Mesopotamia and Peru. Nevertheless, as a nation of islanders, the Japanese found it easy to develop myths making themselves the center of the world, the ultimate result of which was a certain distrust of, and snobbery toward, anything foreign or alien.

When Buddhism was first introduced to Japan from Korea, the Japanese, being a nation of Shintoists, were initially hostile to this foreign religion (not so much because of doctrinal differences but because Buddhism was foreign). Although the conflict between Buddhism and Shintoism continued for hundreds of years, non-Japanese, in particular westerners, may find this surprising since the religious milieu of modern Japan is very much pluralistic and synchronistic in that it promotes the harmony and blending of Shintō, Buddhist, Daoist, and Confucian beliefs—none of which, we must keep in mind, are particularly opposed to such a blending or, more importantly, to pluralism itself.

Now when Christianity was first introduced to the Japanese by Dutch Protestants and Portuguese Catholics in the sixteenth century, the new religion initially appeared as though it would go the way of Buddhism in Japan—at first feared and then, centuries later, accepted in one form or another. In fact, Christianity even looked more promising than Buddhism since the Catholics quickly succeeded in winning the friendship of Oda Nobunaga, who was the most powerful man in Japan at the time.

However, Christianity in Japan faced one problem that Buddhism never did: conflict, brought on by orthodox Christianity's exclusivist claims, between religion and politics. That is, despite their desire for western guns and technology, the Japanese began to see that European expeditions into Asia were resulting in western colonization and so the Japanese came to believe that Christianity was the means by which European powers softened up countries that they intended to conquer. In their own case, the Japanese thought that when the European Christians discouraged people from acknowledging the divinity of the Japanese emperor (among other orthodox Christian prohibitions), the Europeans were promoting complete disobedience to the Japanese government:

> The Christian band have come to Japan, not only sending their merchant vessels to exchange commodities, but also longing to disseminate an evil law, to overthrow true doctrine [such as the Shintō doctrine that the emperor is the son of a god], so that they may change the government of the country and obtain possession of the land. This is the germ of great disaster, and must be crushed. (C.R. Boxer, *The Christian Century in Japan, 1549–1650*, p. 318)

The ultimate result of this Japanese fear was that Christianity was declared illegal in 1606. Shortly after this, in 1637, Christians in the Shimabara region of Kyūshū revolted when they were asked by the intolerant Japanese pluralists to renounce their beliefs. This revolt resulted in the massacre of some 37,000 Christian peasants, and, a few years later, the Japanese government in Edo (Tokyo) established the Office of Inquisition for Christian Affairs, which gave Buddhist temples, among others, the power to sniff out any hint of Christianity and other "evil," subversive religions.

Now it's commonly known that anime generally avoids discussion of real-world religions (*shūkyō*), and this is certainly true of Christianity, particularly as it pertains to Japan's first encounter with it. Nonetheless, there are a few exceptions. For instance, *Nemuri Kyoshiro* tells the tale of a blue-eyed swordsman whose Japanese mother was raped by a devil-worshipping Portuguese priest; *Ninja Resurrection* follows the story of a young Christian named Shiro, who is prophesied to become the messiah who will lead the Shimabara Christians to victory, but who instead becomes the incarnation of Satan; and *Samurai Champloo* is largely about a sword-for-hire living around the time of the Shimabara Rebellion, who, among other things, refuses to step on a *fumie* or a picture of Jesus or Mary, not because he is a closet Christian but rather because he "hates being told what to do." What one can gather from these three series is the common theme that when Christianity was first introduced to Japan, it was largely seen as something alien and either ludicrous, as in *Samurai Champloo*, where the grandson of Francisco Xavier, the first missionary to Japan, is an unhinged megalomaniac, or dangerous, as in *Ninja Resurrection*, where the Christian revolt leads to massive bloodshed as a result of "Christian sorcery" (incidentally, the idea of prayer as magic or the manipulation of an impersonal force, and not a request to a divine being, is a common Japanese Daoist misunderstanding of Christian prayer).

While there are a number of series set in the present or future that encode certain aspects of Christianity in, if not an orthodox, at least a more positive light, such as *Ode to Kirihito's* Scripture-quoting dog-nun, Sister Helen Friese, or *Go Go Heaven's* resurrected Catholic schoolgirl, Shirayuki Kogyoku, some depict Christianity as a dangerous, alien religion. Bypassing *Angel Sanctuary, Roots Search*, and *Chrno Crusade*, all of which depict God as either apathetic or downright evil, and *Sins of the Sisters*, which makes the Pope the equivalent of a child-murderer, an anime series which deals with Christianity as a dangerous, alien philosophy is *Neon Genesis Evangelion*.

Neon Genesis Evangelion (or *Eva* for short) alludes to the Bible in its very name, which means something like "the gospel of a new beginning." The series makes explicit use of orthodox Christianity (the book of Revelation), but also Jewish mysticism and Gnostic Christianity. Examples include the names of the angels who attack the Earth (for instance, Samchel, the angel who allegedly guarded the Garden of Eden), Lilith (Adam's alleged first wife, who refused to submit to her husband—though in *Eva* is one of the angels), and the tree of the *sefirot* (the tree that is related to creation and engenderment and, in *Eva*, a picture of which decorates the ceiling of Gendō Ikari's office).

In keeping with orthodox Christianity, *Eva* focuses on the angels who are sent to the Earth to smite it and who will eventually herald the way for the creation of the New Earth (Revelation 8–9, 16, 21). However, whereas *Eva* never mentions any divine hand behind the angels' attack on the Earth, the Bible puts Jesus front and center. Or again, while *Eva* depicts the destruction and rebirth of the Earth in monistic terms (that is, where all things are mere appearances of a single reality), the Bible shows the judgment of the Old Earth to be a matter of justice and the creation of the New Earth to be a place where the just can find sanctuary. Consequently, it's clear that *Eva* was not intended to be a serious engagement with orthodox Christian theology despite what some may think. Indeed, Kazuya Tsurumaki, the producer of *Eva*, said Christian themes were employed in *Eva* "because Christianity is an uncommon religion in Japan [and I] thought it would be mysterious" (Dani Cavallaro's *Anime Intersections: Tradition and Innovation in Theme and Technique*, p. 59). As a result, one possible reading of *Eva* is to see the angels' attack on Tokyo-3 as an allegory of Christianity's impact, as an alien, hostile religion, on

Japan. This reading is simplistic and ignores many factors; however, the general sense of *dangerous* and *alien*, which the Japanese were taught to associate with western powers and Christianity, can be found in *Eva*.

And this leads to another, closely related issue: how Japanese anime artists have appropriated three key biblical narratives—the Flood, the Tower of Babel and Armageddon—and have related them, particularly Armageddon, to the atomic bombs the Americans dropped on Japan during World War II, which, according to Takashi Murakami, is the "engine that drove the great manga and anime [in the past]" (Rolland Kelts's *Japanamerica: How Japanese Pop Culture Has Invaded the U. S.*, p. 175).

Introducing the End of the World

The biblical flood narrative, wherein God sent a massive deluge to destroy all the sinful people on Earth (Genesis 7–8), appears in many different anime series, such as *Ulysses 31*, *D-Grayman* and *Spriggan*. Setting aside *Ulysses 31*'s interesting science fiction blending of Incan mythology and Judeo-Christianity in regard to the flood, *D-Grayman* and *Spriggan* both deal more explicitly with the biblical flood, yet both share the unusual and unorthodox premise that Noah himself *caused* the flood! For instance, in *D-Grayman*, the gray-skinned, superhuman Clan of Noah—that is, the thirteen descendents of Noah (the Bible lists fewer)—want to wreak divine havoc on the world as their father Noah had done. Or again, in *Spriggan*, Noah's Ark (which is named "Noah") is found on Mt. Ararat, the same resting place indicated by the Bible. Yet, according to *Spriggan*, *Noah* is an alien spaceship that landed on the Earth and, due to its power to control weather, was the cause of the flood and the subsequent ice age. In both of these series, the flood story is reinterpreted in anime but still carries with it the central theme that was originally foreign to the Japanese prior to their contact with the West: worldwide destruction.

This epic theme of worldwide destruction is present in other anime series like *Gilgamesh* and *Babel II* as well as the aforementioned *Ulysses 31*. In particular, the Tower of Babel, the symbol of God-defying unity and cause of the fragmentation of the brotherhood of man as a result of inordinate pride (Genesis 11) is alluded to—often with humanistic overtones alien to Christian orthodoxy—in *Ulysses 31* (where Circe wants to build a literal tower of knowledge so that she can rival the power of the Olympian gods), *Metropolis* (where the Red Duke's Ziggurat eventually crumbles under human arrogance) and *Gilgamesh* (where the institution at Delphys is referred to as "the Tower of Babel" since it is not only a tower in ancient Mesopotamia but also the site where people discovered the demigod Gilgamesh's body and were attempting to discover the secret of immortality through its DNA and subsequent cloning). But the Tower of Babel as a symbol of destruction is the most prominent in *Babel II*, whose creator, Mitsuteru Yokoyama, simply took the name Babel and made it the name of a powerful alien entity which awakes in a young boy named Koichi to allow him to fight a world-threatening disaster. As a result, while the biblical account of the Tower of Babel certainly conjures up the idea of the destruction of human *unity*, the anime *Babel II* is largely about the destruction of the physical world and hence is more closely linked with the gods' judgement of Achilles's Spring in *Big Wars* (a take on God's judgement of Sodom in Genesis 19) or with one of the most important biblical themes in anime: Armageddon, which, though a place, is often understood simply as the global war between the forces of good and evil (Revelation 16:16).

Given that the whole concept of global destruction is an idea that Japan got from the Christian West, it makes sense that when the Americans dropped the two atomic bombs on Japan during the Second World War, the Japanese—not to mention most of the world—often understood this in apocalyptic terms. Of course, since most Japanese weren't Christians, they didn't literally see World War II as Armageddon (nor the reverse: Armageddon as nuclear war), but certainly the biblical ethos was in the air and acted as a source of dark inspiration, often departing from Christian orthodoxy, for many future anime artists (not to mention a few 'Harmagedon' cults, such as Aum Shinrikyō).

Take *Chrno Crusade*, for example, which is set just prior to World War II. It deals with the spiritual—specifically, Christian—events that foreshadow the Second World War and its greater association with cosmic warfare (hence, Revelation 6:12–14 and 18:10 are quoted at different times throughout). The theology in this series is, as to be expected, problematic, for it primarily centers on a three-way war between God and his followers, the devils who are satisfied with the status quo between Heaven and Pandemonium, and the devils who want to overturn the balance of good and evil in order to achieve "freedom."

The premise of the series is that if the balance between good and evil is disrupted, then either good or evil will be destroyed or at least will lose their meaningfulness. Of course, the idea that there is a balance between good and evil is *I Ching* philosophy (which predates both Daoism and Confucianism) and not Christianity. The *I Ching* seems to support Dualism or the belief that good and evil are both *positive*, co-eternal substances, whereas orthodox Christianity maintains that God, who is Goodness itself, only made good things, and so evil must simply be the *absence or privation* of a good that should be present (for instance, when a person steals something, there is a lack of proper self-control in the will).

Or again, the solution to universal religious war as it is presented in *Chrno Crusade* is that since such a war is based on simplistic conceptions of good and evil (such as the *I Ching* and Christianity), Armageddon can be thwarted or at least creatures can recover from its ill-effects by recognizing that good and evil, especially in their bare metaphysical forms, are not what they seem: hence, God appears somewhat apathetic; the only angel in the series, Ewan Remington, hangs up his wings; and the devil Chrno, à la *Hellboy*, is not diabolical at all. However, according to orthodox Christianity, the end of conflict cannot be achieved by seeing through good and evil, as Buddhism teaches when it says everything is *anātman* or "no-Self," meaning that there is no substantial Reality behind appearances. Rather, orthodox Christianity teaches that conflict can only be averted when all submit to the established order that the perfectly Good God has made. The basic idea is that if God created everything and knows (because he is perfectly good) what will make everything happy, then creatures can only achieve true freedom and happiness by conforming to the Good, not by pretending it is an illusion (Buddhism) or that there is a positive alternative to it (*I Ching*).

Finally, the ethos of Armageddon is especially strong in many futuristic anime and manga series, such as *Harmagedon*, *Apocalypse Zero*, *Demon-Beast Phalanx*, *Tokyo Revelations*, *Appleseed*, *Earthian*, *Trinity Blood* and *Akira*, to name but a few. While *Harmagedon*, *Apocalypse Zero*, *Tokyo Revelations* and *Akira* are not directly related to the Christian apocalypse and *Earthian* seems to lose its focus on this early on, *Demon-Beast Phalanx* was inspired by the book of *Revelation*, *Appleseed* quotes Revelation 12:4 in its introduction, and *Trinity Blood* is set just after Armageddon, when the world is divided into two groups: the humans, led by the Pope in Rome, and the vampires, led by the vampire Empress in Byzantium. Yet none of these anime series are very orthodox in regard to Armageddon.

Trinity Blood, in particular, is problematic in its treatment of the Christian conception of Armageddon. For instance, according to Revelation, Armageddon is supposed to pave the way for the establishment of the New Earth, which is to be peopled by the righteous; but in *Trinity Blood*, the post-apocalyptic world only breeds new divisions between humans and vampires. And, to make matters more confusing, the humans in *Trinity Blood* are not identified with the righteous (even though they are led by the Pope) nor are the vampires identified with the unrighteous (as would traditionally have been the case in western vampire lore). Certainly orthodox Christians are able to appreciate that the visible church is not identical with what St. Augustine inclusively calls "the City of God" or the totality of the righteous. That is, orthodox Christians can appreciate that names and physical makeup mean little when it comes to righteousness—the City of God can be composed of Catholics from Rome and Eastern Orthodox from Byzantium, humans and vampires from Earth, and angels from Heaven. And if this is what *Trinity Blood* is really saying, that conflict between good and evil can only be resolved by submission to the Good, then I think *Trinity Blood* is one of the most orthodox Christian anime series around. However, I suspect that by equating humans with Christianity and vampires with non-Christianity and then depicting some humans as evil and some vampires as good, the overarching theme in *Trinity Blood* quickly becomes that of pluralism (all views about Ultimate Reality are equivocal) and Buddhist-Shintō relativism (good and evil, and all categories for that matter, are merely conventions and conflict can only be overcome by seeing past these).

Why Catholicism Is Better than Protestantism . . . for Anime

After reading the past few sections, some might feel that I have too quickly glossed over something vital: that while Japanese pluralism itself is philosophical (and perhaps philosophically problematic), Japanese pluralism as it manifests itself in anime is more literary or symbolic—after all, I've said it is more about the "spiritual mood" than anything else. Although all cultural products, including anime, are inextricably linked to some philosophy, when the Japanese deal with Christianity in their anime, it is more for literary effect than for philosophical argument: symbols, more than syllogisms, are what most Japanese anime artists are concerned with. For instance, in *Golgo 13*, the protagonist is an assassin known as "Golgo 13," which refers to Golgotha, the hill on which Jesus was crucified, and the alleged day—Friday the thirteenth—when Jesus was killed; but beyond the common feelings of death, sorrow and loneliness which both Jesus and Golgo 13 felt or feel, there is nothing else in common between these two. Or again, in *Rave Master*, Shiba's sword is called the "Ten Commandments," which shares the idea of judgement with the biblical commandments but nothing else.

One of the things that follows from this is that, agreeing with C.S. Lewis's claim in his essay "Christian Reunion: An Anglican Speaks to Roman Catholics," Catholicism is a "jungle" of symbols and Protestantism is often a "desert" of bare platitudes (*C.S. Lewis: Essay Collection and Other Short Pieces*, p. 396), when Japanese anime deals with Christianity, it tends to gravitate toward Catholicism. For instance, setting aside the myriad of anime series featuring crucifixes, angels, and demons, all of which are common to both Catholicism and Protestantism, many Japanese anime series make mention of six things that either are uniquely Catholic or Catholics put unique emphasis on:

1. exorcists or priests, such as in *Ghost Sweeper Mikami* or *Puri Puri*;

2. nuns, for example, in *One-Pound Gospel* or *Holy Virgins*;

3. Catholic schools, such as in *St. Lunatic High School* or *La Esperança*;

4. Purgatory, as in *Purgatory Kabuki*;

5. the Virgin Mary, for instance, in *Maria-sama ga Miteru* or *Wicked City*; and

6. angelic hierarchies, such as in *Angel/Dust Neo*, whose android emulates are loosely categorized according to Pseudo-Dionysius's hierarchy of angels (for instance, Musia is a mere "angel," whereas Leia is a "virtue"), or *Soul Rescue*, wherein Renji, a rogue archangel, has to rescue ten thousand souls before he is allowed to return to Heaven by God

(whose omnipresence is wonderfully depicted by a myriad of wires going into His head).

Besides being symbolically richer—and hence better able to create a "spiritual mood"—than Protestantism, Catholicism is also more likely to be featured in Japanese anime because many of the western, biblically-inspired stories that the Japanese have drawn from and encoded in their anime were set in Europe at a time when there was no Catholic-Protestant divide and so have typically been thought of as Catholic. Consider three examples:

1. Dante Alighieri's *Divine Comedy* influenced *Devilman*'s portrayal of Satan being frozen in ice;

2. the Arthurian legends influenced *Fate/Stay Night*'s use of the Holy Grail (but in the legends it is the blood of Christ, whereas in the anime it's more a generic term for a powerful object that grants wishes); and

3. stories about Joan of Arc have been extremely popular in Japan and have inspired many anime, such as *Jeane, the Kamikaze Thief*, in which Joan of Arc is, oddly, a reincarnated Christian hero.

Moreover, the entire Gothic genre itself, with its sympathetic vampires and the like, was largely a product of the Romantic Movement, which, though it began in Protestant countries, combined the Protestant emphasis on freedom with Catholic imagery. This Romanticism, in turn, influenced countless anime, such as *Vampire Hunter D*. Indeed, when Japanese anime present unorthodox Christian views, these views are not always the product of Japanese pluralism but are sometimes Japanese appropriations of Romanticism's unique conceptualization of Christianity; hence, John Milton's Satan (though a villain in *Paradise Lost*) became a hero to many Romantics and this Satanic heroism, wherein Satan and his minions are seen as passionate freedom-fighters, consequently inspired the countless antiheroes that we find in anime such as Alucard in *Hellsing*, Akira in *Devilman*, Setsuna/Alexial in *Angel Sanctuary*, and Sapphire in *Earthian*. And in *Maria-sama ga Miteru*, when a lesbian schoolgirl asks the object of her affection, a potential nun, "Are you choosing God over me?" we can see, even here, the typical sentiments of Romanticism.

Gay Angels, Female Cardinals, and Bishōnen Popes

Whatever the pre-Japanese thought about gender before they arrived on the island of Japan, by the time they did arrive, their religion of choice was Shintoism, which shared with world-shamanism the common belief in goddesses and the importance of priestesses to serve them. However, with the advent of Confucianism, the position of women in society and religion dropped to some degree. Nevertheless, because Confucianism is fundamentally a socio-political philosophy with little or no metaphysical foundation, it was never able to ground its views of gender and sex. Consequently, any deep metaphysical speculation about gender and sex were ultimately rendered meaningless by the antirealist metaphysics of Shintoism, Buddhism, and Daoism, all of which claim that as with everything, gender and sex are not intrinsically stable concepts, but are as illusionary and changing as everything else.

So it comes as little surprise that when we look at Japanese anime, we are bombarded by innumerably different presentations of gender and sex, including those having to do with major Christian figures, such as angels, demons, priests, cardinals, nuns and popes. For instance, in *Earthian*, the two protagonist angels, Chahiya and Kagetsuya, are not only partners in evaluating humanity, but are also shown to be gay lovers since both are in male form when they have sex. Or again, in *Trinity Blood*, the head of the Catholic Church is a *bishōnen* ("beautiful boy") pope, who is flanked by a female cardinal.

Most of these encodings don't reflect orthodox Christianity, which has traditionally claimed that while sex belongs to the body, gender belongs to the soul or spirit; and because the higher affects the lower, the soul or spirit determines the sex of the body. As a result, when orthodox Christians call God 'He' and not 'She,' they mean to say that God is *essentially* masculine, even though He, of course, has feminine attributes. Or again, female bodies point toward feminine souls and male bodies point toward masculine souls, and even though females should have some masculine attributes and males should have some feminine ones, neither sex should engage in any activity, such as cross-dressing or homosexual love, that would confuse or blur the essential differences between men and women.

Moreover, while angels and demons don't have bodies as we understand them and hence are sexless, it doesn't follow that they don't have genders since gender belongs to the soul or spirit. It's based on a theory of gender such as this, coupled with the belief that God made all things to function in certain ways, that most orthodox Christians have held beliefs such as the masculinity of God (John 3:35), male headship in marriage (Ephesians 5:32), the unnaturalness of homosexuality (1 Corinthians 6:9), the lack of sexual marriage in Heaven (Matthew 22:30), the importance of gender for church office (1 Timothy 2:12), and condemnation of cross-dressing and the like (Deuteronomy 22:5). As a result, orthodox Christianity would take issue with *Earthian*'s gay angels and *Trinity Blood*'s female cardinal, and would see potential danger in anime's general tendency to over-feminize men; for instance, masculine, spiritual authority is poorly represented by *Trinity Blood*'s *bishōnen* pope.

Perhaps more than any other issue, this sort of treatment of gender and sexuality demonstrates that Japanese pluralism has penetrated deep into the minds of Japanese anime artists. The ultimate result of this is that when these artists produce anime, they encode their pluralistic interpretations of Christianity into their works. And because pluralism has little use for propositional truths or religious doctrines, when Japanese anime presents Christian teaching, it is almost always rendered inaccurately. Nevertheless, this isn't to say that such anime is valueless to the orthodox Christian (or anyone else for that matter). If the orthodox Christian can appreciate the spiritual mood of the unorthodox appropriation of Christian themes in anime, he can often afford himself a pleasant enough aesthetic experience.

9

Why Nice Princesses Don't Always Finish Last

DANIEL HAAS

Hayao Miyazaki's post-apocalyptic masterpiece *Nausicaa of the Valley of the Wind* raises questions about a myriad of topics including humanity's relationship with the natural world and whether it is ever morally justifiable to torture an innocent. But at the heart of the film are two women, Nauiscaa and Kushana, and their conflicting beliefs about how one ought to conduct oneself during times of political, social, and environmental upheaval.

Kushana, princess and military leader of the Tolmekian Empire, believes that one can and should do whatever it takes to survive in a war-torn world while Nausicaa, princess of the Valley of the Wind, believes that there are restrictions on how one ought to behave, even after the collapse of civilization. Examining these two contrasting approaches, and linking them to similarly conflicting ethical theories, will help us to determine whether the aim of survival is, ultimately, the only relevant moral consideration.

Soon This Place Too Will Be Consumed by the Toxic Jungle

Whether it's meteorites crashing into the Earth as in *7 Seeds*, the nuclear catastrophe of *Desert Punk* or *Barefoot Gen*, or the melting of the polar ice caps and the shifting of the Earth's axis as in *Neon Genesis Evangelion*, destroying the earth is a fairly common pursuit for anime creators.

A global bio-nuclear war that kills most of humanity and radically alters the earth's ecosystem is Miyazaki's apocalypse of choice in *Nausicaa*. The war culminates in a catastrophic event known as

"The Seven Days of Fire," in which man-made living weapons turn on their creators. These creatures, capable of breathing fire in a way reminiscent of a nuclear explosion, scourge the earth, making much of its surface inhabitable.

The film picks up a thousand years later, by which time a toxic jungle full of giant mutated insects thrives among the ruins of human civilization. Greatest of these insects are the Ohmu, giant, sentient pill-bugs that have the ability to communicate telepathically. The spread of the jungle has pushed the remnants of humanity to small pockets of the planet where ecological conditions are still favourable to human survival.

The Valley of the Wind is one such community, an idyllic pastoral society whose people have learned to live in relative harmony with the jungle and its insects. Its people use windmills to harness strong winds from a near-by sea to limit the poisonous gases of the toxic jungle. Save for burning the occasional jungle spore that threatens their farms, Nausicaa's people leave the jungle alone and it, in turn, leaves them in peace.

This is a stark contrast to life outside the valley, where nations engage in endless warfare vying for scarce resources and trying to strike a decisive blow against the jungle in order to return humanity to its place as uncontested rulers of the Earth. The conflict between two of these nations, Pejite, a desert kingdom, and the previously mentioned Tolmekian Empire will play a crucial role in the events that transpire as the anime progresses.

In a pivotal event, the kingdom of Pejite unearths one of the living weapons that devastated the earth during the "Seven Days of Fire." The weapon was buried beneath the city of Pejite in deep hibernation. Tolmekia learns of this discovery and, hoping to capture and use the weapon for its own defense and to destroy the toxic jungle once and for all, Kushana is dispatched to leads an assault force on Pejite. Her attack is successful but victory comes at a high cost, and most of the people of Pejite are killed in the battle. With the weapon hibernating in the cargo-hold of a Tolmekian airship, Kushana and her army begin the voyage back to Tolmekia with the Pejite princess as hostage, to discourage any retaliation.

Kushana's invasion of Pejite raises an important issue. Her motives for this attack are understandable, even admirable. She believes, with some justification, that Tolmekia is better prepared militarily to control a weapon as great and dangerous as the sleeping creature discovered in Pejite. And with the creature's power, it seems entirely plausible that Tolmekia could destroy the jungle forever allowing the human race to return to its former glory. And taken in this context, the loss of a few human lives might be an unfortunate but necessary step on the road to humanity's restoration. So was Kushana right to attack Pejite for the purpose of promoting the welfare of the entire human race?

We're Doing This for the Good of the Planet. You've Got to Understand That

Many people, were they to find themselves in an apocalyptic environment, would be willing to do whatever it takes to survive. This is perfectly understandable. After all, the end of the world is probably not the ideal time to be considering what ethical obligations people are under. People quite reasonably concern themselves with doing what it takes to survive in times of great upheaval. And is there really anything wrong with this attitude? Surely, people who are willing to go to any lengths for the survival of their families, friends, nations, or even the entire human race are admirable and praiseworthy. If morally questionable means, under extraordinary circumstances, are necessary to get to an end result that is highly desirable, why be concerned? And what could be more important than the survival of the entire species? A soldier such as Kushana is on morally solid ground even if she needs to kill a few innocents, isn't she?

Someone sympathetic to this line of reasoning will find many allies in the philosophic tradition. One influential strand in ethical theory is known as Consequentialism. In its simplest form, the basic idea behind consequentialist ethical theories is that "The right act in any given situation is the one that will produce the best overall outcome, as judged from an impersonal standpoint which gives equal weight to the interest of everyone. . ." (Samuel Sheffler, *Consequentialism and its Critics*). This is a straightforward enough idea. If you want to know what the morally appropriate thing to do, you need only to consider the consequences of a proposed course of action. Provided that the action is the one that produces the best results for everyone involved, then it is the right thing to do.

We see Nausicaa use consequentialist reasoning fairly early in the narrative. On the return flight from Pejite, Kushana's airship crash-lands in the Valley of the Wind. As the citizens of the Valley rush to put out the burning airship and assist those injured in the crash, Kushana's army invades the Valley of the Wind to ensure that the ancient weapon is not discovered or seized by the people of the Valley. In the attack, the king of the valley, Nausicaa's father, is killed. Upon seeing her dead father, Nausicaa picks up a sword and in a moment of blind rage nearly kills a Tolmekian soldier. Warned to stand down by her uncle, Lord Yupa, Nausicaa reconsiders her action and realizes that if she goes through with killing the Tolmekian soldier, not only will she be killed, the Tolmekian army will massacre the people of the Valley in response. She surrenders and gives a public speech telling her people to cooperate with the Tolmekians. Nausicaa believed that the best consequence for everyone involved is to stop fighting. Allowing the soldier to live was the only way to achieve this outcome.

With this consequentialist moral framework in mind, we can return to Kushana's actions. Her end game is noble enough—unite the surviving humans under one ruler so that resources can be pooled and destroy the toxic jungle and the mutant insects that threaten to drive the human race into extinction. As far as Kushana is concerned, the attack on Pejite and the subsequent attack on The Valley of The Wind are unfortunate but necessary prices to be paid for the survival of humanity. Sure Kushana is willing to do some fairly cruel and inhuman things to accomplish her goals, but her goals are admirable and, considered from an impartial standpoint, they even seem to be in the best interest of the human species. So, Kushana's actions look to be justified on consequentialist grounds. But is that the end of it?

You're Not Saving the Planet! You're Killing My People

At first glance, Kushana's consequentialist approach seems perfectly reasonable. Sometimes we find ourselves in horrible circumstances, and we do what we have to do to survive even if that means a few innocents get hurt or we spill a little blood. Indeed, the fact that it is so easy to sympathize with and understand a character like Kushana is a testament to Miyazaki. A lesser director might have portrayed Tolmekia as an evil empire whose leader, Kushana, had been seduced by the dark side of the force. While a story about a band of rebels fighting an evil emperor would make for an exciting tale of good versus evil, it's not very true to real human behaviour. What Miyazaki recognizes is that no one ever truly sees themselves as a villain or intentionally does what they believes to be morally wrong. Kushana is a villain, not because she is inherently evil, but because she is willing to do anything to do bring about what she believes is the best overall outcome, even if it means harming others to do so.

And herein lies the problem with responding to war, terror, apocalypse and severe hardship with a "whatever it takes" attitude. A typical feature of any ethical system that focuses on the consequences of one's actions as the sole determinant of whether what one does is morally permissible or not is that the action, in and of itself, is not morally relevant. This seems to allow for the use of any means necessary to achieve a desired end, so long as that end itself is, on balance, the best outcome. Consider Pejite's response to Tolmekia's invasion. Using the capital city of Pejite as a testing ground (because it's been nearly deserted after Tolmekia's invasion killed the majority of Pejite's citizens), Pejite develops a cruel method for luring the Ohmu to attack human cities. Using the telepathic abilities of the Ohmu against them, the Pejite have discovered that if they capture and torture a baby Ohmu, the Ohmu will stampede in order to rescue the infant or at least to kill those who tortured the baby insect.

After successfully testing this on the capital city, Pejite kidnaps a baby Ohmu, brutally tortures the insect, and flies the dying baby towards the Valley of The Wind. They figure the inevitable Ohmu rampage will destroy the Tolmekian army and allow for the retrieval of the hibernating weapon. Because Pejite sees Tolmekia as an evil nation, they believe the weapon is far too dangerous to leave in Tolmekian possession and that only the people of Pejite can be trusted to use the weapon to destroy the toxic jungle.

Pejite's actions are easily on par with the destructive path that Kushana leaves in her wake, if not worse. And yet, they're justifiable, perhaps even morally required on strict consequentialist grounds. If our only concern is bringing about the best consequence, it is hard to see how we could justify not using the baby Ohmu to bait an attack on the Valley of the Wind. If we really believe that Tolmekia is an evil nation, too reckless to handle the ancient weapon and that the destroying the toxic jungle is the only way to ensure the survival of the human race, it seems a simple calculation to determine that the suffering and loss of life that this attack involves are a lesser cost than the suffering that will occur if

Tolmekia is left to do whatever it wants with the weapon. It looks like the consequentialist ought to support the torture of the baby Ohmu and the attack on the Valley of The Wind, but surely torturing a child and causing the death of thousands of innocents should not be what one is ethically permitted, let alone required, to do. What's gone wrong here?

Too Much Fire Gives Birth to Nothing

The worry just raised is about the moral significance of the ends overriding that of the means we employ the reach them. This can easily be extended to Kushana's actions. She has committed countless atrocities in the name of saving the human race. She's ordered the annihilation of cities, the execution of innocents, and even resurrected one of the ancient weapons that destroyed the earth. All Kushana's horrific acts, although they are done in the pursuit of the greater good, seem to lead to a never-ending cycle of endless tragedy. Perhaps the central worry here is that when we focus all of our attention on the goal we're trying to achieve and not on the actions we take to get there, we can readily justify any act, regardless of how perverse. To make matters worse, we might even disregard something fundamentally important—When we look only to the consequences of our actions, we lose sight of the nature and significance of those acts themselves. We ignore the ways in which all of our everyday actions allow for the possibility of significant human values such as compassion, generosity, and recognition of our shared humanity with those who are affected as the result of our actions. In short, we devalue our relations with others by treating them merely as means to our desired ends.

What a Mysterious Power She Has

Where does this leave us? If doing whatever it takes to survive leads to endless atrocities, how ought one to behave in a war-torn and shattered world? Are we forced to choose between our humanity and our survival or is there a third option?

The people of the valley of the wind, and Nauiscaa in particular, take a different approach. Nausicaa and her people seek an end to war and suffering through a deeper understanding of the world around them, and a harmonious relationship between humanity and the jungle's insects.

In a pivotal early scene, Nausicaa befriends a small animal known as a fox-squirrel (a temperamental rodent that looks exactly like its name suggests). As Lord Yupa is thanking Nausicaa for saving the Valley from an Ohmu attack, the fox-squirrel pops out of his satchel and starts growling. Yupa warns Nausicaa that these little animals can be quite ferocious, but Nausicaa reaches out her hand in friendship. The fox-squirrel leaps from Yupa's bag, runs up Nausicaa's outstretched arm, and with its hair rising, hisses at Nausicaa in anger. Calmly, Nausicaa tells the little rodent that there's nothing to fear, and slowly brings her hand towards the angry animal. It lunges at her, biting down on Nausicaa's finger hard, drawing blood. Nausicaa winces, but waits, continuing to tell the fox-squirrel that there's nothing to fear. A tense moment passes, and as the animal realizes that Nausicaa means no harm, it relaxes, releases Nausicaa's finger, and begins to lick her bleeding wound. Both the fox-squirrel and Nausicaa have made a new friend.

As the princess runs off to greet Yupa's ostrich-like mounts, Yupa ponders: "What a mysterious power she has. . ." Nausicaa's "mysterious power" is her near-mystic ability to communicate with non-human animals whether they are fox-squirrels or Ohmu. But of course, there's nothing mysterious about her power. She simply pays attention to the animals and the world around her and in doing so, understands the motives and needs of creatures that are often fierce and unpredictable to her less observant companions.

This scene is significant because it illustrates Nausicaa's general approach to the world and why she is fundamentally different from someone like Kushana. Whereas Kushana focuses on her end goal, paying little attention to her everyday interactions (other than as means to her chosen end), Nausicaa revels in each moment of her day, and takes her interactions with others, whether they're human or fox-squirrel, as fundamentally important. It's not the consequences of her actions that are most important to Nausicaa, but the actions themselves. This is not to say that Nausicaa isn't concerned with survival or the consequences of her actions. It's rather that the means she takes to get there are at least as important as the end goal itself.

You're Nothing Like Our Princess

But how does this translate into a robust ethical view, or even a strategy for adapting to and thriving in a post-apocalyptic environment? Isn't it a little naive to think that the way to thrive in a hostile world is by being concerned about those around you and by respecting the environment in which you live? Well, not necessarily. Nausicaa's approach has several things going for it that Kushana's end-goal directed behaviour does not. Most importantly, Nausicaa's focus on her environment and those who share it with her always places her attention on the way in which her actions affect others. Rather than using a desired goal to determine what action to perform, her regard for others effectively restricts the sorts of actions that she would undertake.

Nausicaa's moral compass is in stark contrast with Kushana's, and is echoed in the philosophic tradition by a theory that contrasts just a sharply with consequentialism. Immanuel Kant developed a conception of morality that is succinctly expressed by his "Categorical Imperative" that we should treat others as ends in themselves and never solely as a means. Not only does treating others as ends in themselves preclude us from disregarding them in the pursuit of our goals, it also requires that we attempt to understand them in order to properly respect their moral worth and measure the impact our actions have on them. While Kant did not necessarily have this in mind, Nausicaa has extended this consideration of other people to include the environment. She seeks to act in ways that respect both the people of the Valley, as well as the Valley itself. And this respect does not stop at the people and places that are familiar and welcoming to her. For Nausicaa, Tolmekians, Pejites, and even the Toxic Jungle and its inhabitants are worthy of moral consideration.

Rather than seeing the jungle as a plague that needs to be destroyed in order for humanity to thrive, Nausicaa sees the jungle as part of the natural environment that she must learn to understand and live in harmony with if she has any hope of surviving. When Nausicaa looks at the jungle, and the world in general, she is not viewing an environment that needs to be conquered, but something to be respected and lived with. This approach allows her to develop a much more nuanced understanding of the jungle than someone like Kushana, and ironically that understanding makes Nausicaa more likely than Kushana to discover the course of action that will lead to the best overall outcome.

Kushana's perspective of the jungle is limited to viewing it as a hostile place full of deadly insects and poisonous spores. When trying to recruit followers in her war against the jungle, she says, "We will put the toxic jungle to the torch and resurrect this land together. . ." To her it is nothing more than a plague that needs to be wiped out. Contrast this with Nausicaa's deeper understanding of her environment. With careful study and exploration of the jungle she has cultivated useful resources for the people of the valley and she's discovered the source of the jungle's poison. In a somewhat ironic twist, Nausicaa discovers that the war that scourged the earth in the first place is what poisoned the soil and the water of the earth and that the plants of the jungle are actually gradually purifying the planet. Kushana' reckless plan to revive one of the ancient weapons to burn the jungle would actually make the planet even more uninhabitable for humans. The jungle is needed if humanity is to have any hope of rebuilding, and this is something Nausicaa would never have discovered were it not for her careful attempts to understand the world she finds herself in and her desire for humans to live in harmony with the jungle and each other.

By paying attention to the animals around her and seeking to befriend them, Nausicaa has also learned that the Ohmu are not mere monsters, but sentient beings that communicate telepathically. They do not seek to annihilate humanity but merely to protect the jungle and ensure that it eventually purifies the planet. This discovery plays a pivotal role during the anime's climax, which I won't needlessly ruin. But suffice to say, that had Nausicaa not known that the Ohmu were sentient creatures, capable of compassion, Kushana's misguided attempt to destroy the jungle and Pejite's attempt to avenge Tolmekia's destruction of the Pejite kingdom, would have been the end of the Valley of The Wind.

One of the most compelling things about Nausicaa's emphasis on how she treats others rather than what she is trying to achieve is that she is able to enjoy her life, even though she lives in an extremely harsh environment. Whereas Kushana sees the world as a miserable and dangerous place that one must always be on guard against, Nausicaa is able to marvel at the world around her. She can appreciate and fully understand her world in a way that Kushana never could. This is not because Nausicaa is naive. It is rather because she pays attention to what she is doing and not just to what she seeks to accomplish.

The Legend Has Come True. The Wind Has Come Back

There needs to be ethical limits on human behaviour, even after the end of the world. Whether fighting zombies, robots, giant insects, or other humans, throwing all restrictions on action out the door and doing whatever it takes to survive leads to a cycle of endless atrocity. Humans are capable of terrible acts in the name of survival, but we're also capable of noble action in pursuit of the same goal. Nausicaa's plea is that we recognize that the best way to ensure that the pursuit of our lofty goals actually has a positive effect on the world is by concerning ourselves not only with what we are trying to achieve, but the way in which we go about accomplishing what we set out to do.

10

Just War Is No Gouf

LOUIS MELANÇON

> Compared to the Earth Federation, the national resources of Zeon are less than one thirtieth of theirs. Despite this how is it that we have been able to fight the fight for so long? It is because our goal in this war is a righteous one. It's been over fifty years since the elite of Earth, consumed by greed, took control of the Earth Federation. We want our freedom. Never forget the times when the Federation has trampled us!
>
> —GIHREN ZABI, 6th October, 0079 Universal Century

The concept of war is not new to the human race. War, whether thought of as the management of organized violence or socially condoned killing, has been occurring for thousands of years. In the vision of Yoshiyuki Tomino, as expressed through the franchise of *Mobile Suit Gundam*, humans are likely to continue to wage war for thousands of years into the future. Whether thinking about reality or the *Mobile Suit Gundam* universe, this shouldn't require a spoiler alert for anyone. Nestled among the battling robots is an insight into the relationship between war and mankind.

There's plenty of fertile ground here to talk about the damage done to individuals in war, such as Kamille Biden at the end of the Gryps War in *Zeta Gundam*—a lost family, a dead love interest, and locked in a vegetative state mentally cut off from the rest of the humanity. While this is compelling, I want to draw our attention to the very intriguing implications in the franchise about the relationship between war and society as a whole—about how we go about waging war.

Our focus will not necessarily be on the tools of destruction (although those mobile suits are nifty), but rather on the legal, moral and ethical mechanisms that are used to conduct war, and perhaps more importantly, the mechanisms which take a society to war in the first place. The Just War Theory (JWT) provides a great mechanism for this in the real world as well as in the Universal Century of *Mobile Suit Gundam*, though the theory does have some problems, which are nicely illustrated through the political landscape of the *Mobile Suit Gundam* universe, most notably:

- If any side in a war can claim just cause, is there truly such a thing as a just war; and

- Have weapons of mass destruction changed the very nature of how war can be waged in a just fashion?

There's More to War than Big Metal Robots

Before we delve too far into this topic, we need to face two basic facts. First, the waging of war, even in a non-defensive fashion, can sometimes be justified. Pacifists would challenge this; but as the US Catholic Conference stated in the 1983 "Pastoral Letter on War and Peace," a core document in modern discussion of Just War, "a totally and permanently peaceful human society is unfortunately a utopia." If conflict will occur, then we can make the assertion that some wars, beyond even those in defense to physical aggression, can be justified.

Second, going to war has to be justified. Realists would say that justification is an unnecessary step; conflict, even to the point of bullets flying, is part of the human experience. And it is true that the need to justify war in certain periods of Western Civilization was less than hip. But there is a solid, clear pedigree from Cicero in the Roman Empire through a series of evolutions which have spawned such things in modern times as the third Geneva Convention and the Hague Protocol. The need to justify going to war is now firmly entrenched in modern society. Let's look at two recent examples.

The first is the Iraq invasion of Kuwait in 1990: Iraq made an argument for justifying the invasion based on economic warfare (slant drilling and refusal to eliminate debts) and a perceived Kuwaiti alliance with countries conspiring to topple the Iraqi regime. Other countries rejected this argument and authorized a United Nations–approved military action to restore the recognized borders of Kuwait. Fast forward to 2003 and the US-led invasion of

Iraq where justifications were also assembled to topple the regime through military action. For now, let's avoid the minefield of whether these arguments were valid or invalid; the point is that the US government at the time felt that it had to offer a justification.

The same is true in *Mobile Suit Gundam*. Look back at the excerpt that started this chapter—it's from Gihren Zabi's "Seig Zeon" speech given at the state funeral of his brother Garma. Even though the One Year War began ten months previously, the leadership of the Duchy of Zeon continues to make a case for why they started this conflict—they claim their cause is righteous. Fourteen years later, in the Second Zeon War, Char Aznable defends his actions against the Earth Federation by once again touting the claim of a justified war due to trampled rights. But is simply claiming justice enough? It is at this point that we can start to see some difficulties with Just War Theory.

Jus ad Londo Bellum

Just War Theory consists of two elements; the first is *jus ad bellum*, or going to war in a just manner. This involves a series of criteria that must be satisfied for a country to initiate a war in a just fashion (if a country is attacked, then the right of defense automatically justifies responding with violence towards the aggressor—the "how" of the response we'll look at shortly). The criteria, as outlined by the US Catholic Conference in the Pastoral Letter are: just cause, competent authority (although there can be exceptions in the event of a "just revolution"), comparative justice, last resort, right intention, probability of success, and proportionality. A few of these are self-explanatory, and rather than going through item by item to see if the Duchy of Zeon or the Neo-Zeon movement fulfilled each one, we're going to look at the most problematic: comparative justice.

This term isn't quite so self-explanatory. For a state to meet the criterion of comparative justice, the injustice that is suffered must be of such significance that the taking of lives in combat is considered appropriate. Basically, one side is more "right" than the other, and this "rightness" allows them to start a war against those who committed the wrong. It may be that one of your eyebrows went up just now. How can "rightness" be measured, who measures the "rightness," and how can one side therefore be more just than the other?

A problem with Just War Theory is that it opens up opportunities for any given regime, especially those that may be aggressive and infused with militarism, to create a hollow case within the Just War Theory framework and initiate conflict without the war truly being just. *Mobile Suit Gundam* demonstrates this very well. In the One Year War, the Duchy of Zeon initiated a war because, as stated in the "Sieg Zeon" speech, the rights of those colonists living in Side 3, also known as the Duchy of Zeon, had been suppressed by the Earth Federation—they were unable to fulfill their potential as spacenoids, humans who had migrated to space and viewed themselves as the next evolutionary opportunity for mankind. This is the comparative justice they claim allows them to initiate the One Year War and attack the Earth Federation. But do these perceived rights infringements really provide a justification for the Duchy to kill billions of people within the opening weeks of the war?

With the glimpses we get of the ruling Zabi family and their decision-making process, it is clear that militarism has a firm hold on the Duchy of Zeon—war would happen, and so they must create a just war argument and the weakness of comparative justice allows them to do this. As shown in the feature film *Char's Counter Attack*, Char Aznable with his Neo-Zeon movement in the Second Zeon War takes the same devious path. In his speech to the members of his fleet, he discusses the injustices thrust upon the colonists and former Zeon soldiers by the Earth Federation and how this permits them to conduct the current conflict in which the primary goal is to change the climate of the Earth in order to make it uninhabitable for humans.

But again, is the claim of justice simply a mechanism that Char can use to manipulate spacenoids to support his ideas and militarism? Of course it is. The story shows that Char's militarism and ego are exploiting not only the people who support him, but an important weakness in the Just War Theory as well. This weakness—the difficulty of measuring the comparative justice of the combatants—raises concerns about the true utility about the theory, as any state can claim justness in initiating war if it supports their less-than-just agenda. But there's more to the theory than just going to war.

Etiquette in War: RSVPs for Bombing?

Jus en bello is the second half of Just War Theory, which deals with the behavior of the combatants in war. The Pastoral Letter identifies two criteria for this: discrimination (acts of war are directed against combatants, and non-combatants are not directly targeted) and proportionality (an attack on a military capability should not result in greater civilian casualties than the advantage gained from the destruction of the military target). However, there is a third commonly accepted criteria, highlighted by Michael Walzer in *Just and Unjust Wars*, of military necessity: military attacks must be intended to assist in achieving the military defeat of the opponent, not simply to cause death and destruction.

To have a just war, a state must satisfy the criteria of both *jus en bello* and *jus ad bellum*. If a state violates *jus en bello*, the validity of their *jus ad bellum* position comes into question. However the converse is not true—a state that conducts combat operations fully within the parameters of *jus en bello* in a conflict that did not meet *jus ad bellum* cannot rehabilitate their position in starting an unjust war.

Let's consider Ramba Ral, the Zeon lieutenant sent to avenge the death of Garma Zabi: a master of guerrilla warfare and mobile suit combat, Ral inspires and heroically leads his men to capture or destroy the Federation's secret weapons of the White Base and Gundam. When encountering civilians in the villages they pass through, he and his men do not spread destruction. When they realize that children are on board the White Base, the assaulting soldiers differentiate their targets; they recognize that children are not combatants and should not be harmed if at all possible in the attack. Though these particular soldiers fought honorably, the Zeon prosecution of the One Year War was still unjust. This isn't particularly problematic until the criteria and linkages between *jus en bello* and *jus ad bellum* are placed in the context of a specific type of weapon: a weapon of mass destruction.

Have Colony, Will Drop

Much thinking on *jus en bello* since the invention and battlefield use of weapons of mass destruction (primarily nuclear, but not let's not forget chemical and biological) has generally centered on the idea that any use of these weapons is unjust as they violate proportionality and likely military necessity. But this is not just use in the offense—it extends to use in the defense (whether in response to the use of a weapon of mass destruction or a conventional attack); the Pastoral Letter explicitly states that use of these weapons in defense is not legitimate and cannot be justified.

What is being said here is that it isn't solely the act of using these very powerful weapons that would be immoral, but that the immorality lies within the weapons themselves. That is a fairly standard line in Just War Theory. The use of these weapons in *Mobile Suit Gundam* seems to support this stance. The One Year War begins with the Three Seconds of Declaration, a three second delay between the declaration of war by the Duchy of Zeon against the Earth Federation and an all out attack with chemical and nuclear weapons against space colonies aligned with the Federation.

The Zeon argument of military necessity starts with the claim that these attacks were against Federation garrisons which would have mobilized and taken to the field of battle against the Zeon forces and so were valid, necessary targets. But the effects of such weapons, especially in the confined atmosphere of a space colony can be horrid, as seen in Shiro Amada's flashback in the *08th MS Team* episode "Reunion" to his first hand experience of the attack. The massive, indiscriminate death and destruction of life due to the enclosed nature of a space colony quickly pushes aside any plausible claims of validity or necessity. The same can be said of the improvised weapons of mass destruction that the Zeon and Neo-Zeon use—twenty kilometer long, dead space colonies and asteroids dropped onto the Earth in the hopes of creating nuclear winter-like conditions. Neither the Zeon nor the Neo-Zeon, as political entities controlling armed forces, conduct themselves within the limits of *jus en bello*—but is this really due to the effect of the weapons, or the intent of the states which used them?

Regardless of the immoral actions of the Zeon and Neo-Zeon in combat, this characterization of a particular weapon of war or use of that weapon as being other than amoral is another weakness of Just War Theory. The assertion behind the characterization of immorality is based on the claim that the damage and destruction caused by these weapons is something unprecedented in human history, and so they are "game changers." It is true that these weapons have the potential to deliver destructive capability on a much wider scale than other weapons, but hasn't mankind used less potent weapons to cause just as much death and destruction in the past? Why yes, we have.

Someone has always found a way to expend that extra effort needed to perform an immoral act with the less powerful tool; be it bombs, machine guns, machetes, or (fictionally) mobile suits—directed disproportionate and indiscriminate killings in times of war have always occurred. Furthermore, it may not be true that there is no possible scenario in which these weapons would be able to meet the conditions of *jus en bello*. I can't think of one scenario in the real world where they could; but I also can't claim to have imagined every scenario. It's highly unlikely, but not impossible, that such a scenario may exist; and *Mobile Suit Gundam* does give a fictional example where the conditions of *jus en bello* are met: Operation Stardust. Here, Anavel Gato, "The Nightmare of Solomon" leads the rag-tag Delaz Fleet in an attack with a nuclear weapon against the Earth Federation fleet review occurring around the space fortress Konpeitoh, formally known as Solomon under the Duchy of Zeon.

Putting aside the question of whether there was proper *jus ad bellum* on the part of the Delaz Fleet, they meet *jus en bello* criteria here: they targeted only combatants (discrimination), and there were few, if any, non-combatant casualties in the attack (proportionality), plus if the Delaz Fleet and the approaching Axis Advance Fleet were to have any hope of militarily defeating or at least stalemating the Federation, it was a military necessity to cripple as much of the fleet as possible while minimizing the damage to their own few ships. Could they have used a more conventional weapon and still achieved their goal? Possibly—this wasn't a job that only a nuke could do—but it was a valid tool here.

It seems more reasonable to say that there is no scenario in which the only possible tool that could be used is a weapon of mass destruction. As such, we should conclude that the weapons are amoral and can be placed alongside more conventional weapons as tools for use—the use only becomes immoral when placed in the specific context of the intent of their use and the judgment of the *jus en bello* criteria. But with these weaknesses in both *jus ad bellum* and *jus en bello,* does Just War Theory remain useful?

Freeing Clausewitz's Soul from Gravity

The short answer is yes—Just War Theory remains a useful framework for not only making sure that a war being entered into is itself just, but also that the goals of the conflict remain clear in the minds of those leading the state into war. That may seem like a ridiculous statement—surely people would understand what they want to achieve in a war and wouldn't lose sight of that goal. But even a cursory examination of the history of warfare demonstrates that this does, in fact, happen. And if we are going to discuss goals in war, we have to resurrect the Dead Prussian. Often, when someone brings up Clausewitz, a call back to realism is assumed; but Realists don't have exclusive rights to him and there is a role within the Just War Theory for Clausewitz.

Carl von Clausewitz, in his book *On War*, is credited for establishing the idea that war is an amoral force—with its own logic and tendencies—tendencies to pursue itself into a self-generating cycle, seeking always for that ever elusive state of the *absolute war*, a pure war with no limits, no measure of control and the goal only of perpetuating itself. Realists often point to this concept of absolute war as a basis for setting aside Just War Theory in pursuit of the concept of *total war*, where any action is acceptable in pursuit of the state's objectives. But there is a problem with absolute war—it can't actually exist for a significant reason highlighted by Clausewitz. War is started to achieve a political goal—while the military goal may be distinct from the political goal, it is shaped, guided, and nested within the political goal. Shaped, guided, and nested: that seems to straightforwardly imply the placing of limits. It does become critical, as war is always seeking to break those limits and achieve that absolute state, that those limits be constantly assessed and adjusted as needed in the context of the political goals. And here is where Just War Theory becomes so useful.

Let's say a state or group of states goes through the *jus ad bellum* criteria (for the moment, even lump in the problematic comparative justice) before initiating a conflict to make sure the war itself, as well as the political goals of the war, is just. This state (or group of states) will then have a clear vision about what it is fighting for. It will also have a clear vision about how it should direct its broader battlefield actions to achieve those larger political goals—the theater of war level strategy it will pursue to achieve those political goals ("We want to occupy this region and add it to our territory"). Now, there is still the requirement to ensure that the tactical battlefield actions are within *jus en bello* ("Let's bomb that military facility, but make sure we don't hit that museum two blocks away"), but it's probably a safe assumption that if the proper homework has been done prior to getting into a war, this will be a manageable situation. This state, or group of states, will then have the ability to ensure that their efforts are consistently geared towards achieving the political goals and, more importantly, that when it has met its goals, it can stop the conflict. The war then would be constrained within just bounds and cannot become disconnected from the political goals that the state is attempting to achieve. If there is a disconnect in execution (a deliberate violation of *jus en bello*) or the goals are allowed to slip away from the initial just criteria (and so a loss of *jus ad bellum*) due to the force of war seeking an absolute state, then how will anyone be able to tell when the goals of the war have been met and victory is achieved?

Isn't this where the Duchy of Zeon finds itself? A lot of the actions can't easily be linked to achieving the political goals of independence. Within the first month of the One Year War, Federation forces were crippled by Zeon action: the vast majority of the Federation space combatant ships were destroyed or too heavily damaged to sail, many naval, air and land forces were destroyed in the environmental aftermath of the colony drop in Operation British.

Militarily, there was no way the Federation could oppose the Zeon, and at the negotiations about weapons of mass destruction in Antarctica, independence for the Duchy could have been established—achieving the political goal. Instead, the Zeon Earth Attack Force is formed and within a week of the conclusion of talks, Zeon forces begin to invade Earth itself, occupying two thirds of the planet within two months. Earth is too tempting to not invade: there would be access to additional resources for building more machines of war, and those resources would be denied to the Federation. But it does not help the Zeon achieve the goal of independence they initially claimed. Just the opposite, in fact: they now have to control and govern all of the land they now occupy, a resource intensive undertaking which sucks away people, materials, funds, and other resources from achieving their political goal.

The force of war has disconnected the military goal from the political goal and made it pre-eminent, shifting actions towards achieving military goals that are nested only within themselves and do nothing to achieve the political end. Soon the Zeon find themselves overstretched with no clear vision for what victory will look like. A small group of space colonies, taking on the rest of the human race in war should probably make sure that it knows what it wants and how it will go about getting it, or it can find itself in a vulnerable position. Because the One Year War is itself unjust when examined through Just War Theory, it's not surprising that the Zeon did not use military force to achieve political goals, but instead had their goals used by that force for its own ends.

It has weaknesses, but Just War Theory provides a framework to ensure the limits placed on war by a state constitute something as close as may be possible to a morally justifiable position. And though the Just War Theory can be exploited by a state in the throes of militarism, it also provides a useful framework for identifying when a state in war may have drifted away from such a position, either as a result of the pull towards total war or the immorality of its leaders.

The Duchy of Zeon and the Neo-Zeon movement both demonstrate this, with their attempts to corrupt the Just War Theory for their own uses. The defeat of both of these elements in the One Year War and Second Zeon War respectively can't be directly attributed to their inability to adhere to Just War Theory, but their attempts to corrupt the theory indicate a lack of understanding of the nature of war itself, as well as what they truly sought to accomplish by starting wars in the first place.

11

The Search for Vengeance

IAN M. PETERS

> Of the characters that run to excess, he that exceeds in fearlessness has no name . . . but a man would be either a maniac or quite insensible to pain who should fear nothing, not even earthquakes and breakers, as they say is the case with the Celts.
>
> —ARISTOTLE, *Nicomachean Ethics*, Book III, Chapter 6

What is courage? Is it defined by what motivates us to perform certain actions or is it found in the actions themselves? It is often said that one man's hero is another man's coward. How, then, do we determine what acts are courageous, and what acts are cowardly? Definitions of each are largely open to interpretation and are usually defined differently by everyone. In Book III, Chapter 6 of *Nicomachean Ethics*, Aristotle explores these concepts and proposes a possible means of determining each state of being. Aristotle argues that courage is determined by how we balance feelings of confidence and fear in relation to death, pain, and loss. It is through experiencing these concepts without giving in to their negative influences that the actions of both a hero and a coward emerge. This struggle for balance, and Aristotle's debate, epitomizes Colin MacLeod's journey in Yoshiaki Kawajiri's *Highlander: The Search For Vengeance*.

In a post-apocalyptic New York, Colin MacLeod searches for Marcus Octavius, a former Roman general and fellow Immortal, who murdered his beloved wife Moya two thousand years ago. In this dark depiction of mankind's future, the twenty-second-century world has fallen into chaos and ruin after a century of terrorism, pollution, and disease. Petty dictators have set up nation states where countries used to thrive, and civilization—as we currently know it—is gone. Tyrants like Marcus Octavius govern over a state's elite, providing them with a clean golden castle to live in, while the lower classes are forced to scavenge in the ruined (and diseased) remains of the surrounding city. Using an army of human soldiers and samurai spider-robots, Marcus governs his kingdom, the remains of New York City, with an iron fist, wiping out any insurrection that may threaten his new "Rome." It was he that released a virus that killed most of the population, and he plans to finish the job with a new, deadlier strain, with any survivors under his control for all time. MacLeod, however, does not care about the state of this new world or anyone living in it. All he cares about is finding the person who killed his wife.

Courageous Crusader or Avenging Coward?

In the *Highlander* universe, first depicted in live-action movies before it was taken up by anime in *Highlander: The Search for Vengeance*, Immortals participate in what is referred to as "the game," where they fight other Immortals in combat to the death (which can only occur through decapitation). By decapitating their opponent, the winner experiences what is known as "the quickening," where the strength, knowledge, and experience of the loser flows into the victor and makes him stronger. The ultimate goal is to be the last Immortal on the planet, where the victor has the strength, knowledge, and experience of every Immortal who has ever lived. Immortals can sense the presence of other Immortals, which acts as a defense mechanism so that one cannot sneak up on another using surprise attacks.

While the majority of the live-action *Highlander* films, TV series, and even the animated series, feature an Immortal descended from the Clan MacLeod, Colin MacLeod is unique to *Highlander: The Search For Vengeance* and has not been seen in any of the franchise's earlier incarnations. This first anime entry in the franchise also presents a vision of *Highlander* that is quite different from most of its previous incarnations, incorporating commonly utilized anime constructs. Kawajiri states that he wanted to "bring out the best . . . that the writer [of the original *Highlander*] had offered . . . while still adding [his] own interpretation" that incorporates the *Highlander* universe into the realm of the anime experience ("A Talk with Kawajiri," *Highlander: The Search For Vengeance*, DVD, 2006; Stars Home Entertainment, 2007).

Colin MacLeod is undeniably a skilled warrior and has overcome great obstacles in his search for Marcus, but is his two-thousand-year quest for vengeance an act of bravery or cowardice? His entire existence for the past two millennia has been focused solely on a quest to track down Marcus and kill him, as he clings to the memory of what he has lost instead of striving to find new purpose in his life. MacLeod continually throws himself into harm's way, risking his immortality in his seemingly never-ending quest. Whether MacLeod's actions are motivated solely by his need to avenge the death of his wife or are a sign that he is too cowardly to live his life without her is open for debate.

Is seeking vengeance for thousands of years an act of bravery or cowardice? Immediately it can be argued, as Aristotle does, that an act of vengeance, which is a product of rage and pain, is not the action of a courageous man. There are, however, other factors that need to be considered before any final conclusions can be drawn regarding MacLeod's situation, as he is unlike any mortal being that Aristotle discussed. Specifically, is Colin MacLeod truly motivated by pain (to seek vengeance) or can his cause be seen as something nobler? Aristotle's argument on courage and cowardice requires an understanding of not only the actions of a person, but of the motives that drive a person to take those actions. For instance, performing certain courageous and "noble" actions, such as fighting in a war, cannot be seen as being courageous if the motivation behind those actions is not "noble" (such as fighting for glory, to escape some other pain, run away from problems, etc.). Therefore, the courageousness or cowardice of MacLeod's quest for vengeance cannot be fully assessed until his motivations are revealed.

War and the Pursuit of Vengeance

Everyone has different ways of defining courage and cowardice, and what one person perceives to be courageous may be seen as cowardly by someone else. Such is the case with Colin MacLeod of the Clan MacLeod, where his perception of himself is oftentimes the opposite of what others see. After spending thousands of years focusing on nothing other than avenging Moya's death, MacLeod is seen as single-minded, selfish, and (sometimes) dangerously insane by those around him. While it is possible that he could be killed if Marcus or another foe cuts off his head, Colin MacLeod is virtually indestructible and therefore his quest for vengeance does not have the same physical implications as it would for a mortal. Death, time, and mortality do not mean the same thing to an Immortal like MacLeod, since he has it within his power to—most of the time—cheat death, the aging process, and the passage of time. So, can his never-ending quest be a courageous act if he is not susceptible to the same mortal conditions as everyone else?

The concept of mortality and how we face its consequences and implications plays an important role in Aristotle's debate on courage and cowardice. He argues that courage is determined by how we balance feelings of confidence and fear, specifically when facing an honorable death. Fear, Aristotle says, is "excited by evil of any kind" and courage is found in walking the line between the "good" that inspires confidence and the "evil" that destroys it.

Since notions of courage and cowardice are oftentimes open to interpretation, Aristotle argues that courage can only be found in facing the most universal fear: the fear of death. Death, which is identified as the most "terrible" fear, "is our limit" since when we are dead, "there is no longer good or evil" inside of us. A courageous person is therefore someone "who fearlessly faces an honorable death and all sudden emergencies which involve death," and the greatest emergency, in this sense, is war. To act courageously in war is to commit oneself to the battle willingly and acting nobly in complete understanding that such a situation could lead to your death.

Can Colin MacLeod's quest for vengeance be contextualized as a war; a great emergency? If nobility can be found in risking your life in what Aristotle argues as a noble cause, then determining the status of MacLeod's battle with Marcus is paramount to understanding whether it is an act of courage or cowardice. MacLeod's quest against Marcus Octavius began during a war, when MacLeod was fighting to protect his people from Marcus's invading Roman forces two thousand years ago. This situation, when applied to Aristotle's criteria, would qualify as being a prime opportunity for courageous action on the part of Colin MacLeod. However, this war is short lived (as MacLeod's army was wiped out during the first skirmish) and MacLeod spends the next two thousand years trying to kill Marcus for what he has done. Can MacLeod's actions qualify as being a continuation of the war that began it all? Others may see MacLeod as fighting not out of a willingness to face an honorable death but out of pain inspired by the loss of his wife. MacLeod, however, may see things differently.

Death, Pain, Rage, and Loss

When determining whether or not MacLeod's quest is courageous or cowardly, we have to look at several specific factors (death, pain, rage, and loss), and how they each affect the Highlander's actions and his uniquely immortal life.

First let's look at the concept of death. MacLeod is virtually immortal, and therefore his "death" is contextually a bit different than what Aristotle had considered in his initial debate on the subject. Colin MacLeod is not restricted to the same limited lifespan of ordinary humans, and his quest therefore can continue indefinitely (unless his head is cut off). Unlike the situations examined by Aristotle, MacLeod's journey began with his death, although that death was not permanent, and he didn't fully understand his immortal status until after the destruction of his village and his initial post-first death attack on Marcus.

In the *Highlander* stories, all Immortals are foundlings who have no knowledge of their origins. They continue to age normally until they experience their "first death," which is the first time they are killed. To become an Immortal, they need to die a violent death (which does not include disease, old age, or other natural causes). After this event, they are revived by whatever mystical forces that give Immortals their power, and from that point on they do not age again. If they're killed (apart from having their head cut off), Immortals come back to life after a few moments (or hours, days, or longer, depending on the extent of the damage) and show no physical sign of their injuries. The only exceptions are if a limb gets cut off or if they experience a major wound to their head, such as the scar running down Colin MacLeod's face.

After having his head nearly cut in half, MacLeod is informed by his spirit guide, Amergan, that he is an Immortal. Since MacLeod first attacks Marcus without knowing of his special ability, is it not possible that MacLeod, at least at the beginning, entered into his quest fully believing that his actions could lead to his own destruction? When it is revealed that he can only permanently die after being decapitated, MacLeod still continues to fight

Octavius, knowing that this man has the ability to end MacLeod's life forever. Does this therefore count as courageously facing death?

Aristotle argues that, in order for an act to be courageous, the person needs to be able to feel pain and, like death, understand its implications. According to Aristotle, "men are called courageous for enduring painful things," for being "insensible to pain" is the sign of a "foolhardy" braggart who hides their cowardice behind false courage. MacLeod still feels pain, which means he is not "insensible" to such things. However, is his tolerance to pain different than that of a normal man since he knows that, barring decapitation, his wounds will always heal?

While Aristotle argues that a courageous person needs to be able to feel pain and, in turn, face it honorably and without fear, he does not specify as to whether or not that pain actually needs to be lethal. As with everyone who dies in combat, a lethal blow is incomparable to a non-lethal blow, as no other wound would carry the same outcome or consequence (being decapitated would bring with it a different type of pain than being stabbed through the chest). While MacLeod will not remain dead from any wound other than decapitation, he still nonetheless feels pain and experiences "death," albeit not a permanent one. The threat of complete and utter death still remains, and MacLeod faces that possibility every time he goes into combat. Therefore, it can be argued that Colin MacLeod is still capable of dying a hero's death in the pursuit of his cause because he willingly puts his life on the line.

While physical pain is necessary to behaving courageously, it cannot be the sole driving force behind that person's intentions. To be moved by pain is to be a "wild beast" or, as Aristotle at one point says, "is the case with the Celts." At the time Aristotle wrote that book, the Celts were considered by many in Greece to be uncontrollable savages, and their motivations were seen as such. While we know that this is not the case, Aristotle's argument that it is foolhardy for someone to be "quite insensible to pain" still has its merits (if we ignore the racial slurs). The existence of pain and how susceptible we are to its sting oftentimes helps us contextualize what is truly at stake in a situation (such as war or combat). However, it is important to remember that pain is not solely a physical construct. To fully examine MacLeod's actions we must also take into consideration how emotional pain can be a driving force in his life and in the pursuit of his quest.

Although he may be fully aware of physical pain as well as the imminent possibility of his (permanent) death, MacLeod's actions can be considered to be the product of his (literally) undying psychological pain and rage. He watched his wife die, and he then attacked Marcus as a result of that pain and fury, which nearly led to his permanent death. Having pain act as a motivator for his actions is not what Aristotle would consider to be that of a "noble" hero but is instead the behavior of a wild beast. Aristotle states that "those who in sheer rage turn like wild beasts on those who have wounded them are [oftentimes mistakenly] taken for courageous, because the courageous man is also full of rage" since "rage is above all things" an eagerness to "rush on danger." While he agrees that rage can be beneficial to the courageous man and provide fuel for his fighting spirit, Aristotle emphasizes that a person needs to be motivated by noble causes and not solely by painful rage in order to be considered courageous.

Over the course of the film, we see Colin MacLeod engage in combat with many different enemies. When he is fighting samurai spider-robots or Marcus's foot soldiers, MacLeod fights in a controlled and disciplined manner that is seemingly devoid of rage (or any other emotion). When confronted by his main nemesis, MacLeod's technique changes. He no longer seems to focus on form and efficiency but is instead driven by a need to inflict as much damage as possible. MacLeod, in these instances, fights like a crazed, enraged animal instead of a skilled warrior. He seems to have little regard for his own life (or too little fear of his own death), which Aristotle would argue is the hallmark of a coward. MacLeod's uncontrollable rage is the prime piece of evidence to support that his quest is indeed for vengeance instead of the continuation of the original war.

While killing Marcus is one possible end result in his millennia-long journey, it is debatable that MacLeod may have other intentions. Is MacLeod using this quest merely as an opportunity for him to die in combat fighting for his cause? As Aristotle says, "to seek death as a refuge from poverty, or love, or any painful thing, is not the act of a brave man, but of a coward," and MacLeod's actions can easily be seen as a means of escape if the end result that he seeks is his own death. Since Moya died, Colin MacLeod's entire existence has been dedicated to this one cause. During this time he fought in what seems like every major war, choosing a side not because of his ideals but because it was against Marcus. While

MacLeod fought and died in these wars, it can be argued that, in his mind, he has been fighting in the same war for the past two thousand years, with Marcus's death his intended goal. Aristotle argues that "the happier" a person is, "the more grievous will death be" for them. Since MacLeod has not been happy since the death of his wife, the end of his own life would have very little meaning to him, and therefore his quest lacks courage since he cannot truly face death courageously.

After crashing a plane into a church[1] during a confrontation with his foe during World War II, MacLeod reveals some insight into his motivations:

> **MARCUS:** Why don't you just give up before your luck runs out?
>
> **MACLEOD:** I loved Moya, and you killed her!
>
> **MARCUS:** I loved Rome. Things die. It is the way of life. All we can do is try to find a reason to go on; build it again. I have found mine. Why don't you find something?
>
> **MACLEOD:** Mine is to bury you.
>
> **MARCUS:** I wonder, who is the bigger fool?

If we are to take what he says in this scene at face value, MacLeod is not motivated in his quest by anything other than anguish over his wife's death. His ultimate goal is to kill Marcus, despite the fact that the ex-Roman general has defeated MacLeod in each of their encounters. Whereas Aristotle says that a "sanguine man," someone who "is confident in danger because he has often won and has defeated many adversaries" is not courageous: neither is someone who is foolhardy. This quest is motivated by the pain of loss, and such motivation is not, according to Aristotle, the way of a courageous person. However, Aristotle also argues that "a man is not to be called cowardly for fearing outrage to his children or his wife."

It seems that the true test of courage, in MacLeod's situation, is trying to find a way to live without Moya, start a new life for himself, and find honor in that life. Unfortunately, MacLeod seems

---

[1] In the *Highlander* stories, it's against the rules of "the game" for Immortals to fight on holy ground. This is a rule that no Immortal will break, no matter how evil his opponent might be.

incapable of doing this as he is still blinded by grief after two millennia. Amergan, who tries to act as MacLeod's conscience, attempts to make the Highlander see the truth to his own existence:

> **AMERGAN:** Did you live with honor? No, because honor was not what you wanted. Over a thousand years there was only vengeance. . . . You died again and again with no thought to what you could have been; what you could have done.

MacLeod seems to have forgotten the words he said to his people before they were massacred by Marcus: fight for "freedom," for "glory," and "in the name of honor." Although fighting for glory is not considered by Aristotle to be courageous, fighting for freedom and with honor is. However, the pain MacLeod felt over the loss of his wife solely fueled his actions. While Aristotle says that pain alone cannot serve as the motivation for courageous action, it is still not cowardly to fear the outrage of your own wife. But the question then becomes, if that "fear" becomes a reality, can that fear act as just cause to fuel a courageous act? Perhaps Colin is a coward, not for fearing death, but instead for fearing life without Moya.

Colin MacLeod's quest can, in some ways, be interpreted as a desire to keep some part of Moya's memory alive through physical action. However, instead of honoring her wishes and building a new life for himself, MacLeod remains trapped in his despondent past, without living in hope of a better future. These, Aristotle would argue, are not the actions of a courageous hero. Instead, MacLeod is a coward since to be courageous a person needs to have confidence, and confidence "implies hopefulness." For thousands of years MacLeod had no hope, and therefore didn't really have any courage.

Redemption and Hope for the Future

Highlander: The Search For Vengeance is a tragic tale that chronicles the long, yet arguably empty life of Colin MacLeod of the Clan MacLeod and his two-thousand-year quest for vengeance. With pain and loss as his motivators, MacLeod used his immortality to pursue a man who had wronged him across the centuries instead of trying to find a new life for himself. But instead of living his life, MacLeod seemed to be looking for a way to die as he had lost all hope for a better future. Aristotle would claim that this is not the way of a courageous man; it is instead the life of a coward.

While the path a person takes can keep them from altering course their entire life, sometimes the journey offers them the possibility for redemption. At the film's end, MacLeod accomplishes what he has sought for so many years when he takes Marcus's head. However, in the process he gains something more; he regains his courage, nobility, and, for the first time in millennia, has found hope. It is all thanks to Dahlia, a young woman who had spent her entire life as an outcast living in the shadow of Marcus's new "Rome." With MacLeod's redemption, however, came the revelation of a new tragedy: since her death, Colin has encountered the reincarnated "soul" of Moya many times in the forms of women, like Dahlia, who love him unconditionally. MacLeod was so hell-bent on his quest for vengeance that he never realized the opportunities for happiness that he had missed over the centuries. In the end, Dahlia (and Moya) helped Colin break out of his endless cycle of hate and remember who he was: a Highland Chieftain who once led a small band of villagers in a fight against an invading force who wanted to destroy them all. That was Colin MacLeod's purpose. It is also his destiny.

History has a way of repeating itself. After centuries of searching, Dahlia helped Colin realize that Marcus was once again attacking a group of "villagers" who had no hope of surviving against the superior numbers of "Rome." His journey had come full circle, and Colin MacLeod finally understood that Marcus has caused more pain in the world than just the death of his own wife. Without MacLeod's help, Marcus would succeed in killing these people just as he had succeeding in wiping out Colin's village two thousand years before. His old foe had to be stopped, not just because MacLeod wanted him to pay for the death of Moya, but because countless other lives depended on it. Through Dahlia, MacLeod saw how selfish his quest had been and how much time he had wasted in his quest for vengeance. While Aristotle would argue that MacLeod lived the life of a coward for the past two thousand years, Dahlia and the people of New York changed all of that. MacLeod became a general in their war, and while he does kill Marcus, it is no longer solely to avenge Moya's death. Instead, MacLeod uses the power of Marcus's quickening to destroy the newly released virus and foil his enemy's plans. Unlike in their previous encounters, MacLeod no longer fights like a wild beast but instead with precision and courage, and these traits led him to victory.

According to Aristotle, courage is found in our ability to face an honorable death during times of war and, in such instances, to behave nobly. While MacLeod did not fear his own death, he did not allow himself to understand its implications, nor the hollowness of his quest for vengeance. Rage, anguish, and pain were the sole motivators for his actions, which resulted in a never ending struggle that existed outside the realm of a noble cause. While it took another war for Colin MacLeod of the Clan MacLeod to once again find courage, honor, and nobility, is it not equally honorable or courageous to find ways of preventing wars? Although MacLeod was able to regain some of what he lost during his quest, does this redemption excuse two thousand years' worth of cowardice? That remains to be seen. Whether or not MacLeod has completely changed for the better is also a mystery, but perhaps now that MacLeod has been reminded of his potential, he will find a more noble purpose to dedicate his life to. While Dahlia is killed during his final battle against Marcus, perhaps MacLeod will one day meet the reincarnation of his beloved wife again and be given the chance to start over, finding peace with himself and with the world around him.

Colin MacLeod's is a cautionary tale of love, loss, death, rebirth, vengeance, and redemption. By building a new life for himself, MacLeod would be able to exhibit true courage. Through that courage he would find strength, and through strength MacLeod may one day find happiness. As *Highlander: The Search For Vengeance* reminds us, a willingness to die is not always the same thing as courage. For Colin MacLeod, dying is easy. It is living that is hard.

12

The Possibility of Perfection

ANDREW TERJESEN

A lot of *shonen* anime series have plots that revolve around major tournaments, such as the *DragonBall* series, *YuYu Hakusho, Yu-Gi-Oh! Duel Monsters, Pokemon*, and even some non-fighting anime like *Hikaru no Go*. Or the story is advanced by a series of extended fight scenes (as occurs in *Bleach, Naruto*, and *One Piece*).

The young boys and adolescents who are the target demographic for these anime find these conflicts exciting, but there's also an interesting philosophical presupposition underlying all these anime: the assumption is that competition will bring out the best in everyone who participates. Although the hero of the anime is usually on a personal quest that requires them to win the fight or tournament, there are always a number of supporting characters who share the goal of Roronoa Zoro in *One Piece*, which is to simply become the best at whatever it is they do. These characters also share Zoro's philosophy: the only way to become better is by competing with someone who is better than you—and winning.

When thinking about the relationship between competition and improvement, two philosophers' names spring to mind immediately: Adam Smith (1723–1790) and Charles Darwin (1809–1882). You might not normally think of these thinkers as philosophers, but Smith was actually a professor of moral philosophy at the University of Glasgow and in his lifetime was more famous for his work in moral philosophy than in economic theory. And in Darwin's time, many people still referred to the biological and physical sciences as "natural philosophy." Today we draw too sharp a distinction between science and philosophy, forgetting that any branch of knowledge involves some reasoning and justification of one's ideas (it's not just looking at the data and seeing the obvious answer). Still, there are important differences between how economics, evolutionary biology, and philosophy approach things.

Smith's theory and Darwin's theory are in conflict with one another, as Smith (despite what you may have been told) favors competition within limits in opposition to the unbridled competition and limitless development of Darwin's theory. Even in a world without a Dark Tournament or chunin exams, it can be important to think about what role we think competition should play in shaping who we are.

And the Winner Is . . . the Best?

Before he encounters Luffy in *One Piece*, Zoro is traveling the oceans looking for Mihawk—the best swordsman on the Grand Line—just so he can test his skills against him. Zoro's quest leads him into conflict with a number of adversaries, but his goal always remains the same: to fight the best in order to become the best. Every fight is just a step on the way to that final challenge. Mihawk shares a similar desire. When the two finally meet in the series, Mihawk is able to defeat Zoro, but rather than killing him, he tells Zoro to get stronger and give him a real challenge someday.

The idea that competition improves the competitors is associated with Smith's masterwork, *An Inquiry into the Nature and Causes of the Wealth of Nations*. Although Smith is writing about the importance of free markets, his reasoning is just as applicable to Zoro and Mihawk. The reason that Smith thinks competition is so important is that without it, people tend to be sloppy and lazy. According to Smith, a monopoly (that is, a situation in which there is no real competitor) "is a great enemy to good management" (p. 163). Fighting someone like Mihawk forces Zoro to dig deep and summon every ounce of skill he has. And while Mihawk is somewhat challenged by Zoro, he knows he needs real competition if he wants to keep his edge.

A good example of how competition brings out the best in us can be found in Zoro's conflict with Mr. 1, a member of Baroque Works. Mr. 1, thanks to the Dice-Dice Fruit, can turn any part of his body into a steel blade. While struggling against him, Zoro states that once he has defeated Mr. 1, he will have learned to cut steel. And that is exactly what he does to defeat Mr. 1. That conflict forces Zoro to reflect back on his sword training and come to a new realization about his technique so that he can cut something which he could not cut before. Zoro's achievement is a form of "powering up"—taking his existing abilities and increasing their capacity.

The reason that competition leads to so much improvement in fighting anime is because the threat of death is a great motivator. Had Zoro failed to figure this out, Mr. 1 would have killed him. Despite what some people might think, not all competition is do or die. *Hikaru no Go* is set in the competitive world of Go. It is not the life-and-death situation of many of the fighting anime, but what is at stake is almost as important to the players, and there is not enough to go around. Hikaru's skills improve remarkably as he plays games against various talented Go players and he improves by leaps and bounds playing with the ghost of Go master Sai. Sai remarks upon the effects of their go-playing on Hikaru and on himself, as he notices that his game has also improved. This makes sense as each challenges the other with new moves that force the opponent to look at the game in a different way. Hikaru and Sai also have to "power up" their gameplay, if they want to keep winning games.

Tsuyoku Naritai (I Want to Become Stronger)

One of the basic principles of Smith's theory is that the extent to which we can compete (and improve) is related to how much we can specialize. People who focus their attention on learning and practicing a specific task will come up with better ways to do that task. Someone who is constantly cutting things with a sword will develop better and more efficient ways of cutting, while someone who is playing Go constantly will figure out better ways to trap their opponents and escape traps set by their opponent. We can see this philosophy evidenced in the fact that Zoro is trying to become the best swordsman, not the best fighter, and certainly not the best swordfighter who plays Go. Effective "powering up" requires narrow attention to the capacity you're trying to develop.

Improving on one's skills by focusing one's training is something that we see in abundance in fighting anime. Consider the early training of Son Goku in *Dragon Ball*. Although he is superior to a human in speed, strength, and so on, it is his constant training that equips him with the techniques to beat "inferior" human fighters (as well as fighters from other planets). In the beginning, he just attacked his opponents with a rapid series of blows. When that proves inadequate, he learns the Kamehameha, and later King Kai teaches him other ways to channel his chi in a fight. He eventually learns to channel not only his own chi, but also the chi of those around him into the devastating Spirit Bomb. Throughout his early training, Goku's focus is on developing fighting techniques that best utilize his abilities. Each new move is a better way of doing what he had done before.

We see a similar development in Yusuke Urameshi in *YuYu Hakusho*. Much like Goku, Yusuke's fighting prowess is not enough for dealing with the tougher opponents he encounters, and he has to learn how to channel his energy in order to defeat stronger opponents. Koenma teaches Yusuke the rei gun technique—allowing him to fire a concentrated blast of spirit energy once a day. As the series progress, Yusuke improves upon the rei gun, so that he can shoot it up to four times a day. Then he learns the rei shotgun, which allows him to shoot lots of little balls of spirit energy so that it is harder to dodge. Eventually he develops the ability to fire two rei gun blasts in a row to create a more powerful blast. Finally he learns to shoot the rei gun at point blank range (his Spirit Wave) to create a devastating attack.

Both Goku and Yusuke are "powering up" their existing abilities by constantly challenging themselves. If Yusuke didn't have to fight higher class demons, he would not need to be able to fire a Spirit Wave. Heck, if he had never become a spirit detective, he would have been happy to beat on his classmates with his fists and not developed his capacity to channel rei energy. This seems so obvious that you might wonder why Smith is still lauded today for "discovering" that idea. What's really important about Smith is that he gave a strong philosophical argument for why we should allow competition and specialization to flourish, even if we have the power to eliminate it. It's possible that one day Zoro will become the kind of swordsman that could kill Mihawk. Mihawk knows this, but rather than eliminate a potential challenge before it has fully developed, he welcomes the opportunity to face a "powered up" Zoro and to keep testing himself because he will be much better for taking on the challenge.

Rock Lee and the Limits of Specialization

What really matters in competition is the challenges it presents that keep us from getting complacent. So while searching out superior opponents is an obvious way to challenge oneself, there are other ways, like those of Rock Lee in *Naruto*. In order to develop his physical skills, Rock wears weights that force him to work even harder to land an effective punch. The result is that when he removes those obstacles, he is an even stronger opponent. In a similar fashion, when Rock opens each of his "chakra gates" he removes one of the limits to his physical abilities enabling him to be an even more powerful fighter.

Rock's focus on his physical abilities is much greater than the typical ninja. A normal ninja learns to use three different fighting methods: physical attacks, "real" chakra attacks, and illusory attacks. Rock is only developing one of these three areas. This is not by choice. Rock does not have the capability to manipulate chakra, and so he can only use physical attacks. His challenging regimen is designed to hone his physical attacks so that his strength and speed far exceed a normal ninja opponent and therefore give him a fighting chance against a more balanced arsenal of techniques. Rock's mentor, Guy, does not lack the ability to use the other two ninja techniques. Instead, Guy chooses to try and win every battle by means of physical attacks. This artificial limit is a challenge that forces Guy to be creative in how he fights opponents.

As a result of this focus, both Rock and Guy are much faster and stronger than the average ninja, but that is because they did not spend time developing their other skills. Their physical attributes are much more "powered up" than their other ninja attributes, and it seems impossible that any normal ninja could match their physical level and also have greater skill in other areas of ninja training. The example of Guy and Rock highlight an important fact about "powering up:" the only way to maximize an ability is by neglecting others. But isn't it possible that some ninja consider Rock to be a wannabe because he can't master the three skills of the ninja? That idea reflects a concern that Smith had about specialization.

When reflecting on the growing tendency towards specialization in factories, Smith expressed the fear that too much specialization could have the result that "all the nobler parts of the human character may be, in great measure, obliterated and extinguished in the great body of people" (pp. 783–84). Focusing too much on one task could cause one to neglect the mental faculties needed to deal with everyday life. Smith was a big proponent of a basic education for all, in order to make sure that we tended to some things other than our job and livelihood. His fear was that too much specialization would mean sacrificing our humanity, including our morality.

Because Smith values the things that he thought made us human, for example a general sympathy for the fortunes of others, he thought there had to be a limit to how much we specialized. That, in turn, meant there had to be a limit to how much we competed with each other.

One of the ideas most closely associated with Smith—that markets left unregulated by the government will achieve a natural equilibrium—is actually rooted in Smith's idea that competition is regulated by human nature (which includes a natural tendency towards the moral, which he explored in his first book *The Theory of Moral Sentiments*). The laws of supply and demand are based upon assumptions that there are limits to human want (such as no one buys or consumes what they don't have a use for), and that the market will only be at an equilibrium if people do not commit fraud or steal from each other. All of these limits come from Smith's ideas concerning what it means to be human. Just like Zoro and Mihawk cannot be the best swordsman if they use other weapons or attack their opponents while they are sleeping. The competition to be the best swordsman has certain implicit limits based on what it means to be a swordsman. Smith thought this was true of all activities, but one of the most basic limits on specialization and competition was our own humanity.

Cell's Game and the Darwinian Model

Smith's limit on competition only makes sense if we think that being a certain kind of person is more important than simply winning. After all, if Rock and Guy could defeat every opponent they faced, why should it matter whether they did it using the full range of ninja techniques? The whole point of the three techniques is to give ninjas a range of options for different opponents. The only reason to criticize Rock and Guy would be because one thinks it is really important to be a "real" ninja as opposed to merely a successful fighter.

In point of fact, Rock is not able to hold his own against ninjas with a more well-rounded set of skills. His inability to fight on a non-physical level results in his being crippled. Rock is proof that "powering up" one's physical abilities is not enough when one is confronted with a different level of fighting. Even Guy recognizes this since he does make use of the other aspects of his ninja training when physical prowess is not enough. Rock was a master of taijutsu, but Guy was a "real" ninja. Rock and Guy are really on different levels, and the only way Rock could ever match Guy would be if he "leveled up" and discovered a way to access the other ninja abilities. Unlike "powering up," "leveling up" is not merely a matter of getting stronger, it's also about gaining access to new abilities and capacities that you couldn't use before. To "level up" requires changing, in some sense, who you are.

The idea that "leveling up" should be about evolution and not improvement is something that seems to have been well understood by Cell in *Dragon Ball Z*. Once you have two competitors who have reached the limits of human capacity, the only way to win is for one of them to become something more than human. Cell starts with a combination of the DNA of several fighters in the *Dragon Ball* series, including Goku and Piccolo. The only way Dr. Gero thought he could beat those individuals was by creating something that combined their attributes. Later on, Cell absorbs the androids in order to improve his fighting ability. As Cell absorbs other fighters, his abilities change and so does his appearance. As the Cell Saga progresses, Cell becomes a different creature with each "leveling up." Each form is a different evolutionary stage as Cell moves towards his "Perfect Form."

There are a lot of commonalities between Smith and Darwin's views of competition, which is not surprising since Darwin stated that his insights were inspired by reading economic theory. However, the example of Cell shows where their views of competition come apart. Smith was worried that specialization was changing the nature of what it meant to be human. The flexibility of the human intellect was, at least in his mind, in danger of being replaced by a more focused, drone-like mind. Smith takes for granted that certain states of being are better than others. Becoming a focused drone is inferior to a relatively well-rounded human. The reason Smith thinks this is that he sees competition in the context of a particular goal: to live the best kind of life for human beings as they existed in the eighteenth century.

Darwin does not share Smith's assumption. To start with, Darwin did not think that there was a clear and unchanging notion of what it means to be human (or any other kind of animal). In *The Origin of Species*, a large part of the book is dedicated to showing that species can change. Only later in *The Descent of Man* does he follow his argument to its logical conclusion and recognize that what it means to be human is also mutable.

Darwin also does not assume that there is a particular way of life that evolution is tending towards. If it turned out that being a focused drone was advantageous, then drones would become the dominant species. If taijutsu could consistently beat other jutsu, then people would stop learning to be ninjas. Evolutionary principles even explain why Rock is a rarity among ninja, since families that did not have much skill in manipulating chakra would be squeezed out of the village by those who were better at it.

From an evolutionary point of view, the only limit on competition is whether something outcompetes everyone else. There are no rules that one has to play by, so if the best way to outcompete everyone is to trick them, then that is favored by the evolutionary environment. And since there are no limits placed on competition, there is in principle (actual limits are empirical questions for biologists) no limit to the kinds of improvements that competition would bring about.

Transcending One's Limits: The Super Saiyan

Cell is able to choose to evolve, but in most anime, people "level up" without intending to do so. The clearest example of this is Son Goku in the *Dragon Ball* series. When the seemingly unbeatable Frieza kills Goku's friend Krillin, Goku's rage triggers his transformation into the mythical "Super Saiyan." He had reached his natural limit as a saiyan while fighting (and failing to defeat) Frieza. His emotions push him over the edge and give him the raw power necessary to beat Frieza. Becoming a Super Saiyan doesn't really alter his fighting techniques, but it gives him a whole new level of power to draw upon and channel into his Kamehameha and other attacks. It changes him into a different kind of being, with different skills and weaknesses (such as being slower in Super Saiyan form and manipulating ki differently); and if he changes back, his old limits reassert themselves. When the Super Saiyan form is not enough to meet the new challenge of the androids, further stages of Super Saiyan power are employed, going as far as Super Saiyan 4 in *Dragon Ball GT*.

Another example of this unintentional "leveling up" is when Yusuke is near death during the fight with Sensui. Yusuke's demon heritage provokes a transformation in him, and from then on he is a different kind of person. He trains to improve his powers in his new form, but never again does he experience such a radical change in what he is. When the challenge proves too great, our hero must become a new kind of being in order to survive.

Darwin recognizes that "leveling up" to meet challenges should not be a directed process. After all, if you try and consciously change yourself to meet a challenge you might make a mistake about what you need to overcome the challenge. In *The Origin of Species*, Darwin distinguished between natural selection and domestic selection (like breeding dogs). The problem with domestic selection is that humans select characteristics based upon human wants and desires, not the needs of the animals being bred. That's how we end up with toy poodles. Natural selection uses a much more objective measurement—what survives is better than what doesn't survive. It's hard to know though what will enable one to survive. Most people in the world of *Naruto* distance themselves from those who host tailed beasts (especially Gaara and Naruto). This is probably because they think they are a threat to their survival. In practice though, these hosts are able to protect their villages in ways that other ninja couldn't. One great example of this is when Gaara becomes Kazekage of his village and uses his abilities to shelter the whole village from attack. He does this despite the fact that many in his village still feared him (and until that moment were uneasy with his presence).

The fact that most "leveling up" occurs unintentionally (at least the first time) in fighting anime reflects the idea that we cannot predict very well what we need to survive. Even those who are able to control their evolution can make mistakes, as Cell does when he makes a transformation that enables Gohan to finish him off. Despite what Cell thinks, evolution does not have a notion of "Perfect Form." What matters is what keeps you alive, but that might change depending on the circumstances. Super Saiyan 2 is perfect for fighting someone like Cell, but the peculiar qualities of the form are exploited by Majin Buu. To defeat Buu, even Super Saiyan 3 is not enough. A different set of skills are needed, and Goku defeats Buu in a "lower" Super Saiyan form (with some help from a Spirit Bomb).

Whatever It Takes? Soul Reapers, Hollows, and Buu

In the anime *Bleach*, Ichigo happens upon his Soul Reaper powers by accident, when they are transferred from Rukia. After he loses those powers, he tries to regain them by training. The end result is that he unleashes his own Soul Reaper nature with much greater power than he can control, and a malevolent "hollow" tries to gain control of his body. Given how much harm he could do, these actions seem reckless. Later on, Ichigo gets the visoreds to teach him how to control his hollow powers. In the end he is successful and achieves a new level of power by donning a hollow mask for short periods of time. The hollowification of Ichigo greatly increases his strength and makes it possible for him to engage with tremendous threats like the arrancars. But he has changed his nature—it seems he is no longer human or Soul Reaper. Moreover, his training was highly risky. He might have failed to conquer his inner hollow and instead have unleashed a great threat on the Earth.

From a Darwinian perspective, it does not matter if Ichigo has "leveled up" and lost his humanity. All that matters is whether he has reached a level that will enable him to survive whatever challenges life throws at him. However, when you think about something like hollowification, Smith's attitude towards competition seems more attractive. Darwin's model is much more open-ended because it focuses on the most basic level of competition—you either win or you don't. Smith is more restricted because all competition is viewed through the lens of human competition. After all, wanting to be stronger (like Mihawk does) is a human trait. If you just want to win then you should simply eliminate the competition by any means necessary. If it means becoming something that could be a threat to friends and family, like Ichigo does when he "levels up," then so be it.

Using a notion of what it means to be human to constrict how much we "power up" allows society to achieve a relatively stable equilibrium, like Smith's economic markets. As long as everyone behaves like human beings, competition will reach a certain level and stay at that plateau. Although it means that humans will not "level up" to a new form, it also means that there is no danger of a free-for-all that could lead to a very undesirable result. Although this seems a pretty strong argument in favor of Smith's notion of competition, the fundamental concern of the Darwinian model—how do we decide what is a desirable result—remains unaddressed.

Don't Be a Vegeta

Whether he's a villain or an ally, Vegeta's main goal in the *Dragon Ball* saga is always the same. Vegeta wants to be better than Goku, which will presumably make him the best. Every time Goku (or Gohan or some other saiyan) unlocks a new Super Saiyan form, Vegeta becomes obsessed with training in order to surpass that level.

On the face of it, this might not seem like a big problem. But consider what it means to try and be the "best" on a Darwinian model. The "best" is whoever survives today's challenges. The problem with that is tomorrow's challenges. As almost every fighting anime illustrates, once you become strong enough to beat your current opponent, you'll be ready to face an even stronger opponent. As long as the challenges keep coming, you can never take a rest or be satisfied with the level you're at. Instead, you become the perpetually dissatisfied and grumpy Vegeta. Vegeta's obsession with beating Goku seems to color all of his relationships. It's sometimes hard to imagine how he got together with Bulma and certainly his relationship with Trunks is rocky. If you're going to achieve any sort of satisfaction with life, you need to have some sense of completion. Otherwise, after each "leveling up," you have to wonder if there is another "level" to achieve. Vegeta's only consistently affectionate relationship seems to be towards his daughter Bra, who was born after he had set aside his obsession with simply being the best.

Smith's model offers a chance to have that sense of completion. Instead of simply trying to beat everybody else, these fighters should focus on being the best *fill-in-the-blank*. The never-ending quest for the next level is replaced with a relatively manageable quest to "power up" as much as you can. To live a satisfying life, it is important to frame competition in such a way that it can be managed and kept from dominating our lives. So even though someone who supported a Darwinian model might object that it is unclear what makes "being human" a desirable goal, they would have to admit that a focus on winning leads to a very undesirable life. Once someone admits that the only desirable kinds of life are those that are framed in terms of being this kind of person or that kind of person, then they are no longer adhering to a Darwinian model of competition. On a Darwinian model there can be no presumptions about the kinds of beings that we need to be when we compete. Darwinian models must be open to an unbridled amount of "leveling up."

Most of us seem to recognize that the Darwinian idea of winning at all costs is not the way to go. And not just because it leads to an unsatisfying life like Vegeta's. Think of Sasuke's quest to beat his brother Itachi in *Naruto*. To reach Itachi's level, Sasuke thinks he needs to acquire the Mangekyo Sharingan which requires him to kill someone dear to him in order to awaken it. Even though he's obsessed with vengeance, Sasuke recognizes that there are certain lines that shouldn't be crossed. Better to lose than to win by "leveling up" into a monster. As in most philosophical debates, even when we think one side is clearly right, the other side has a point.

The Darwinian model challenges the Smithian idea that we can be certain about what kind of life is desirable. Looking at some of our examples, we can see that people do make mistakes when distinguishing "heroes" from "monsters." Many people treat those who are the hosts of tailed beasts as monstrous beings and shun them. They do this even though some of those hosts, notably Naruto and Gaara, have been the only ones who are at a high enough "level" to protect their village. Similarly, in the world of *One Piece*, most people who partake of the Devil Fruit (look at its name) are regarded as monsters and ostracized. Once again, some very good people, like Monkey D. Luffy, Smoker and even Nico Robin, use their abilities to fight for people when no one else can. Those who champion the Darwinian model remind us that even if it is better to take a Smithian perspective on competition, we cannot let our notion of "the kind of person we ought to be" close off the possibility of change and improvement in the kind of person we can be. Any major changes in our ideas of what it means to be "human" must be carefully considered. And certainly any change in the kind of life we ought to pursue must be supported by moral arguments. Certainly, that is what Smith does in his books when he presents a certain vision of how humans live together.

However, even though we should be open to the possibility of revising our ideas concerning the kind of competitor we ought to practice being, we should not embrace the Darwinian idea that "winning" a competition is all that matters. The argument in favor of the Smithian way of thinking about competition is based upon both the level of personal satisfaction it offers and the fact that trying to shape ourselves into the kind of beings that we think will win can backfire. Becoming Super Saiyan 4 might work great in one circumstance and lead to your defeat in another. It is far better to focus on being a great human martial artist than on simply being a winning fighter.

This does not mean we should stop debating what it means to be human or a great martial artist. Certainly modern economists do not share Smith's ideas concerning human nature, and thus they tolerate an environment of competition that contributed to the global economic crisis that began in 2008. What it does mean is that we should concentrate on something more than winning or simply improving a specialized set of skills. Perhaps the kind of person we are trying to be.

13

Alchemic Heroes

BENJAMIN CHANDLER

Our heroes define us. They represent the best of us. In attempting to determine how they might reflect the society from which they emerge, a variety of methods have been used: the functional approach, which examines what heroes do within a narrative and how they do it; the psychological approach, which looks at why heroes act the way they do; and the archetypal approach, which identifies recurring patterns of heroic characteristics. These methods often complement each other. The functional and psychological approaches can help identify heroic archetypes, while the archetypal approach can give us a deeper understanding of the psychological and functional approaches and how these might reflect any cultural nuances inherent in a heroic character.

In applying these methods to an analysis of the heroes in Hiromu Arakawa's *Fullmetal Alchemist* [*Hagane no Renkinjyutsushi*] and its movie-length sequel, *Fullmetal Alchemist: Conqueror of Shambala*, we can explore how its heroes might represent certain aspects of Japanese culture. Edward (Ed) and Alphonse (Al) Elric are two brothers devoted to the study of alchemy in order to fulfill their quest for redemption. As a pair of heroes they function as what I label a *dual-hero*, the quintessential Japanese heroic archetype that embodies the fundamental principle at the heart of Japanese philosophical thought. As students they epitomize the Japanese student hero, which reflects the importance of and focus on education throughout Japanese history. As seekers of redemption the brothers represent the wandering redemption seeker, one of the most common Japanese heroic figures, symbolic of the influence of Buddhism on Japanese thought and society.

These three inter-related methods can tell us a lot about the Elric brothers, and how they might reflect aspects of Japanese culture, but there's another method of analysis that we can use to deepen our understanding of these heroes. This new method grows out of the functional, psychological, and archetypal approaches and focuses on how these elements—what a hero does, how they do it, why they do it, and who they are—are combined to form a complete character. I call this the *compositional approach* to understanding heroism because the focus is on the nature of the composition that defines a hero, and how that particular composition might reflect something of the society from which that hero emerges.

A combination of the functional, psychological, archetypal *and* compositional approaches is ideal for examining the figure of the alchemic hero because its defining characteristic is its composition. The alchemic hero is an archetype formed by the combination of other heroic archetypes. Ed and Al are alchemic heroes, because they bring together a number of archetypes: the dual-hero, the student hero, and the redemption seeker. They also bring together other Japanese heroic archetypes: the young boy seeking acceptance amongst his older peers, the super strong boy, and the *shōjo*.

The Dual-Hero

When we think of the hero, we tend to think of a single person, of individuals like Beowulf or Superman. Some of our heroes take on sidekicks, but even the name "sidekick" implies they are lesser than the hero to whom they lend a hand. Even when our heroes group together to form crime-fighting, Earth-saving, wrong-righting super teams, like the Knights of the Round Table or the X-men or the Justice League, we still tend to think of them as groups of individuals rather than as a single entity. In part, this is what makes them so interesting. Each part is separate, distinct, and though the heroes might all be pulling in the same general direction, tensions often arise between them. Tension breeds conflict, conflict breeds drama, and so on.

Things are different in Japan. There are individual, partnered, and teams of heroes in Japan, too, but there also exists a peculiar Japanese heroic identity that I have come to call the dual-hero— two individuals so irrevocably linked that they function within the narrative as a single entity, a single hero.

This uniquely Japanese heroic construction is rooted in Japanese culture, mythology, and philosophy. In the Japanese creation story, two gods—Izanami ("Female-Who-Invites") and Izanagi ("Male-Who-Invites")—come together to create the world. They are two opposing yet equal principles, male and female, which together make a whole. Although it's unclear, it is possible Izanami and Izanagi are modeled on the principles of *yin* (darkness, female, passivity) and *yang* (light, male, activity) in Chinese philosophy. Although the forces of *yin* and *yang* are opposites, they each hold the essence of the other within themselves. This is the exact opposite of the Judeo-Christian mythology, which involves the splitting of a whole into two parts: God creates Adam and then takes something from him in order to make Eve.[1] One being becomes two. In Japan, two forces come together to create the universe: two beings become one. This manner of creation is reflected in the heroism of each culture. Western heroes are often divided within themselves, while Japanese dual-heroes bring together two separate entities.

Ed and Al form the dual-hero in *Fullmetal Alchemist*. They are both alchemists, able to transmute one substance into another by analysing it, breaking it down into its component parts, and then reassembling it into a new form. In many ways they are opposites: Ed is brash, easily agitated, and aggressive (the *yang*), while Al is reserved, calm, and passive (the *yin*). Yet they each possess elements of the other at their heart: Al actually fights better than Ed, and Ed is capable of the sustained study necessary for mastering alchemy, which requires the ability to remain calm and focused. In this way the brothers embody the principles of *yin* and *yang*.

This alone is not enough to make them a dual-hero. What truly forges the brothers into a single function is their common goal. During an ill-fated attempt to resurrect their mother, the Elric brothers lose their human bodies in a perverse act of equivalent exchange, which is the underlying philosophy of their world and the guiding principle of alchemy. Instead of bringing their mother back to life, they birth a monster and, in doing so, Ed loses his right arm and left leg, and Al loses his entire body. Ed is able to fuse Al's soul onto a suit of armor and later replaces his lost limbs with automated ones, called auto-mail. The Elric brothers then embark on a quest to discover the Philosopher's Stone that allows

---

[1] On the difference between Japanese and Western origin myths, see Joseph Campbell, *The Masks of God: Oriental Mythology* (1976), pp. 9–13.

alchemists to transmute objects from nothing, circumventing the law of equivalent exchange. They no longer wish to resurrect their mother but to return their bodies to normal. This is more than a common quest or goal shared by two heroes. It is the same quest, and neither brother wants more nor less than to reach their goal. It is this utter singularity of purpose that fuses the two brothers into a dual-hero.

Student Heroes

The dual-hero has been present in Japanese myth, legend, and folklore since Izanami and Izanagi first came together. If the Elric brothers were simply a dual-hero, they wouldn't be anything new. What makes them so interesting is that they also bring together a number of other Japanese heroic archetypes in a fusion almost alchemic itself in nature. One of the components of that alchemic fusion is the dual-hero. Another is the student hero.

Like the dual-hero, the student hero can be traced back through the Japanese narrative tradition. Descended from the samurai culture of the Bushido Code, which stressed the importance of training the body and mind to be always ready for death, the Japanese student hero devotes him or herself to intense study and training. It is the intensity of this study and training that sets Japanese student heroes apart from other heroes, or even from student heroes from other cultures. Ed and Al both study alchemy from a very young age, but once they lose their mother and decide to bring her back to life, they devote themselves entirely to mastering alchemy. If anything, once they have failed and begin instead their quest to return their bodies to normal, their pursuit of knowledge becomes even more intense and focused.

Although Ed and Al's father is a great alchemist, there is never any question that their abilities are anything but the result of hard-earned knowledge. They did not inherit their powers from their father, nor gain them from some other source like a nuclear reactor or genetically modified spider bite. Ed and Al are great alchemists because they sacrifice everything to study alchemy. They even go searching for a teacher when they realize they won't be able to gain the knowledge they need on their own.

Their teacher is Izumi Curtis, a woman who, like the brothers, attempts a forbidden resurrection. Izumi puts the Elric brothers through intense physical as well as mental training in order to improve their alchemy. The brothers already had a desire to study hard, but under Izumi they learn to hone their bodies as well as their minds. A part of this training involves stranding the brothers on a deserted island to fend for themselves for one month, with no food, while a masked man terrorizes them constantly. Izumi won't agree to train the Elrics unless they survive and, in the process of overcoming this great physical ordeal, discover the secret at the heart of all alchemy—all is one and one is all. During their training they learn that the mind and body are inexorably linked.

The study of alchemy is also a form of spiritual study. The laws of alchemy are governed by equivalent exchange: nothing is ever gained without first giving something else up in exchange. This is also the underlying philosophy of the culture in which the Elric brothers grow up, and so the study of alchemy is partly a study of the way that culture functions. By bringing together and focusing so intently on these three forms of study – mental, physical, and spiritual—the Elric brothers epitomize the figure of the Japanese student hero.

Wandering Redemption Seekers

Another Japanese heroic archetype is the wanderer seeking redemption. These wanderers are usually warriors who seek to atone for a past life of sin and typically come to the path of redemption later in life. The youth of the Elric brothers makes them somewhat unique in this tradition—Ed and Al are fifteen and fourteen-years-old respectively during the events of *Fullmetal Alchemist*—but their quest to restore what was lost to them, not their mother but their bodies, is classic wanderer fare. They are seeking to make up for their past wrongs, to make a clean break from the errors of their past. Increasingly, the brothers' quest sees them trying to break away from the errors of the older generations as well.

Wandering redemption seekers have a strong history in Japanese heroic narratives. Often Samurai warriors have laid down their swords to pursue a spiritual life or have turned from a blood-thirsty past to use their swords to protect the weak and innocent. Such wandering warriors inevitably stumble across helpless innocents along their travels and take time out of their quest for redemption to stop and help those less fortunate. The true heart of their redemption lies in these small acts, though often the hero does not realize this, instead focusing on some ultimate, often unattainable goal, never realizing they are constantly moving towards redemption in everything they do.

Alchemy has few laws, but they are absolute. Do not create gold. Human transmutation is forbidden. For something to be gained, something of equal value must be given up. In attempting to resurrect their mother, the Elric brothers have sinned. They are spurred to find the Philosopher's Stone to nullify that sin, to replace what was taken from them. They are actually looking for redemption, but they don't fully grasp what that means. Their goal is to attain the Stone; that is all they see, but along the way they commit a number of redemptive acts without realizing the significance of those acts. They expose a fraudulent holy man, freeing a town from a man bent on raising an army. They liberate a coal-mining town from a corrupt state official. They restore an entire town to good health by destroying the well of toxic red water they could otherwise have used to make a Philosopher's Stone. Ed refuses to murder a group of convicted criminals even though he could use their life energy to make the Philosopher's Stone. They gain a reputation for supporting the innocent and helping the weak. Ed and Al bear a heavy burden, especially for children their age, but they do not shirk their responsibility, devoting themselves to their quest for redemption as many Japanese heroes have done before them.

Al-Chemy

Edward and Alphonse draw together three other Japanese heroic archetypes: the young boy struggling for acceptance amongst his older peers; the super-strong boy; and the unthreatening *shōjo*. These archetypes are interrelated and find a fusion in Al's character. In the process they are slightly altered but still maintain their essential elements.

The young boy seeking to find his place in a world of older, more mature children is a common theme in Japanese fiction, as noted by Tom Gill ("Transformational Magic: Some Japanese Super-Heroes and Monsters"). In a way, both Elric brothers are seeking their place. Ed becomes a State Alchemist at the age of twelve, the youngest person ever to achieve such a position. As such, he's constantly acting as though he is a grown up, while others in the military often comment that he and his brother are still children and should leave dangerous situations to the adults. The Elric brothers refuse to do so, often finding themselves in situations far more dangerous than their elders. The boys' advanced knowledge of alchemy, gained through intense study, also places them above most of the people they encounter, but still, however much they act like adults, they are only children. Ed is constantly trying to make those in the military see him as an equal.

Ironically, Al doesn't seek to be treated as an adult, but since his soul is attached to a giant suit of armor, people are constantly mistaking him for his older brother, whose codename as a State Alchemist is "Fullmetal." Unlike his brother, Al automatically achieves recognition as an adult, but he regards this as a mistake and rejects it. In Episode 16, Major Armstrong treats the Elric brothers like children, insisting that they need minding. Ed takes offense, but Al is overjoyed, as it is the first time since losing his human body that someone actually treats him like the child he knows himself to be. Al presents a twist on the young boy who seeks acknowledgement, a result perhaps of the fusion in his character with two other heroic archetypes—the super-strong boy and the *shōjo*.

The super-strong boy, like the student hero and wanderer, is strongly rooted in the Japanese heroic tradition. Such boys, like Momotaro the goblin-slayer and Kintaro the Golden Boy, possess incredible strength that is easily the match of the far older and more dangerous villains they face. Emotionally and mentally Al remains eleven-years-old—the age he was when they attempted to resurrect their mother and he lost his body—but his new metal body is almost invulnerable. Like Momotaro he is incredibly strong, and like Kintaro he is skilled in martial arts. Ed comments regularly that he is never able to defeat Al in a fight, and Al often intimidates full-grown men. He is even able to beat up the serial killer Barry the chopper, both when Barry is human and then again after Barry's soul is also attached to a suit of armor. Even though, as suits of armor, both Al and Barry should be perfectly matched, as neither possesses tendons, bones, or muscles, Al has little trouble defeating his older foe.

This super-strength is balanced by Al's naïveté and gentle disposition, the *yin* aspect of his nature. Ed, too, is a kind of super-strong boy, though he has far more human limitations than his brother. Ed's auto-mail compensates for his body's weaknesses and allows him to compete with the big boys, but it is his knowledge of alchemy, his student hero nature, that truly sets him above the adults around him. Al is a much more precise application of the super-strong boy heroic archetype.

Ironically, Al is also connected to the *shōjo* tradition described by Susan Napier in "Vampires, Psychic Girls, Flying Women, and Sailor Scouts: Four Faces of the Young Female in Japanese popular culture." The *shōjo* is an idealized young girl who never grows up. She is seen as non-threatening because she is essentially sexless. Al is definitely not a young girl, but he is a young *boy* who has had his soul attached to a suit of armor, which means he has no sexual organs and is therefore sexless. The fact that the *shōjo* is also sexless allows for a male version of this archetype.

Equivalent Exchange

Being alchemic in nature, and keeping in line with the law of equivalent exchange, something must be lost in the formation of an alchemic hero. Certain attributes relating to the individual component heroic archetypes must be forfeited in order to create this new type of hero, the alchemic hero. This is particularly true when those types, like the young boy seeking acceptance, the super-strong boy, and the *shōjo*, are so intricately linked. Al is accepted by the older people around him, but in being accepted he must bear an adult's share of responsibility. He also loses the protection his age might otherwise grant him; his age becomes a non-factor when Al deals with dangerous people.

This is also one of the things Al sacrifices from his male *shōjo* character archetype. The *shōjo*, being essentially harmless, often inspires feelings of protectiveness in others. Though it is true that certain characters, such as Izumi and Major Armstrong, feel the need to protect the Elric brothers, there's a sense running throughout the series that they can largely fend for themselves. It's worth noting that, in Episode 16 when Major Armstrong treats the boys like children by offering to protect them, Al has had half of his body disintegrated, and Ed has lost his auto-mail arm. Without his arm, Ed loses the only tools that allow him to stand up to the grown ups around him—he cannot fight or perform alchemy—and Al's loss of the right side of his body means that he, too, is incapable of defending himself. It is only when they are completely helpless that others step in to protect them. At other times, they handle things on their own.

In being bound to a suit of armor, Al must sacrifice all sensation. He cannot taste, smell or feel anything, though he can apparently see and hear. Why he is able to use some of his senses and not others is never made clear, but part of the reason the Elric brothers are so intent on restoring Al's body is so that he can regain the senses he has lost. Although the brothers are trying to restore both their bodies, Ed never expresses much of a desire to replace his own lost limbs. There is a sense that he is doing this for Al, whose loss is far greater than his own. While enduring the pain of having his limbs replaced, Ed comments that Al's pain is far worse, as he has given up all sensation. As the second half of the dual-hero, Al wants to restore Ed's body first.

Al also loses the benefits he might have gained through the struggles involved with puberty. In not going through that developmental process, he doesn't really mature, remaining an immortal adolescent. This immortality also puts him at the mercy of Greed, one of the villains of *Fullmetal Alchemist*. Greed is a homunculus, an artificial human being, who longs for true immortality and believes he can gain it by copying the process that attached Al's soul to the armor. This makes Al one of Greed's targets, and Al is kidnapped in Episode 33 so that Greed can learn how he achieved his immortality. This process involves something called a blood-seal, an alchemic seal of blood that binds Al's soul to the armor. The seal provides Al with his only weakness, his fatal flaw, as it is the only thing keeping him tethered to the mortal world. If the blood-seal is destroyed, Al dies. This is proved in Episode 21 when another armor-bound soul destroys itself by crushing its own seal. This fatal flaw sets Al apart from other Japanese super-strong boys and aligns him more closely with Western comic book superheroes like Superman, who is rendered defenseless when exposed to kryptonite.

Alchemic Heroism

The Elric brothers, as alchemic heroes, fuse together a number of disparate heroic archetypes and meld them into a single, coherent whole. And this new type of hero reflects something of the nature of Japanese culture. Japan has a long history of drawing together disparate external elements and somehow incorporating them into its own cultural integrity. When Buddhism was incorporated into Japan, it became *bukkyō*, a Japanese form of Buddhism that melded Indian and Japanese Shinto beliefs. The same process of assimilation can be seen in the way Chinese beliefs, such as Confucianism and the philosophy of the *yin* and *yang*, were incorporated into the Japanese culture. This alchemic process is reflected in the Japanese narrative tradition. When Confucianism and Buddhism were introduced via mainland China around the fifth and sixth centuries, Japan did not import the narratives of China and India wholesale and complete. Instead, they retold these foreign narratives in their own way, changing the settings and characters into Japanese ones while retaining something of the original themes. Aspects were lost; sacrifices were made in the fusion, but somehow Japan managed to retain its own individual, homogenous national identity.

The element of sacrifice in the alchemic hero also has its roots in the nature of Japanese heroism, and it tells us a lot about the underlying traits that influence the development of Japanese heroes. The samurai, Japan's warrior class, form the basis of Japanese heroic literature. The term "samurai" refers to a class of people who serve the nobility. They adhere to the Bushido Code, which demands that they be always ready for death, to sacrifice their own lives in service to their lord. No matter what they are doing, the samurai are *always ready* to die for someone else. This willingness to sacrifice themselves is as inherent in Japanese culture as it is embedded in the composition of the alchemic hero. We can see at work in the composition of the Elric brothers the Japanese tendencies of assimilation and sacrifice.

By examining the combination of functional, psychological, and archetypal elements at work in the formulation of the Elric Brothers as "alchemic hero" in *Fullmetal Alchemist*, a compositional analysis gives us the opportunity to gain a deeper insight into Japanese cultural traditions as they relate to heroism and the hero in anime. But more importantly, this compositional approach allows us to better understand who our heroes are, and how they might represent us.

14

Astro Boy and the Atomic Age

ALICIA GIBSON

Meanwhile man, precisely as the one so threatened, exalts himself to the posture of lord of the earth. In this way the impression comes to prevail that everything man encounters exists only insofar as it is his construct. This illusion gives rise in turn to one final delusion: It seems as though man everywhere and always encounters only himself.

—Martin Heidegger

. . . the sign that *remains*—in the form of a literal being-there, an externalization and an exhibition—in the aftermath of a process of sacrifice, whether or not the sacrifice has been witnessed or apprehended as such. Mimesis is the (visibly or sensorially available) substitute that follows, that bears the effects of (an invisible or illegible) sacrifice.

—Rey Chow

Originating as a Japanese manga series from 1951, the television program *Astro Boy* was broadcast in Japan between 1963 and 1966. The original Japanese title, *Mighty Atom* (Tetsuwan atomu), illustrates more clearly than its English counterpart the central role played by atomic power in the cartoon series. The hero Atomu (Atom), a young robot created in the form of a human boy, is powered by nuclear energy. The animated series gained widespread international popularity throughout the Cold War period and was remade in the 1980s (when it was given its English title), and again in 2003. Atomu, with his peaceful use of atomic power, embodies the latent utopic possibilities of the atomic age—nuclear power can be used to save rather than to destroy. Yet in order to turn this technology into a life-saving power, humanity, here represented by a precocious Atomu, must learn to wisely manage the tremendous power it has discovered. Humanity must likewise first make it through the painful "baby steps" of the atomic age and learn how to use the power for "good" before unwittingly destroying that which it would save.

Atomu is both the one who must learn to control his atomic powers, and he is also that power itself. Much of the drama of the television series centers on this ambivalent position. Atomu is after all not human. He is a robot built in the exact likeness of another child, one who dies as the show begins. Although he has the external structure of a child, he is a machine. And despite his good intentions and willingness to sacrifice himself to save others, he is continually cast away. Beginning with the show's first episode, the robot-boy finds it impossible to live up to the expectations of the human subjects who create and manage him: his desire to do good cannot wholly overcome a world predicated upon the instrumentalization of his power.

Atomu's ambivalent positioning as both subject and object provides most of the series' narrative drive. The concept of *mimesis* allows us to examine the ways in which, despite its utopic longings, *Astro Boy* re-enacts the violence of the atomic age and exposes the sacrificial logic of the nuclear order. Mimesis refers generally to the act of imitation and has long been used to describe the relationship between art and life: the power of aesthetic representation lies in its ability to reflect (or imitate) the conditions of human existence. As such, mimesis is the generative source of artistic creativity. However, in an age in which destruction has "gone global," and humankind's greatest achievements are measured by kill-power, we must confront the possibility that artistic reproduction of the conditions of human life is now marked by destructive, rather than productive, forces.

From Horsepower to the Power of a Thousand Suns

Due to a complex integration of atomic, mechanical, electrical, and (in later releases of the show) digital technologies, Atomu flies with supersonic speed and battles forces of destruction with strength the equivalent of a "one hundred-thousand-horsepower" engine. In the early 1950s when Osamu Tezuka first created *Astro Boy*, the robot's famed "one hundred thousand horsepower" was meant to represent an order of power at the limit of human imagination. Yet, given the actual power unleashed in an atomic explosion, and its escalating potential power in the Cold War Era—measured by reference to the power of the sun itself—Atomu's "one hundred thousand horsepower" was oddly obsolete even at the time of his inception. This slippage highlights the difficulty audiences had integrating the terrifying reality of a world gone nuclear with previous conceptions of technological power. A bomb described rhetorically as comparable to the energy of a thousand suns was dropped over Hiroshima. The forces unleashed on Hiroshima and Nagasaki exponentially outpaced the projections of even the scientists who created the bomb. This magnitude was simply too frightening to confront. Designed for an audience of children facing a future where entire cities could be destroyed in seconds, Atomu's "hundred thousand horsepower" served as a representation of atomic power that provided a more manageable reference for a new audience of children whose utopic dreams of nuclear power might just as easily turn to nightmare.

In keeping with this more benign reference for atomic power, one wrapped in a cuddly package, *Astro Boy* also offers a positive example of atomic power's possible uses. Although technically a weaponized robot (powered by nuclear fission, he has laser beams and machine guns that shoot out of his rear-end), Atomu is not used for the destruction of the world's cities, but rather their salvation. As he awkwardly discovers his new capabilities, he represents not only atomic technologies, he also represents humanity itself as we learn to properly use this new power. Just as a troubled humanity struggles with a new form of power and its attendant ethical dilemmas, Atomu's control over his capacities is not complete: he has the strength of a superhuman, but only a boy's control of his awesome powers. In the manga and anime series, his foibles largely play to comic effect. When asked to clean the robot tigers until they shine, he scrubs off even their stripes, leaving them gleaming white; when left alone in an airship cabin, he accidentally rips pipes from the walls, breaks the legs off chairs, and generally embarrasses his handler's attempts to integrate him into "normal" society. The boy's overwhelming strength becomes his liability and exposes his imperfection. Behind the comedy lies a serious message: we must learn to control the atomic power we have awakened.

The Death of Tobio—The Birth of Atomu

As aesthetic device, the robot serves as a figure in which the mimetic impulse found in artistic practices and technological advancement converge. The robot is a copy of the human, one that is not subject to the same laws of mortality and one that allows the human to project the fantasy of eternal life. This fantastical construction is also the dream of the technological supplement of divine or natural law: from the construction of the machinic form of life, human beings go beyond mere reproduction of the species and become Creators in their own right. Yet from his very inception, Atomu illustrates the ways in which the mimetic impulse that characterizes the atomic age is fraught with disillusionment.

According to the storyline presented in the first episode, "The Birth of Astro Boy," the robot-boy is meant to mask the death of another. In the episode's opening scenes the audience confronts the "original" Atomu, Dr. Tenma's son Tobio, who dies in a violent accident. The death scene and subsequent moments of remorse quickly transform into a "birthing" scene as Dr. Tenma decides to tempt fate and replicate the divine mysteries of life and death by creating an exact replica of his dead child, this time in the form of a new robotic weapon: Atomu. Shadowed in darkness and secrecy, a distraught Dr. Tenma pushes forward with his scientific experiment, which is laid out in its monstrous steel shell on an operating table. In a puddle at his feet lies the robot's outer covering, a bio-mechanical breakthrough that camouflages the steel that lies just below the surface and makes it possible for Tenma to achieve his vision. Tenma delicately pulls the suit over the unrecognizable machine. As he reaches its head, he moves his hand across what appears now to be the face of Tobio, gently smoothing away the flesh-like wrinkles of the suit as though comforting a child to sleep. Here the line between creation and destruction blurs. Tenma "clothes" the robot in silence, bringing to life his new "son." And yet the scene also takes on the tone of funeral rite. Above all, the body lying on the table symbolizes a grieving father's inability to face the absolute law of mortality; he cannot say goodbye.

What are we to make of this melancholic beginning of a children's cartoon series? Within the very first minutes of the show as we are introduced to the larger story-arc and foundational narrative, we encounter the death of a child and the birth of a machine.

The life of the robot-boy is forever tied to the life of this first child, the "real" boy. As an inert and lifeless carcass awaiting Tenma's life-giving touch, Atomu must first re-enact the boy's death before coming to life—the father acknowledges as much in the silent gesture made in the darkness of the laboratory. While the family dog (named Jump) does finally accept him as the young master returned from the grave, his "father" eventually does not. Atomu faithfully studies the relationship between words and things, and earnestly embarks upon the project of becoming Tobio. However, he is forever trapped within the steel cage of Tenma's making: he cannot grow. With every passing year his now too-faithful replication of the "original" son as he *was* serves only to remind Tenma of his ultimate failure. Moreover, his internal nuclear reactor makes him much more powerful than the human Tobio could ever be.

Imitating the Power of the Universe

The confused mixture of emotion Atomu encounters in the humans among whom he lives reenacts the ancient anxiety over "original" and "copy," "life" and "art," "master" and "disciple" first problematized by Plato in the *Republic*. Plato's suspicion of mimesis stems from a fear of the rhetorical power embedded in art practices that not only reflect the world "as it is," but also shape that very world. Mimetic practices—the act of mimicking, imitating, copying, aping, and parody—create an impassable rupture for any concept of Truth as an absolute, and unsettle the corresponding insistence on the perfect correlation between reality as a concrete material world and as a set of ideas about that world. If the purely fictional does not act passively as mirror but also as a crucible for the new, there emerges a radical opening to possibility that brings with it also a terror. This terror is not unlike that encountered at the dawn of the atomic age in the images of destruction from Hiroshima and Nagasaki, and in Harry Truman's claim of mastery over "the basic power of the universe" (*Papers of the Presidents*, p, 197). In this moment the possibility of radical potential meets that of radical end.

Theodor Adorno and Max Horkheimer described this phenomena in philosophical terms as the dialectic of enlightenment: technological mastery over nature—what we call progress—gives way to destruction in the increasing rationalization and abstraction of all that is. When all things (including human subjects) are assigned a numerical equivalence or treated as items of exchange in the name of utility and efficiency, then their elimination becomes a mere keystroke or final step in an equation. Writing after the genocide in Europe and a war that threatened to turn the entire world against itself, they wrote of a lingering anxiety prevalent in everyday attitudes:

> The noonday panic fear in which nature suddenly appeared to humans as an all-encompassing power has found its counterpart in the panic which is ready to break out at any moment today: human beings expect the world, which is without issue, to be set ablaze by a universal power which they themselves are and over which they are powerless. (Max Horkheimer and Theodor Adorno, *Dialectic of Enlightenment*, p. 29)

The nuclear bomb, with its ability to replicate the fiery forces of the sun, exemplifies the kind of universal power referred to by Adorno and Horkheimer. Tragically, exposure to this new form of terror springs not simply from a desire to destroy, but from a desire to know, to create, and to exert some measure of control over the conditions of human existence. The bomb and the achievement of nuclear fission represents the highest technological advancement and expresses this complicated desire—to no longer be at the mercy of, but to control the essential productive capacity of the universe.

Artistic representation cannot escape the contradictions of the atomic age. Technology and art are both ways of engaging the world in order to create new conditions for existence. Moreover, it is from the mimetic faculty—the ability to present the world with a mirror—that art finds its power. As Adorno explains in *Aesthetic Theory*, from its reflection of the concrete experiences of any given historical moment, art makes its claims to relevance. The advent of the atomic, however, represents a fatal implosion of scales of power, the point at which the twinned desire to create as well as to control turns back upon itself. Technology, which is meant to secure the meaning of human life, becomes instead the latest weapon of mass destruction, the easiest means to an end and the ultimate threat for the continuation of that life. Mimetic representation in the wake of the atomic bomb cannot help but express this anxiety of a world at once full of technological promise but shadowed by this universalizing terror.

Existing *Otherwise*

Atomu pays a price for his inability to seamlessly integrate his atomic power with his life among humans. Even though advanced robotic technology enables him to look nearly identical to the child he is modeled after, he is in the end an artifact of the atomic age, one that touches upon a lingering anxiety that his human counterparts can only express alternately with awe and disgust.

As artifact Atomu is both human and non-human. Most obviously, he appears at surface-level as a human. He is also human in the sense that as a human creation—in this instance a nuclear-powered weaponized robot—he bears the history of human technological progress and its deadly underside in his physical structure. Ultimately, his existence has little meaning outside the human world of which he is the product. And yet he is also non-human, for despite his external replication of the human form, he is never considered truly human. As machine he is only a tool for worldmaking, a non-human object by which the human world structures its atomic future.

Thus Atomu's life is structured by a two contradictory requirements: he is expected to live among humans, according to their rules, however unlike the other boys that Atomu goes to school with, it is he alone who is ruled by the categorical imperative to save his human companions at any cost to his own structural integrity. Episode 3 (of the English version), "Save the Classmate," offers an early example of Atomu's problematic status. After rescuing a group of school bullies from certain death in a roller-coaster accident, and nearly fatally shorting his own circuitry in the process, the story ends with Atomu physically separated from the humans he has served, looking on as the boys are reunited with their relieved (though angry) parents. While some of the more friendly children accept Atomu's sacrifice and reconcile themselves to his presence in their class, the parents of the saved classmates are the very ones who, early in the episode, want to see Atomu removed from class. These parents, who are also the school's benefactors, do not acknowledge Atomu's efforts or notice the injuries he receives while endangering himself on their behalf. In their minds, his sacrifice is expected as a robot created to serve their human ends.

Martin Heidegger argued that the future of humanity rests on an ability to understand our relationship to modern technology. He put the dilemma in simple terms: atomic energy "can be released either for destruction or for peaceful use." While Heidegger refused to be wooed by the fairy tale ideology of atomic utopia, he acknowledged that technology is essential to any definition of what it means to be human, as such it is much more than merely "a means and a human activity." Although the use of technology is a defining characteristic of the human, in the events of the twentieth century Heidegger identified a shift in the way technology is used. Not only is technology a way of using objects to the benefit of man, technology has become a way of "unlocking" the energy stored inside objects.

Objects are thus not things belonging to this world encountered and used, but a representation of human virtual power. Just as a pirate seeks his secret treasure seeing only the wealth it will be converted into at some later date, human beings create a relationship with objects, and the world itself, as mere means for human enrichment. The world and everything found therein only exists as something to be mined, resources to plunder. When this happens the things of this world are no longer *objects*, a category of being that for Heidegger implies an autonomous existence and an otherness outside the confines of human experience. They become, rather, that which properly belongs always at the ready for human control, what Heidegger calls *standing-reserve*:

> The danger attests itself to us in two ways. As soon as what is unconcealed no longer concerns man even as object, but does so, rather, exclusively as standing-reserve, and man in the midst of objectlessness is nothing but the orderer of the standing-reserve, then he comes to the very brink of a precipitous fall; that is, he comes to the point where he himself will have to be taken as standing-reserve. Meanwhile man, precisely as the one so threatened, exalts himself to the posture of lord of the earth. In this way the impression comes to prevail that everything man encounters exists only insofar as it is his construct. This illusion gives rise in turn to one final delusion: It seems as though man everywhere and always encounters only himself. (*The Question Concerning Technology and Other Essays*, p. 27).

Each object, turned standing-reserve—now a disposable representation of universal power—serves as a mirror for human achievement. As this power grows and copies of the human appear in every reflection, so grows the impoverishment of the world. By forcing an image of the human on all that is encountered, a kind of coerced existential mimicry becomes the ruling logic of modernity. Objects do not exist as objects but as potential forms of human power.

Herein lies the melancholy of *Astro Boy*. Atomu is an object turned standing-reserve; his value as a being in this world is measured by how well he fulfills his function and by how well this functioning resembles or mimics the universal power that humanity seeks to master. And yet particularly striking is that the series goes to great lengths to create an affective relationship between the viewer and the robot, Atomu. As he silently casts his glance downward, head bowed with every scene of abandonment, we are induced to sympathize with him and shed the tears that he cannot. In his innocent curiosity and delight in the people and things he encounters, Atomu embodies a form of subjectivity preserved only in the early years of childhood. Tenma's rage can be understood in this light, for Atomu's inability to grow is also an inability to "grow up." This inability acts as a kind of refusal of the ruling social order and thus serves as an implicit critique of a human world defined by increasing levels of mastery.

In Atomu's imperfect mimicry of the human, and in our ready identification with his constant exclusion, we better understand Heidegger's argument that the transformation into standing-reserve is not limited to objects. In a world that exists only for command and control, a world in which utility is the highest form of measure, the human being also becomes standing-reserve. Every individual instance of the human is already marshaled for that same ultimate purpose awaiting the life of all things: the production and reproduction of power. In this way, each of us is virtually robotic, a truth which explains *Astro Boy*'s cult status as well as the constant anxiety present in the show's more "human" characters.

The Sacrificial Lamb

From its inception, *Astro Boy* reflects the tragic conditions of the atomic age. Like every good television show, each episode ends in minor triumph. Despite his abandonment and exclusion, Atomu proves his worth by sacrificing his own body for the humans, who refuse to acknowledge his existence as something other than their inferior copy or their machine. Yet, the larger crisis remains. One is left with a sense of profound sadness as Atomu looks on at a world to which he does not belong. Rey Chow offers a conception of mimesis that may help us understand the seemingly strange confluence of living and dying, inclusion and abandonment, the human and the non-human in *Astro Boy*:

> . . . mimesis, one may argue, is the sign that *remains*—in the form of a literal being-there, an externalization and an exhibition—in the aftermath of a process of sacrifice, whether or not the sacrifice has been witnessed or apprehended as such. Mimesis is the (visibly or sensorially available) substitute that follows, that bears the effects of (an invisible or illegible) sacrifice. ("Sacrifice, Mimesis, and the Theorizing of Victimhood (A Speculative Essay)," *Representations* 94, p. 137)

According to the conventional definition of mimesis as aesthetic representation, mimesis is essentially productive and has been present in human civilization since its most ancient beginnings. Chow provocatively suggests that sacrifice is in fact the destructive analog to the creative faculty, and that both mimesis and sacrifice underlie the very processes through which we make meaning of our world.

In a fully rationalized world, sacrifice now represents the violence we are willing to submit ourselves to in our quest to fully master those forces that belonged to a non-human world. As the secret of the atom—what we have long held to be the "building block of the universe" or in Truman's term the "basic power of the universe"—is unlocked and mobilized, so what was a universal power becomes more properly, though no less terrifyingly, human power. Mimesis was then in its primitive form a non-violent repetition of nature's violence. However, in a world in which human beings claim themselves masters of the universe, and the sphere of the non-human diminishes in its ordering as standing-reserve, mimesis becomes the repetition of *human* violence.

Astro Boy then offers unique insight into the historic conditions of existence in the atomic world. Written and produced in the decades following Hiroshima and Nagasaki, *Astro Boy*'s episodes mimetically re-enact a sacrificial logic whereby the new world order—announced dramatically with the deployment of the atomic bomb—rises from the ashes of the burning cities. With every subsequent revision and translation for global audiences, what emerges in the robotic version of the young boy is a nostalgic, static vision of an innocence no longer possible in a world turned nuclear.

The darker side of the atomic age is visible most clearly in the death of Tobio, a death that marks the birth of Atomu's narrative. Traces of this founding violence haunt the show in every failed attempt to reconcile the utopic possibilities of the age with what we might call an atomic diegetic demand: the world can only be saved with the sacrifice of the abandoned.

15

Grave of the Child Hero

HAL SHIPMAN

Set in Japan during the last days of World War II, Isao Takahata's *Grave of the Fireflies* tells the poignant tale of two orphaned children, Seita, and his younger sister Setsuko. The children lose their mother in the firebombing of Kobe and their father in service to the Imperial Japanese Navy. As a result, they have to try to survive amidst widespread famine and the callous indifference of their countrymen, eventually striking out on their own in rebellion against a distant family member. Both children die of malnutrition, demonstrating that the consequences of wars are not only violent.

Though not a commercial success when it was first released, *Grave of the Fireflies* has become one of the most critically acclaimed anime films, due to its graphic and truly emotional depiction of the consequences of war on all people. As such, its relevance resonates even today as we hear about the impact of armed battle on civilian populations in places like Iraq, Afghanistan, and Gaza. But *Grave of the Fireflies* tells us as much about the prevailing ideas regarding the nature of childhood development and adolescence within mainstream anime as it does about the damages of war.

Natural States

Anime largely relies on the trope of the child hero, most often an adolescent (pre- or newly pubescent), who is thrust into a dire situation and sometimes even responsible for saving the world. Often, the children succeed specifically in spite of the adults, who ignore or disregard the insights of the protagonists, forcing these young heroes to take action on their own, for the salvation of us all. Adults are

sometimes advisors or support, at best, but the children are ultimately left to their own devices to solve whatever problem is facing
them. This perspective that children are capable of facing the challenges of the world—even a fantasy world—on their own is based
in an ignorance of the concept of "adolescence," which only began
to break down in Western thought at the end of the Middle Ages.

Up through the Middle Ages, the notion of childhood development, including the concept of adolescence, simply did not exist.
There was a clean break between early childhood and adulthood.
The ability to reason, to make sound choices, was assumed to be
granted in one big lump once adolescence began. Someone like
Seita should be perfectly capable of succeeding in his goals. And if
he were in any other anime film, he probably would. The overwhelming majority of anime films and series focus on children, up
through their teens, who are clearly able to make sound choices.
These characters are supposed to be of adolescent age, visually distinct from the films' adults, and yet their capabilities are on par with
adults. Despite being children and adolescents, they are hyper-com-
petent and capable, literally saving the world many times over. These
are fantasies, almost exclusively centered on a romanticized version
of medieval concepts regarding the essential nature of a child.

But unlike most of his filmic peers, Seita does not succeed. His
story more closely reflects a perspective of childhood proposed by
Aristotle, who suggested that the child is "unfinished" in regards to
its development of "human nature," meaning adulthood. The qual-
ifier "unfinished" implies that while the human [adult] nature is not
yet fully realized, it will be realized as long as it is properly provided for and protected from harm and random influences that
could deflect or damage its natural growth. In other words, actual-
ization as a human comes through the progression of development
from nature to habit to reason.

The role of the parents is to temper the child's wildness, the natural state, through nurture and discipline. Aristotle even believed
that children are incapable of happiness (which can only be
achieved through reason) as they have not yet developed the ability to use their intelligence to guide their actions. The child's actu-
alization as a person, a fully realized human being, only comes
when the child attains the ability to reason. This fundamental concept is the core of modern childhood development theory and our
modern understanding of how children develop the capacity to
make thoughtful choices throughout their teens.

Like Adults, Only Smaller

Despite anime adventures often depicting a child's natural state—wildness, innocence and/or a purity of spirit—as the key to solving the problems that face his or her world, many cultures now see it differently. American culture doesn't recognize children as being able to make decisions on their own behalf until they are at least eighteen years old, and this maturation includes an individual's ability to decide to live on his or her own. It is this specific trope of anime that falls apart under the modern lens and which *Grave of the Fireflies* most directly argues against. As modern adults, we understand that a child living on his own, without an adult, will most likely have a tragic existence including life on the streets, drug addiction, and prostitution. If a child strikes out on his own, he leaves the protective, nurturing sphere of the family while unprepared to make healthy choices. Seita demonstrates the importance of this preparation throughout the film, through the negative examples of making unhealthy choices time and time again. Fundamentally, *Grave of the Fireflies* is a cautionary tale about a child's inability to make these choices precisely because he isn't yet old enough to reason.

Though it seems obvious to us now, the development framework Aristotle recognized and espoused was ignored until the beginning of the Early Modern period. In his book, *Centuries of Childhood*, Philippe Ariès describes how concepts of childhood have varied through history. The very notion of a child, he argues, is historically and culturally conditioned and was at its lowest ebb in the west during the Medieval period. The concept of "child" as an innocent to be protected and nurtured didn't really exist until the end of the Middle Ages, when Descartes and Locke first returned to Aristotle's notion of the development of reason. Instead, children were thought of as little adults, with no awareness of the need to develop the capacity to reason. In medieval cultural artifacts, most often paintings, children as we know them simply don't exist. Ariès points out that the children look and dress exactly like adults, only on a smaller scale to indicate their age.

Since the idea of adolescence as an interim stage in growth was unknown, the medieval assumption was that children progressed directly from an infantile state to adulthood. Once a child displayed the very first signs of physical maturity, they were considered, for all intents and purposes, to be adults at that instant, with no regard to the many years of further physical and emotional growth that are

needed. Though smaller in stature, once a child was able to articulate himself coherently and read fluently, if he were educated, he
was considered as capable of reason as any grown-up.

Within this framework, the door is opened to the range of adult
experiences at an age we in developed societies consider to be
wholly inappropriate. Such situations include putting a child to
work (even in extremely dangerous situations such as mining), sex
and marriage (by not recognizing a minimum age of consent) or
the intersection of the work and sex trajectories, in prostitution.
Unfortunately, we still see this potential at work today. Though
most first world countries recognize the age of majority and condemn child labor, many parts of the world turn a blind eye to the
situations of the conscription of children for war and the child sex
trade.

The Ability to Reason

Grave of the Fireflies can be seen as taking the position that this
medieval attitude regarding childhood and the nature of children is
completely wrong. When the protagonist, Seita, takes on the role
of the anime hero in the film, he starts down a path that leads
directly to his own death and the death of his sister, Setsuko. For
his initiative, instead of saving himself and his younger sister, he
dooms them both because he is simply not capable of making
choices, those that we would consider to be rational and adult, or,
in philosophical terms, applying the capacity to reason.

The popular anime notion of child as hero is placed in direct
contrast with our modern understanding of childhood. *Grave of the
Fireflies'* emphasis on the importance of the ability to reason is
rooted as much in an Aristotelian philosophy as it is in modern
developmental psychology. Traditional anime, like its medieval attitude counterpart, simply ignores this need for emotional and rational growth. *Grave of the Fireflies* demonstrates just how dangerous
this approach can be. Seita completely and utterly fails in his mission: to care for his sister and himself. Aristotelian concepts of the
nature of children and the limits of their capabilities are reinforced
through negative examples, demanding an awareness and application in our world. The two philosophies of childhood come into
their most direct conflict over the idea of reason.

The child or adolescent in anime puts a romantic spin on the
medieval notion. Seita, the apparent hero in *Grave of the Fireflies,*

is about the same age as most anime adventurers. In these animated series or movie fantasies, children succeed in their struggles to gather dragonballs and cards or win tournaments through hope and dogged determination in the face of insurmountable odds. We see over and over again that the fantasy children in anime don't need adults as nurturers. Intrepid children constantly strike out on their own, without any guidance or supervision. Children in series such as *Dragon Ball*, *Pokémon*, *Yu-Gi-Oh!*, and *Fullmetal Alchemist*, wander the countryside from adventure to adventure with no adults around, frequently failing to address the most basic issues of food and shelter, unless the plot specifically calls for those issues as McGuffins.

While there are cases such as Hayao Miyazaki's *Spirited Away*, where the goal of the child's journey is to save her parents (whose absence is part of the plot), the dangers of unaccompanied travel are ignored, at best. One might believe that there would be no problems in running away from home. Seita certainly believes that he is as capable as any adult and that he, like other child heroes, can succeed. He takes his first step on his own journey of adventure by taking Setsuko and leaving the home of their aunt.

Defying Conventions

We now understand that a child needs nurturing and guidance from adults throughout adolescence. They are not realized as people and, most significantly, not capable of reasoning, of making their own decisions for their own or others' welfare. Our modern notion is informed by the rise of developmental psychology but is also rooted in the Aristotelian concepts of childhood that predated the medieval notion.

Grave of the Fireflies warns the viewer as soon as it begins that this will be no ordinary anime, providing a few feints before the direction of the tale is made clear. The starkness of the opening scene in the train station seems to indicate that this will be an adult tale, of mecha-grittiness perhaps. As the candy-tin spills open, the *rei* (spirit) of Setsuko rises out of cremated remains[1] and the *rei* of

---

[1] The real-life maker of this candy, Sakuma, now sells candies in these tins as a *Grave of the Fireflies* licensed product, with Setsuko's picture on the tin. Apparently, the fact that the tin is her cremation urn is not seen as a barrier to marketing.

Seita steps out of the train station. The softness of their features and
the deliberate cuteness of the little girl then hint that this may be
some type of spirit fantasy along the lines of Miyazaki's *Princess
Mononoke*. But, an instant later, the realization of what we've just
seen crashes down as it becomes clear that this story is going to be
told in flashback and isn't going to end happily. The impending
tragedy indicates the first break from classic, child-centered anime.
The specific anime genre in which *Grave of the Fireflies* works isn't
clear in the introduction, but the death of the cute child doesn't fit
within any of them.

Over the course of the tale, we see Seita act like a classic anime
youth, believing that the medieval perspective will hold true, and he
will be capable of succeeding in his mission. Seita makes several
choices which, in the lens of the traditional anime world, would
seem daring and empowering. These decisions seem perfectly reasonable to him at the time. They are made at moments where
adventures tell us that plucky determination will win out. But these
ill-informed choices lead directly to the deaths of the children.

The focus of these choices is the aunt with whom the children
stay while their mother is in the hospital and after her death. To a
certain degree, the aunt is taking the role of the wicked stepmother
from western fairy tales. She is an adult, somewhat related, so com-
mands a certain amount of respect, but not immune to criticism like
a parent or grandparent would be.

Nothing she does is particularly evil. She is unpleasant, to be
sure, but there is no actual abuse. She makes rather pedestrian
complaints such as demanding why Seita doesn't get a job and help
the community and their home? She complains about Setsuka's cry-
ing. She grouses when Seita leaves all of his dirty dishes in the sink,
after the children start making their own food. That being said,
there is nothing fundamentally unreasonable about what she's asking of the boy. Show respect for the others you live with. Clean up
after yourself, contribute to the household, and let others get their
rest. Where some might see these parameters as the minimum
behavior expected for a roommate, especially in wartime, these
demands cast her as the adversary in Seita's eyes.

His reactions to her demands are childish and spiteful. While
she's obviously unpleasant, she never threatened to kick them out
of the house or deny them food. All she really wanted was at least
"a single word of apology." But he ignores her, offers no response
to the suggestions that he work, and he starts cooking his own

meals in her house out of spite (and, again, leaving the dirty dishes). The implicit refusals to contribute to the household are compounded when it's revealed that Seita has access to fairly large amounts of money in the bank. Finally, in his pride and the plucky determination of an anime hero, Seita strikes out on his own with Setsuko. But let's face it, Seita is striking out in defiance of an adversary who, at the end of the day, is at worst only a mean aunt.

This is the first and most major decision by which he dooms his sister and himself to death. To live without an adult is the clearest demarcation of adulthood, which Seita assumes for himself without any thought of the real consequences. The decision, though, is framed as that of the classic anime hero. Seita rebels against his adversary, the mean authority figure. Or, at least, this is how it is justified in Seita's mind.

The aunt is clearly not faultless when the crucial turning point is reached. When Seita announces that the two are leaving, she asks "Where are you going?" and he tells her, "I don't know for certain, yet." The aunt doesn't express a great deal more concern for their decision. She simply says, "Well, be careful," without trying to stop them from their misguided adventure.

The Offer of Help

Anime is littered with adults playing the role of advisors, who give the heroes bits or information or tools they need in their quests. Their input is always friendly and helpful, though they notably don't ever take in the children or join on the quests in order to protect them. Seita is so sure of his ability to command his situation, his ability to reason for himself, that he ignores these adults, particularly when they point out his need to be nurtured. The farmer with whom he tries to trade for food directly tells Seita to rely on his relatives, his family. Seita claims, "Well, . . . I can't get in touch with them," as if to imply the other relatives in Tokyo that the aunt referred to earlier. But the farmer apparently recognizes that Setsuko is hiding the truth. "Then it's better for you to go back to that house. Besides, everything's rationed now. If you're not part of a community group, you can't eat. Apologize and ask them to let you stay."

In this one moment, Seita is specifically told where he needs to go and what he needs to do in order to survive, but he consciously chooses to take another path. His ability to reason as an adult is inadequate. Seita does noticeably pause when the farmer lays out the situation, and he seems to consider, but ultimately disregard, the option. "Sorry to have bothered you. I'll try other places." Seita clings to his idea that he is a man, not a child, ironically demonstrating that he, in fact, is only a child.

The medieval spirit rears its head again as Seita deals with his sister's health. Over the course of their time in the wilderness, Setsuko becomes weaker and sicker. When Seita finally takes her to get some help, the doctor tells Seita that Setsuko is malnourished. At this point, the boy simply cannot comprehend the impact of his neglect and demands that the doctor fix the problem with a shot or some medicine, as if there is literally a magic quick fix. Even at this crucial point, when he has been explicitly told of the problem, Seita doesn't consider returning to the aunt's house, out of childish pride. It is this final decision that ultimately dooms Setsuko.

The Aftermath of Tragedy

As adults, we can look at every single one of these decisions by Seita and see how they led to the deaths of the children. Our understanding of children tells us that they simply can't take care of themselves, but the framework of the anime adventurer does not allow for any alternatives.

It's hard to imagine that the film's director, Isao Takahata, and Studio Ghibli, intended for the film to be a criticism of anime's depiction of childhood, given their respective artistic and commercial interest in the genre. However, it is equally hard to imagine that the comparisons did not occur to them.

This disconnect is noticeable particularly in light of the fact that Studio Ghibli released and marketed the now-classic, more traditional anime feature, *My Neighbor Toturo*, alongside *Grave of the Fireflies* as a double feature. Miyazaki's *My Neighbor Toturo* is more of a "spirit" anime—an exploration of the Japanese concept of the spirit world—rather than an adventure story, but still it evokes the broad range of children's fantasy anime. In pairing the two, the producers beg a comparison between *Grave of the Fireflies* and the other films in the genre.

In fact, the pairing was initially a commercial failure because *Grave of the Fireflies* was so completely different from the expectations set with the marketing campaign, which indicated that the story was suitable for children.[2] The fact that it was initially a commercial failure points to its uniqueness in the medium and how the public simply wasn't prepared for that perspective.

Grave of the Fireflies is an adaptation of the semi-autobiographical novel of the same name by Akiyuki Nosaka. Nosaka says in interviews that he wrote the story as a personal apology to his two sisters who died of malnutrition during World War II. Referring to the younger of the two, Nosaka says, "My sister's death is an exact match with the novel." He feels responsible for her death. His reaction is classic survivor's guilt, but he is also fully aware that his own immaturity was a factor in his sister's death.

The real-life tragedy behind *Grave of the Fireflies* resonates with even more power in animated form where the genre conventions tell us to expect a happy ending and capable children. The director makes Seita's failure that much more poignant by implicitly placing the boy next to anime heroes such as Yugi Mutou, Ash Ketchum, and Son Goku. If the boys of *Yu-Gi-Oh!*, *Pokemon* and *Dragon Ball* can succeed in their tasks over and over again, what does this say about Seita? If these heroes can save the world, why can't Seita save one little girl?

The answer lies in that he is simply a normal young teenager who does not have the reasoning ability or maturity to adequately care for himself or others. Seita is an adolescent in the Aristotelian mold. Even when you strip away the fantasy elements of the adventure stories, most anime heroes can be seen as personifications of romanticized medieval ideals of children. Their fantastic powers and tools are independent of the coping skills needed for their travels. Seita, too, had resources of money and family available to him, just not the judgment needed to use them.

Perhaps this additional layer of meaning is exactly why Seita and Setsuko's tragedy was not first told as a live-action film.[3] The realities of the story conflict with the conventions of anime, demonstrating that much more intensely how the medievalist attitude regarding children really is unworkable in real life. While the story of *Grave of the Fireflies* reminds us of the horrors of war, telling that story in anime raises questions about the very elements that frequently define the medium. Anime often romanticizes the idea that

---

[2] Studio Ghibli was only saved from financial ruin thanks to the extreme popularity of *Torturo*-licensed toys.

a child striking out on his own will discover a world of thrilling adventures with little personal consequence. How many children viewing these anime adventures might come to believe the same delusion? While the odds of such an influence are extremely low, Takahata's film works as an effective counter-balance to these unrealistic depictions of the capabilities of children in anime. *Grave of the Fireflies* reminds us that, while the cockiness and bravado of adolescence may try to fool us, a child's ability to reason and to make sound decisions is not ready-made but instead takes years of development, guidance, and nurturing.

---

[3] A live-action version was produced for Nippon TV in 2005, based on the critical success of the anime.

Devils

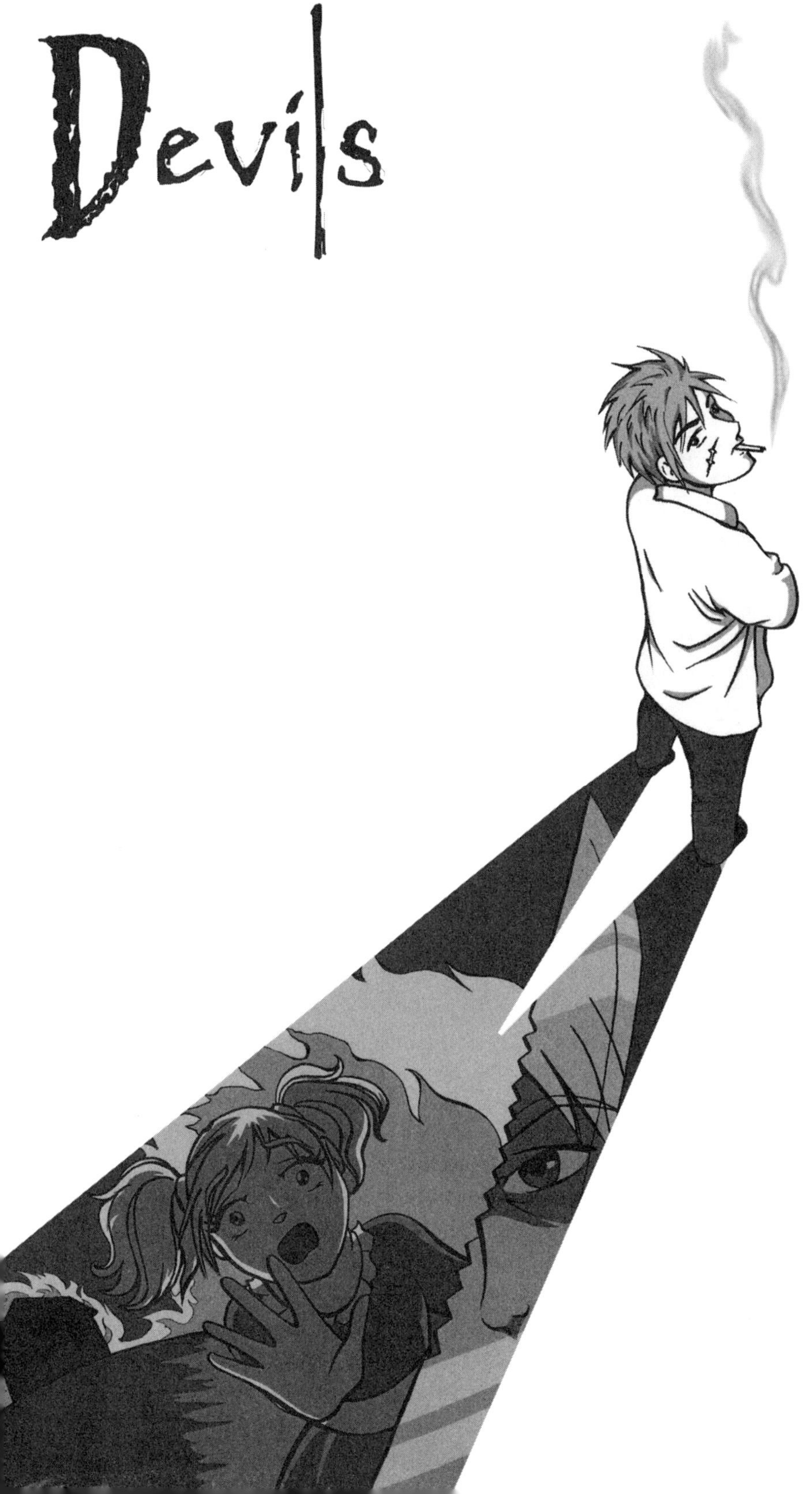

16

Human Alchemy and the Deadly Sins of Capitalism

D.E. WITTKOWER

> Humankind cannot gain anything without first giving something in return. To obtain, something of equal value must be lost. That is Alchemy's First Law of Equivalent Exchange.
>
> —Alphonse Elric, *Fullmetal Alchemist*

The law of equivalent exchange might express a number of different basic beliefs we have about the world. As a Law of Alchemy, it expresses a scientific rationality—both the beauty of an ordered, knowable universe, and the sorrows of a world where not everything is possible. A world where there is final, permanent, and insoluble loss. As a moral law, it expresses an ideal of justice—both that none should benefit without having done something to deserve that benefit, and that no sacrifice should ever fail to receive some kind of compensation in return. A religious perspective binds these meanings together. In a world created by a just God, the world would work according to fair and knowable laws—both that we would know there is a price to be paid for our desires and sins, and that there are some things for which we must never strive. Things beyond the reach of humankind.

How are we meant to interpret the meaning of the law of Equivalent Exchange? As with any central theme in any really interesting work of fiction, there are many ways, and we shouldn't claim that there is a single right—or even a best—interpretation. But I'd like to speak of it as telling us something about our contemporary form of alchemy: *economics*.

Economics is a form of alchemy; it transforms goods into one another, and turns productive elements into gold. It dreams too of the Philosopher's Stone—a way of escaping equivalent exchange and creating profit. And it too has the same fundamental problem: How can you have a process that ends up with more than you started with? And the answer for economics is the same as it is in *Fullmetal Alchemist*: only by sacrificing human lives.

It's Not a Miracle, It's Science

In a basic alchemical transmutation all the parts there at the end must be present at the beginning; the change has to do simply with a useful reorganization of those parts. For example, when Alphonse fixes a radio in "Those Who Challenge the Sun," he doesn't create anything new, but only rearranges the parts so that it's a working device again, instead of just a collection of detached radio parts.

This is basically the way that any artisan or craftsman creates value. The usefulness of something comes from both its raw materials and its organization, and neither is useful without the other. You can't make soup out of a stone any more than you can squeeze blood from a turnip, but, on the other hand, a perfectly ripe and nutritious basket of berries is of no use to you until someone bothers to go into the forest and pick it. In the same way, it's through taking some suitable raw material (cotton or wool, yes; dirt or milk, no and ew) and reorganizing it in a proper sort of way (yarning and weaving, yes; burning and shredding, no) that we get clothing. And it's the same with all the basic goods of life: clothing, food, shelter, and so on.

Here, there is a kind of equivalent exchange—raw materials go into and are used in the finished product. There is, of course, another kind of equivalent exchange that takes place when the product is brought to market. The berries I gather can be traded for the clothing you've made. And in this, we *both* stand to gain, *even though* there is an *equivalent* exchange.

How is this possible? If I spend a full day gathering berries, a basket worth will have cost me less time to gather than it would cost you to do so yourself. By spending the day out there, the time spent per basket is far less, because I only have to walk there and back and find a good patch once. Similarly, each coat you make costs you less time than it would cost me to make my own, if you make many of them, get raw materials in bulk, and if I can be saved the expense and effort of getting a loom and learning how to do a good job of it.

And so, even with simple equivalent economic exchanges, there can be profit and improving standards of living, just through specialization and economies of scale. When we work on our own trades, and exchange products, we have more and better quality goods in our lives. Like alchemy, it seems almost like magic if you don't understand it, but it's a science, based on equivalent exchange.

Turning Lead into Gold

The Philosopher's Stone, in the historical tradition of alchemy, was held to either allow the user to transform other metals into gold, or to grant immortality. Why these two very different things? The reason is simple: because they are not so different, really.

Gold was believed to be the purest of all metals, and was associated with the sun. To turn a base metal, such as lead, into gold was to make it pure and incorruptible—no longer subject to change and decay. So it made some sense that such an elixir would make the flesh pure and incorruptible as well, and thus save the alchemist from aging, decay, and death.

From *Livre des figures hiéroglypiques* (1612), reportedly written by Nicolas Flamel. Look familiar?

According to legend, Nicolas Flamel (born 1330, died 1418 according to some) succeeded in both through his use of an ancient lost book that he gained possession of. In *Fullmetal Alchemist*, there are characters very similar to Nicolas Flamel and his wife Perenelle, who were—in some legends—believed to have escaped aging and death together through an elixir of life made using the Philosopher's Stone. The couple in *Fullmetal Alchemist*, however, can only do so by taking the bodies of other people.

In economic terms, there is a similar connection between gold and eternal life—and one which involves the extension of the days we may spend upon the earth by gathering together and sacrificing human lives, just as in the case of the red stones or the Philosopher's Stone itself.

Gold and the Philosopher's Stone

Gold, or money more generally, is nothing but a distillate of lives lost. Eighteenth-century philosopher John Locke helps us see why in his *Second Treatise of Government*.

Locke argued that, as we are all equally descendents of Adam, God gave us all the world in common equally. This helped him explain why it was wrong for kings and barons to own all the land in Europe, while everyone else owned none and had to serve these, their masters. The idea brings up a different problem, though: If God gave us all the world in common, then how is it that any of us ever gain the right to own anything? If God gave everything to all, how could I ever presume to call anything my own and not yours?

The answer is simple, although a little strange: While God gave us all the world in common, he gave us each our own bodies. It cannot be doubted that I alone own my body, for without it I cannot (and would not) exist at all.[1] And so, whatever I mix my body with becomes mine, for my body is clearly mine alone. Now, when we produce goods of value, we take raw materials and reorganize it so that it is useful for human life. So when I weave cloth or gather berries, I mix myself, through my labor, with those goods given to us all in common. It is again equivalent exchange: I lose the hours of my life spent in labor, but I gain ownership over the valuable good made through those lost hours.

Through trade, as we mentioned before, it is possible for us to specialize and increase our productivity. If you produce clothes

---

[1] At least, unless I have a blood seal.

only, and I only pick berries (and someone else only makes automail, and so on) then we are each able to produce a particular good (item of clothing, basket of berries, automail leg) in less time than it would take someone else to make just one for themselves. If it takes you less time to make an item of clothing than it would take me, and if it takes me less time to pick a basket of berries than it would take you, then we actually have more time left in our days if we produce for each other and trade than we would if we made everything ourselves. And so, by specializing our labor and trading with each other, we can actually, in effect, extend our lives!

There is, though, a limit to how much of our lives we can transmute into luxury, wealth, and longevity, because there's a natural limit to how much useful work we can do. There's only so much clothing, and so many automail limbs that I need at a given time. If we imagine, as Locke suggested, a desert island where there is nothing of value except food, water, and simple clothing, we would see that this would result in a life where a few hours would be spent in the morning gathering provisions, and the rest of the day spent in leisure. What other work is there to do? Gather more food than you need for the day? There's no point—it will go bad, and you'll have just as much spare time the next day to gather food anyway.

With money, this changes. Money has no use, and never spoils. As a result, I can never have too much money, or more money than I can make use of. And so I can work all day if I choose, converting the hours of my life into wealth at an ever more efficient rate as I work longer hours and more days.

With enough money, I can even employ others to work for me, and, just as working long hours on a single task makes production of individual goods more efficient so too does employing many people on a shared production process increase efficiency further. By working on different parts of the production process, they can specialize even further. And I don't have to pay them back for every bit of value they produce—they will agree to work if I pay them only a bit more than what they need to survive from day to day and month to month, especially if I happen to be the only major employer in town, like Lieutenant Yoki and his coal mine in "Be Thou for the People."

And so, money allows me to bind together the hours of my life spent in labor, but money is also the concrete residue left by distilling the lives of others spent in wage-labor. If labor is necessary to the creation of goods and services of value to human life, then money is nothing but the concrete form of hours of labor already lost. In the alchemy of economics, money is that most temporary and ever-passing thing—the hours we each have to walk upon the earth—purified and made permanent and undecaying, just like lead turned to pure and incorruptible gold. But, like the creation of the red stones, there is a moral price to be paid as well.

Money, Power, Corruption

Of course, another way of saying that I can never have *too much* money is to say that I can never have *enough* money, and the knowledge that wealth leads to corruption is as old as economics itself.

Our word "economics" comes from the Greek *οικονομικός*, meaning, more-or-less, "how to run a household." For Aristotle, the first person in the Western tradition to write about this systematically, running a household wasn't about gaining wealth, but gaining virtue and happiness. Aristotle, ever a realist, recognized that it's much easier to be a virtuous and happy person—to help others, for example—if you're at reasonably well-off, or at least not poor. At the same time, though, he warned that wealth should never be pursued for its own sake.

Aristotle claimed that "there are two sorts of wealth-getting . . . one is a part of household management," such as farming, fishing, or raising livestock, "the other is retail trade: the former is necessary and honorable, while that which consists in exchange is justly censured; for it is unnatural, and a mode by which men gain from one another."[2] The question, for him, is whether we understand that coins are not true wealth. He asks "how can that be wealth of which a man may have a great abundance and yet perish with hunger, like Midas in the fable, whose insatiable prayer turned everything that was set before him into gold?" True wealth is that kind of abundance that serves true human needs: the wealth of objects and tools, food and wine, land and honor. This is a *human* wealth; the kind of wealth which allows for human flourishing.

Those who mistake coin for true wealth live impoverished lives, for "the whole idea of their lives is that they ought either to

---

[2] All quotes from Aristotle are from his *Politics*, Book I, Chapters 9 and 10, Benjamin Jowett translation.

increase their money without limit." Aristotle believed that "the origin of this disposition in men is that they are intent upon living only, and not upon living well"—that is, living a balanced, healthy, and virtuous life—"and, as their desires are unlimited, they also desire that the means of gratifying them should be without limit."

And so, from even the earliest thoughts about economics, it seems we've always recognized that money leads directly to corruption; that money pulls us towards greed, pride, sloth, envy, gluttony, lust, and wrath. When do these deadly sins emerge from our simple use of money? Exactly when it happens in the world of *Fullmetal Alchemist*: when we attempt to create human value through economic exchange.

Deadly Sins and Capital Vices

In *Fullmetal Alchemist*, human alchemy is forbidden. When considering the horrifying abominations created through the attempts at human alchemy, we might ask why it is forbidden. Aren't the horror stories of those who have tried sufficient to teach alchemists that such things should never be attempted?

Of course this isn't enough. Time and again, alchemists think they'll be able to do it in just the right way, or perhaps they think that they—unlike those before them—will succeed because they are willing to make the massive sacrifices and pay the costs that others have refused to pay, or have tried to avoid. They believe this not because those others who tried were not brilliant, or unwilling to make sacrifices. They believe this because they are unwilling to give up the idea that their desires truly are beyond their reach. Because they are unwilling to accept limits placed on their desire. The result is bringing deadly sin into the world, in the form of homunculi. So too does economics bring vice and degradation into the world when it seeks to create or replace human value using mere coin and exchange.

The seven homunculi take their names from what are often called "the seven deadly sins," or in the language of the great Catholic theologian, St. Thomas Aquinas, the seven "capital vices." The word *capital*, Aquinas tells us, comes from the Latin *caput*, meaning "head," the part of the body that controls and motivates the rest of the body. This is why these vices are called *capital* vices:

they are the vices that motivate and drive us towards all lesser forms of sin and viciousness.[3]

Every sin, he tells us, has its root in the capital vice of Greed, and its beginning in the capital sin of Pride. Greed, the desire for money and material wealth, is called the root of all evil, for money is to sin as roots are to a tree: Greed provides food and support for the pursuit of all vice and sin. As Aquinas says, "by riches, man acquires the means of committing any sin whatever, and of sating his desire for any sin whatever, since money helps man to obtain all manner of temporal goods, according to *Ecclesiastes* 10:19: 'All things obey money'" (*Summa*, I–II, Q. 84, p. i).

And yet, though the root and means of sin are supplied through Greed, it is Pride that begins all movement towards sin. Pride is the self-interested desire to become something greater than one is, and is a sin and vice for it disparages what God has provided, seeking always something greater for oneself—to serve oneself rather than serving God, and living by his will, and within the means he provides. Aquinas's understanding of Pride as an unwillingness to accept limits is just the same turning away from God that the Ishbalans see in alchemy.

To seek money is to seek power for oneself over things and people, and to seek power for oneself is not far from pridefully standing against the will of God. Karl Marx, the great critic of capitalism, noted this well: "By possessing the *property* of buying everything, by possessing the property of appropriating all objects, *money* is thus the *object* of eminent possession. The universality of its *property* is the omnipotence of its being. It therefore functions as the almighty being" (*Economic and Philosophic Manuscripts of 1844*, p. 136.) As with Father Cornello's deception of the desert city of Lior, there is a seductive but false divinity in the promise that, if you work hard and accept your place in society, you will be rewarded with the satisfaction of all your earthy desires. And what could be more prideful than the worship, possession, and service rendered to that earthly almighty being: money?

Marx also agrees with Aquinas in the claim that not only is money possessed of a false and earthly sort of almighty power, but it is also the root of vice. In the very next sentence, we read:

---

[3] *Summa Theologica*, I–II, Q. 84, iii. All Aquinas quotes are from the translation by the Fathers of the English Dominican Province.

"Money is the *pimp* between man's need and the object, between his life and his means of life." But worse yet, "*that which* mediates *my* life for me, also *mediates* the existence of other people *for me*. For me it is the *other* person." This is human alchemy: money is the pimp that brings to me whatever I desire—and if what I desire is *someone else*; their time, effort, good opinion, work, or respect . . . well, money buys me all that as well.

Human Alchemy

As Marx claims, if I am lame, money buys me horse and carriage; if I am ugly, money makes me desirable; if I am stupid, money buys me advisors; and if I am dishonorable, money makes me honored nonetheless. If I wish a particular food, can't money make it for me? If I don't want to leave the house, can't money have it delivered? He asks, "if *money* is the bond binding me to *human* life, binding society to me, binding me and nature and man, is not money the bond of all *bonds*? Can it not dissolve and bind all ties? It is the true *agent of divorce* as well as the true *binding agent*— the *galvano-chemical* power of Society" (*Economic and Philosophic Manuscripts*, p. 138).

Money transforms my deficiencies into fullnesses, my failings into virtues. Money brings objects to meet and fuel my desires, and brings other people to serve, honor, value, and praise me even as I become ever less deserving of all of these things. Money—stored, accumulated, dead labor; the red stones—is the Philosopher's Stone which allows me to perform human alchemy by controlling and changing others, and to perform human alchemy by transmuting myself as well.

Surely, money used merely as a means to transmute what I have produced into a needful thing—used in the simple transmutation of berries to clothing—does not have this dire effect. According to Aristotle, Marx, and Aquinas as well, this only happens when money comes to moderate relationships, not just between things, but between people as well, and to govern our own self-regard and happiness. In a society where all things are for sale and all people strive and sell themselves for money, a society where money is both our almighty earthly god and master, "visible divinity," and also "the common whore, the common pimp of peoples and nations" (Karl Marx, *Economic and Philosophic Manuscripts*, p. 138.)—in *that* kind of society, money becomes the means of human alchemy. It's no wonder that people who believe fervently in the irreplaceable value of humanity—whether Ishbalan, Muslim, Christian, Jewish, Socialist, or Humanist—find themselves troubled by a society where our most fundamental relationships are determined by market forces.

When we allow money to moderate the way that we think of ourselves, we begin to steadily lose touch with our humanity. Like Alphonse, whose bond to the world is through an alchemic seal rather than a human body, our connections with others begin to appear calculated rather than genuine, and we start to lose a sense of purpose and meaning in our lives. (This is a threat to Alphonse throughout the series, but "Heart of Steel" is where this comes out most clearly.) Alchemy and economics, when allowed to determine or define our human relationships, does not just threaten how we think of ourselves and others, but how we treat them as well. Whether, for example, we might come to think of others simply as ingredients for our projects.

Usury and Human Ingredients

At the heart of capitalism is capital. Capital can be defined as money used to make more money, rather than money expended in purchasing objects of use to us. The consensus throughout most of history is that as soon as we use money to make more money, rather than expending money on human needs, we begin to exchange human value for profits, and to fall into the most loathsome and destructive sorts of sin. The clearest and simplest form of use of capital to extract profit from others is to charge interest on a loan. This act used to be known as usury.

Usury was not infrequently compared to robbery or murder, both in the severity and in the nature of its immorality. Writers including Aristotle, Cato, Cicero, Seneca, Plutarch, St. Basil, St. Ambrose, St. Jerome, St. Augustine, St. Thomas Aquinas, and Martin Luther have claimed that usury is a great moral wrong for a variety of different reasons, including that money should serve humanity, not humanity serve money; that it involved selling the time of human life; that it preyed upon the poor by making them pay more because of their poverty; that it was charging a price without providing a product; and that it was a form of dishonesty, for it made the recipient further impoverished while pretending to give aid. Protestant reformer John Calvin wrote that usury was "in the same rank of criminality" as murder, for the goal of both "is to suck the blood of other men" (*Commentary on the Book of Psalms*, p. 213). We may be beginning, today, to return to something like this view, after having seen how the great accumulation of wealth through usury in the form of no-income no-asset loans, credit-default swaps, and mortgage-backed securities has threatened to break the back of our global economy.

Usury makes dead labor—labor expended and bound alchemically into gold—the master of living men. It makes the borrower the servant of the dead. In this necrocracy, we see the epitome of human alchemy; the approach to human life as a resource to be used up in the service of gathering power; the use of human life—whether of the poor in the case of usury, or of prisoners in the case of the hidden Laboratory 5—to create artifacts of control and domination. And so, it is fitting that human alchemy should be both the origin and the goal of the homunculi.

Homunculi and the Deadly Sins

Homunculi have a human form, but no humanity. They are brought into the world when alchemy is used to realize human goal by going against human limitations. And in just the same way does our use of economics to attempt to replace human value bring the sins for which the homunculi are named into the world.

When we use humans in the service of economic value, rather than using money and profits to increase and realize human values, we quickly lose our humanity, becoming akin to homunculi. In business, we treat humans as mere commodities to be paid as little as possible and dismissed when profits can't be further extracted from them. In love, we mistake purchases for affection. When our relationships take place in the context of greed and prideful, self-serving desires, the other capital vices are sure to be borne in the wake of our actions. Lust and Envy, Gluttony and Wrath, and Sloth as well—the vice closest to the Elric brothers.

Sloth is perhaps the least obvious of these capital vices. Why is Sloth a capital vice, and why is *she* the vice that the Elric brothers bring into the world with *their* forbidden act?

Sloth is not a mere laziness, or at least this is not the sense in which Sloth is a capital vice. As a capital vice, according to Aquinas in *Summa*, II–II, Q. 35, Sloth is a feeling of weariness when faced with the knowledge of how much work it is to do good in the world, and to act in a right manner. Sloth, then, is opposed not to activity or to liveliness, but to charity and care for others. And so Sloth is the servant of Pride, in life as in *Fullmetal Alchemist*, for both are self-interested and avoid and shirk the difficult work of living within the limits of an honest and virtuous life. And it is perhaps right that she should be the product of the Elric brothers' action because they were unwilling to accept and take up the difficult burden that fate laid upon them.

While Greed is the root of evil, and Pride is the beginning of sin, Sloth is the attendant of all vice. It is Sloth that keeps us from taking the hard road and accepting the responsibility of treating others well and working within the limits we find ourselves in. Sloth is the dream of the quick fix, the get-rich-quick scheme, and the attempt to solve a human problem through technology. Along with Greed and Pride, she is the third of the most essential of the deadly sins of capitalism, and of all other forms of alchemy as well.

Equivalent Exchange

> But the world isn't perfect, and the law is incomplete. Equivalent exchange doesn't encompass everything that goes on here. But I still choose to believe in its principle: that all things do come at a price; that there's an ebb and a flow, a cycle. That the pain we went through did have a reward and that anyone who's determined and perseveres will get something of value in return, even if it's not what they expected. I don't think of equivalent exchange as a law of the world anymore, I think of it as a promise between my brother and me; a promise that someday we'll see each other again.
>
> —ALPHONSE ELRIC, *Fullmetal Alchemist*

Simple economic equivalent exchange brings us eventually to great imbalance, loss, and injustice. Safety regulations are cheated—some estimates put the number of work-related deaths at one every five minutes in the United States alone. Children are hungry and

---

[4] That's Dennis Kozlowski. Google him! Of course, he's only a single famous example, but the ultra-rich make similarly outrageous choices all the time.

cold in the same nation where others buy shower curtains made of gold and fifteen-thousand dollar umbrella stands.[4] Free and fair equivalent economic exchange brings about conditions which are not fair, and in which we are not free. The reason is simple: in our world, unlike the Elric brothers', we have allowed economic exchange to transmute human values; we have not adequately protected people's freedom, opportunity, health, and welfare from the transmutations of markets and money. This is the "truth behind truths" of our economic structure: the power to profit without work and to purchase whatever is desired is able to disobey the law of equivalent exchange only because capital is built up by human sacrifice. The secret ingredient in capital is the same as that of the Philosopher's Stone.

If the market will not make good on its promise of equivalent exchange, we too must come to treat it as an incomplete law, and we too must think of it as a promise that we must make to one another. A promise to respect each other, to be fair, to care for each other and strive for our common good. Most of all, a promise to oppose and always guard against Greed, Pride, and Sloth: a promise to be charitable and to accept that the hard work of helping others is our responsibility. In this way, we can strive, *within* a capitalist economy, to avoid the capital vices of the alchemy of money, and use our economic alchemy to support humans within humane limits, rather than to rage against those limits in a selfish, abusive, and exploitative manner.

Alchemist and capitalist both: Be Thou for the People.

17

Everything You *Never* Wanted to Know about Sex and Were Afraid to Watch

ANDREW A. DOWD

Sexual Decisions. That was the name of the first college-level sex-ed textbook to make its way to the islands of Japan. 1985 was the year.

At the time, any graphic depiction of the naked male or female form was expressly forbidden. This fledgling volume, a translated version of a very tasteful, contemporary American text, didn't reach campuses in all its original glory. Many of the drawings and photographs within the book—the detailed sketches of genitalia and the full-frontal model diagrams—were unceremoniously excised. Those that weren't got black boxes plastered over them or were airbrushed into blurry obscurity. Sex could finally be studied and talked about in a Japanese university classroom. Students just had to use their imaginations a little. This, again, was 1985. This was Japan.

My, what a difference two decades can make! To say that Japanese culture has become more, shall we say . . . *permissive* of sexually explicit materials is to understate the point. Images that would have gotten their purveyors locked up in the 1980s now adorn the covers of magazines, staring out from wire racks in airports and convenience stores. Stroll down the right avenue in Tokyo and the city becomes a smut aficionado's playground, with pornographic video vendors and adult bookstores on every corner. Sex sells, and it's everywhere.

There's manga, that intrinsically Japanese brand of comic book, the kind whose best-selling titles now seem split almost evenly between kid-appropriate action fantasy and full-on, no-limits erotica. These books fly off the shelves, into the hands of any and all age groups, parental discretion neither suggested nor required. In Japan, the taboo has become commonplace, private desires have become public domain, and we all have a pretty good idea of what keeps sons rising in the Land of the Rising Sun. As web columnist Jon Wilks puts it, in his tongue-in-cheek, (almost) complete *Dictionary of Japan Sex*, "without hentai and its associated pictorial success the world would know little of Japan's outlandish sexual practices." The dirty secret's out. Proof's in the Gokkun pudding.

But what happened to the puritanically repressed Japan of legend, that nation of prudes, of functional and strictly missionary sex? Did this place ever really exist? Have things changed or are we just now seeing the *real* face of Japan? Either way, attitudes have certainly shifted. The unconvinced need look no further than one of the country's most profitable and prevalent cultural exports, manga's younger cousin, those same wild fantasies put into herky-jerky motion. Got a strong disposition and a stronger stomach? Plug "hentai" into an Internet search engine. For kicks, pepper in a few choice keyboards, like "tentacle" or "bondage" or "dismemberment." Go ahead, I dare you. What you'll find waiting at your fingertips would make Larry Flynt blush and give the Marquis de Sade pause. Forget slasher movies, those perpetual scapegoat texts of the Moral Majority. This here is *actual* torture porn, Grand Guignol in the master bedroom, the *real* return of Robin Wood's infamous repressed.

"How'd you like your hymen broken by a horse speculum?" someone asks a bound, gagged, and hung upside down sex kitten early into *Pigeon Blood*. It's a rhetorical question, of course. Girl doesn't really have much of a choice. In this twisted fable, a bored hedonist oversees a mansion of sex slaves, young girls he makes crawl on all fours, lick up puddles of fresh urine, and serve at the whim of his cruel, sadistic sex drive.

The ten-part *Night Shift Nurses* is worse still. Here, a hulking horndog of a doctor is hired to "break in" the virginal nursing staff of a secluded hospital, to train them in the arts of erotic pleasure. Except there's nothing particularly erotic or pleasurable about the horrors he inflicts upon these fragile, bright-eyed waifs. Sick monster starts by raping each of them, then steadily escalates the intensity of his "training," creatively incorporating stress positions and the systematic insertion of strange objects into uncomfortable places. The young victims are then left in quivering heaps, alone in the dark, often soaked in their own fear-and-pain-induced bodily fluids. Rough stuff. And then there's Tentacle Rape, the always popular, deeply peculiar depiction (popularized by such titles as *La Blue Girl* and *Twin Dolls*) of colossal squid beasties penetrating sweet young things with their phallic feelers. Compared to the episodic atrocities of *Night Shift Nurses*, such oddball sci-fi flourishes seem kind of comical, if still predicated on some pretty nasty business.

Of course, adult anime isn't all violence and viscera, monsters and mutilation. It's the graphic stuff that grabs the headlines and sets the message boards aflutter, but a Google search of *hentai*, minus any grisly qualifiers, will unearth a much wider and more eclectic range of "mature" animated entertainment. Hardcore and softcore, gay and straight, underage and old age, fetish and comparably tame "sensual fantasies"—here in the States, "hentai" is about as specific a signifier as "porno." Really, it's a broad distortion of a precise distinction. What we call *hentai*—basically, any and all pornographic anime—the Japanese refer to as *ero* (erotic) or *seinen* (adult). They also use the single letter "H" (pronounced *ecchi*) in much the same way the Western world uses "X" or "XXX." *Hentai*, to the Japanese, is a slight or an insult, comparable to *pervert* or *weirdo*. Thus the animated pornography actually classified as hentai in Japan is the *really* bizarre or extreme kind: the rape fantasies, the pedophilia porn, the slimy tentacle titillation, the sadomasochistic snuff films. In a market that caters to the every whim and desire of its clientele, these are the only movies that still carry any real measure of stigma or taboo.

True hentai, in other words, *is* the hard stuff. And from here on out, when I use the term, that's what I'm referring to. This is the obscenest of the obscene, the seedy underbelly of Japan's burgeoning sexual revolution, repellant to all but the most jaded of carnal connoisseurs. It's pretty tempting to outright condemn these films, on moral *and* social grounds, as the sick and twisted outgrowth of a sexually deviant, misogynistic culture. (Animated or not, is there any viable defense to be made for, say, the simulated torture and gang rape of a schoolgirl?) Yet to disgustedly denounce these controversial texts, with no consideration of what inspires them and from what deep cultural crevices they seep, is to deny the real *value* they may possess—potentially, *theoretically*, as a safe outlet for a society's darkest desires, its pent-up frustrations, and its most unusual curiosities. Steady your resolve, stifle your gag reflex, and dive headfirst into the mad, mad history of hentai.

Abnormal Conception

If the pictures are to be believed, giant sea beasts were making amorous advances on young Japanese women as early as 1814. That's the year that a painting called *Diver and Two Octopi* appeared in Katsushika Hokusai's art collection *Kinoe no komatsu*. The picture, tame by today's anything-goes standards but quite provocative at the time, depicts a skinny-dipper being pleasured by two enormous squids, their tendrils roaming freely over her naked body. Though it's difficult to infer whether this interspecies love pairing is consensual or not—the girl's eyes are closed in what *could* be construed as ecstasy, and she doesn't appear to be fighting off the horny monster's affections—this popular image struck some kind of chord in the national psyche. It's often cited as the very first known example of Tentacle Rape erotica.

That tentacle-in-cheek history lesson aside, the *real* birth of hentai can be traced back to Japan circa the 1920s. It was then that a number of academic journals sprung up, their express purpose to examine the growing phenomenon of "perverse sexuality" or *ero-guro-nansensu* ("erotic, grotesque nonsense"). Cheaply printed and accessibly written, titles like *Kisho* ("Strange Book") and *Gurotesuku* ("Grotesque") tackled the psychology of perversion through ultra vivid description, indulging in the kind of sensational sexual fantasy they were supposedly dissecting. Predictably, if rather ironically, these journals gained popularity outside of academic circles, appealing more to the folks they purported to study than to those doing the studying. In a culture deprived of the sexual imagery it craved, the analysis of the demand *became* the supply. Sales spiked, a cult of interest was cultivated, and the Japanese government became increasingly suspicious of the "educational value" of these publications. They pulled the plug on the study, but the journals continued to circulate, no longer beholden to any sort of dubious academic obligation. It was during this time that the word "hentai" first entered the Japanese lexicon.

Printing of these now-underground fetish magazines was suspended during World War II, when any and all paper supplies were devoted to the war effort. It was well into the 1950s, after the postwar American occupation, that they resurfaced with a vengeance. This was a tumultuous time for Japan and its culture, one divided between strict reinforcement of moral codes and a growing desire, on the fringes of society, for freedom of sexual expression. The market for hentai grew through the 1960s and 1970s, but it remained underground, out of the line of fire, its writers and publishers operating just out of reach of the long arm of the law.

The fusion of hentai and *shunga* (Japanese erotic art) was a natural and obvious progression, one that flourished in the pages of underground manga. Some of the desired fantasies were so bizarre and extreme that they more or less *had* to be drawn. Can't find any actual multi-limbed creatures to suggestively photograph? Don't really want to murder and mutilate a living woman? In the world of hentai manga, the pen really is mightier than the sword. As with all sexually explicit material in Japan, these publications hovered well below the mainstream. It wasn't until the late 1980s, when the tide began to shift dramatically in favor of legalizing pornography, that adult manga began to really take hold of the public consciousness. Almost overnight, these books became a sensation. It was as though the proceeding sixty years of black-market wheelings and dealings, of sordid stories scribbled across forbidden pages, had all been foreplay. Here, at last, was the explosive orgasm. The Age of Hentai had finally arrived. And manga was at the forefront of it.

That is, until someone had the bright idea of putting those lewd drawings into *motion*. It was during this period of radical social upheaval, when laws prohibiting pornographic materials fell like dominoes with each passing year, that hentai anime first reared its randy head. The loosening of media content restrictions dovetailed neatly with the proliferation of VHS and the fledgling years of the international anime boom. Hentai found its way into anime via the new medium of OVA, or Original Video Animation. These were serialized fantasies, distributed exclusively on video, usually one episode per tape.

Lolita Anime, released in 1984, was not just the first hentai OVA, but also, broadly speaking and per most estimations, the very first animated hentai. It was an anthology series, with no real narrative thread tying together its various tales of adultery, underage intercourse, and sexual humiliation. Many of the genre's hallmarks were introduced in the OVA's six-episode run: bondage fantasies, scandalous encounters with clergymen, *yuri* (or lesbian sex), and more. Even more influential was *Cream Lemon*, released later that same year, another anthology that helped shape the popular hentai template. This series introduced more surreal elements to the formula, setting its graphic sex scenes against a constantly changing backdrop of bizarre genre tropes and convoluted melodrama. In an exemplary episode, a schoolgirl overcomes her history of sexual abuse by masturbating in front of her classmates . . . a development that immediately inspires a mass orgy around her. (Offensive or empowering? YOU be the judge!)

The overarching framing device, loosely employed on an episode-to-episode basis, involves a brother and sister inching ever so slowly into an incestuous relationship. Here, in the dialectic between this reoccurring narrative and the one-off short story snippets it bridges, is a "something-for-everyone" pornographic democracy: instant gratification for some and a meticulous, deliberate build in erotic tension for others. Though they upped the ante in outrageousness, extremity, and elaborate sci-fi affectation, few of the OVAs *Cream Lemon* subsequently inspired could boast such a complicated *modus operandi*. Nor could they lay claim to such classically beautiful animation, reminiscent of mainstream 1970s anime. Before or since, rarely have such outlandish sexual situations been so elegantly, artfully depicted. *Cream Lemon* set a standard of taboo-smashing almost-artistry, basically laying a foundation for the entire hentai movement. Alas, it also set a queasy precedent: the dependence of one gender's sexual liberation on another's complete degradation. There's a reason, in other words, that girls just don't watch this stuff.

Bi-Cultural Attraction

So where do these fantasies *come from*? A budding cultural theorist with a degree in psychology and a tolerance for exquisitely, colorfully rendered depravity could make a career out of answering that question. Many have, I'm sure—if nothing else, hentai is among the most revealing and psychologically loaded brands of smut available. It might seem appropriate to place the burden of baggage on the creators of these films, the writers dreaming up each boundary-pushing scenario, and the animators bringing them to ever so vivid, oh so lurid life. Yet hentai, like all pornography, is more a product than it is an art form. In fact, it's a multi-million dollar industry. Those making this stuff are meeting a demand, plain and simple, and they're certainly not operating in some kind of cultural vacuum. Forget bedroom politics. You could map a complete cultural history—the complicated gender relations and collective sexual insecurities of a whole nation—onto the prevalent images and reoccurring motifs of this gruesome genre.

Hentai's most obvious explanatory scapegoat is sexual repression. This is the notion that one's strangest and most grotesque desires stem from ignoring biological urges, from denying oneself the gratification of regular sexual release. It's one of Freud's most influential principles: that abnormal or dysfunctional sexuality can be traced to the repression of healthy, natural desire. The problem with this theory as it pertains to hentai is that it hinges on the popular belief that Japanese culture actively *encourages* the repression of sexual drive. Historically speaking, this is a vast and troubling oversimplification. Like just about any nation with at least a couple hundred years under its belt, Japan has seen a periodic sway and shift in its core values. This habitual push-pull between conservatism and progression sometimes manifests itself in seeming inconsistencies. For example, pornography was illegal until the late 1980s, yet erotic art has been a celebrated staple of Japanese culture for centuries. What appear at first like inherent contradictions in the country's moral makeup are merely telltale signs of a malleable culture, one that's steadily changing and constantly evolving.

Some of Japan's most striking cultural dichotomies can be traced back to an era in which two separate moral frameworks seemed to be operating at once. During the Tokugawa Period (1603–1868) differing attitudes about the role of sex in everyday life were drawn cleanly down class division lines. On one side you had the ruling class, the feudal Samurais, whose strict code of personal conduct was heavily influenced by the rigid tenets of Confucianism. For these prisoners of the aristocracy, passions of the flesh were severely restricted, often outright forbidden. *Any* form of romantic expression was generally frowned upon in the upper echelons of Japanese society. You had to slide much further down the totem pole, to the powerless peasants and toiling merchants of the working class, before you'd encounter uninhibited sexual pursuit. Shinto was the dominant faith *these* people clung to; among the major world religions, it remains unique in its celebration of carnal desire as a healthy, essential component of human nature. Buddhism, the other organized religious faith of the Japanese proletariat, promotes a similarly *laissez-faire* attitude toward sexual expression.

Japan's aristocracy eventually crumbled and collapsed, resulting in the gradual collision of these two very different sets of cultural ideals. Opposing values, long segregated into separate social strata, began to bump up against each other. The end of Japan's lengthy isolationist period brought an influx of fresh ideologies. These new ways of thinking scraped up roughly against occasional periods of imposed "moral decency," such as the one that accompanied the post-war American occupation. The right hand and the left hand were suddenly and consistently at odds. Modern Japan thus seems less defined by a unilaterally conservative attitude about sex and more by a complicated and sometimes confused relationship between warring perspectives on the matter. It's from this fissure, perhaps, that hentai was spawned—mixed signals curdle into sexual revenge fantasies, the viewer transposing his frustration with a culture constantly in transition upon onscreen surrogates. The big-eyed, squeaky-voiced, pony-tailed kind.

Hate Fuck

Is hentai therapeutic—as some kind of psychosexual spectatorship, a means of channeling more deeply entrenched anxieties? Perhaps it functions that way for men. But for the "fairer sex?" So much of the medium speaks to a deep resentment of women and to a fear of the changing role they play in contemporary Japan. Workplace equality, political ascendancy, sexual liberation—Japanese women may still occupy a position of relative social subjugation, but baby, they've come a long way. Now take a look at the nubile vixens traipsing through your average hentai. They're blushing, obedient virgins, ripe for the deflowering. Secretaries and nurses, wide-eyed servant girls, and naive co-eds—these are the desirable archetypes of adult anime. If ever a strong female figure should appear onscreen, you can bet that either (a) she's going to make some shy girly girl her submissive sex slave or (b)—and this is much more common—she'll be knocked down a peg or two, literally or symbolically stripped of her power. In *Night Shift Nurses*, it's the innocent young med students our "hero" dutifully corrupts and defiles. Yet his first conquest is actually the power-suit-clad dragon lady who hires him. She's a no nonsense businesswoman, a real ball-buster, so naturally she has to be broken. (Minutes she's on screen before dropping to her knees: roughly four.) Even hentai that employ a female protagonist, an intergalactic traveler or sexy warrior princess, eventually subject the heroine to some violation or horrific sexual ordeal. Here the appeal of strong women lies in the promise of their comeuppance. These Supergirls won't be so super once the Octo-Beasts get their loose limbs upon them.

In her seminal essay "From Reverence to Rape," cultural theorist Molly Haskel proposes that, on the whole, contemporary cinema offers only two prevailing notions of womanhood: the Madonna (or pure, saintly mother figure) and the Whore. As a nation that has long established the rigid role and responsibility of its female citizens—as mothers, daughters and housewives, mostly—Japan has veritably overdosed on its centuries-old Madonna complex. Hentai could be seen as a reactionary revolt against that standard, though certainly not one that benefits, via representation, the women compelled to adhere to it. These films transform Madonnas *into* Whores, dragging the sacred image of the chaste, loyal über-woman into the down-and-dirty muck. (Hence, also, the nun raping in *Advancer Tina* and its shocking ilk.) Hentai often reads like a lashing out against *all* women: the mousey and traditional Madonnas, the promiscuous Whores, and the independent career women, for whom the support of "good men" scarcely seems necessary anymore. No getting around it, these are fundamentally misogynistic texts.

And yet one has to wonder if all this rage and violence is really even *about* women. Let's can the euphemisms: hentai *is* rape porn. Ninety percent of the time, the sexual aggressor is forcing his/her/itself onto an unwilling partner. When this isn't the case, the films still traffic in fear, shame, degradation, and agony. What could possibly inspire someone, *anyone*, to find any such extreme states of mind or states of being sexually arousing? Well, psychologically speaking, rape isn't really about sex, but *power*. And that leads us to the problematic notion of Japanese Inferiority. This fabled complex—excessively evoked, though not necessarily without *some* merit—proposes that a century of military defeats, compounded by the unfathomable tragedy of Hiroshima and Nagaski, has effectively emasculated the character of the Japanese nation. Theoretically, one might read hentai as a fantasy reclamation of that lost power, that compromised "manhood." Certainly, the mere *physiology* of the male figures in hentai speaks to a kind of wish fulfillment. If the women are wiry, petite, demure little numbers, the men are tall, dashing, muscular Alpha Males. They tend to be exceptionally well endowed, their genitals sketched epically large, to only-in-porno proportions. And when they orgasm, the ejaculation is often hilariously explosive, like some erupting volcano or geyser. That kind of machismo distortion of the human form is common in most adolescent male fantasies, not just the Japanese variety. Insecurity—about one's body, one's manhood and one's power in relation to others—is a pretty universal malady of the modern man.

Hentai, then, is at least a *superficially* empowering medium. It's also a revolt against good taste, a subversive transformation of the sacred into the profane, and a canvas on which to boldly splash, without reproach, one's anger and fear and frustration. Hentai is fantasy, and fantasy has value. But how much value, this extreme and vicious variety? Do these films really cleanse their viewers of their dangerous desires or instead merely articulate, finally and with appetite-stoking clarity, the depth of their depravity? Put another way: does hentai satiate the raping, tentacled monster within or does it give it the taste for human flesh?

How Dirty Boys Get Clean?

The argument about *catharsis*, generally defined as a *purging* of the mind or spirit via sensational art or entertainment, can be traced back to long before cities were wicked, bibles were black, or the Overfiend had a legend to speak of. It was history's foremost Great Thinkers, the granddaddy heavyweights of philosophy, who first took sides in that endless debate. Aristotle, in his famous *Poetics*, proposed that some works can actively "cleanse" the emotional palette of those experiencing them, offering a recognition and sub-sequent release of pent-up feelings, anxieties, or frustrations.

This conclusion was written in direct and purposeful opposition to one posited by Plato, in his own magnum opus, *The Republic*. It was Plato's contention that works of dramatic sensationalism encouraged men to be irrational or hysterical, to lose control of their feelings. These philosophers were writing of poetry and the-ater, not animated skin flicks. And the "feelings" they referred to were those you have in your heart, not the ones that rise in your loins. Regardless, this ancient sparring of theses is the foundation of a very modern debate. Does violent art and entertainment instill in each of us a greater need or desire for *real* violence? Or do such works offer a healthy, harmless, and periodic outlet for anti-social behavior, a play fantasy way to get all of those messy impulses out of our system?

The latter notion, referred to today as the Theory of Catharsis, was revived and popularized for the Media Age by Seymour Feshbach. His 1955 essay, "The Drive-Reducing Function of Fantasy

Behaviour," offered a fervent defense of television and movie violence, suggesting that such materials defuse latent aggression by placating viewers with small and safe doses of vicarious violence. In other words, those that occasionally stoke their own biological bloodlust with the power of make-believe are then less likely to take it out on the "real world." Sounds reasonably convincing, except a number of theories sprung up afterwards that actively challenged Feshbach's findings. There was Leonard Berkowitz's Theory of Disinhibition, which stated, in affect, that violent media lessens our inhibitions about behaving aggressively and can also confuse our sense of what is or is not "aggressive behavior." This is somewhat related to the Theory of Desensitization, wherein prolonged exposure to *fake* violence conditions us to think of *real* violence as "normal" or "natural." And then there's Social Learning Theory, a.k.a. the hypothesis that since we all learn how to behave from observing others, watching dollops of violent media—especially at a young and impressionable age—teaches violence as an acceptable mode of interpersonal relations (Nancy Signorielli, *Violence in the Media: A Reference Handbook*, pp. 16–22)

Those last three, roundly summarized as the Anti-Violent Media theories, have gained a lot of traction in the last few decades. Catharsis, on the other hand, has been rather roundly dismissed by psychologists and cultural theorists alike. B.J. Bushman and L.R. Huesmann, two vocal proponents of the Disinhibition Theory, rather brashly asserted that "there is not a thread of convincing scientific data" to support the Catharsis theory ("Effects of Televised Violence on Aggression," *Handbook of Children and the Media*, p. 236). What they meant, of course, is that controlled group studies of catharsis, the kind that virtually "proved" the Anti-Violent Media theories, yielded no such accreditation from the medical or psychiatric community. As far as most of academia is concerned, catharsis just doesn't fly. And yet it still routinely pops up in the critical conversation, a few rouge theorists fighting the good fight on behalf of this (mostly) discredited theory.

Most of those "successful" studies looked at sample groups, tracking the various reactions of various individuals in a controlled environment. Few of them examined "real world" data. And almost none of them measured the effects, positive *or* negative, of violent *sexual* media—"rough" pornography. But that's exactly what University of Hawaii PhD candidate Milton Diamond did in 1998. In his thesis "The Effects of Pornography: An International

Perspective," Diamond tracked the correlation between the increase in quantity or availability of pornography in Japan and the nation's yearly sexual assault statistics. The results were surprising: from the early 1970s to the mid-1990s, a period defined by the rapid legalization and proliferation of pornography, the rate of sex crimes in Japan went *way* down, steadily and continuously. This included both the number of rape victims (1,500 in 1995, down from 4,677 in 1972) and the number of rape offenders (1,160 in 1995, down from 5,464 in 1972).

Pornography goes up, rape goes down, and the theory of catharsis holds water. Case closed, right? Not so fast. First of all, correlation does not imply causation—there are any number of factors that could have contributed to that steady decline in sexual assaults. At best, the study suggests that violent pornography doesn't actively *cause* more rapes or *create* more rapists. But it sure doesn't prove that it curtails those kinds of criminal sexual desires. One has to also consider that rape is a crime that depends on an official complaint being filed. Japan may have made great leaps and bounds in its social progression, but it's still a Shame Society, one that's historically controlled its citizens by instilling in them fear of bringing shame upon themselves or their family. How many of the country's actual sexual assaults go unreported every year? Experts sometimes project as many as five to ten times the number reported (Yoshiro Hatano and Tsuguo Shimazaki, "Japan," *The International Encyclopedia of Sexuality*). How many of the rapists tried every year beat the system? In a country still slanted towards the dominance of the male authority figure, that number can't be too insignificant either. Diamond's magic decline may have been little more than a beautiful lie, at best a half-truth. If this is the most convincing case one can dig up for catharsis, Feshbach and his faithful proponents need to start showing their work.

Textually Transmitted Disease

"Pornography is the theory and rape is the practice," feminist author Robin Morgan famously declared in her 1980 essay, "Theory and Practice: Pornography and Rape." Yet no conclusive link has ever really been made between pornography and sex crimes. Really, even the popular theories regarding violent, *non*sexual media—Disinhibition, Desensitization, and Social Learning—remain mostly speculative. Hentai, which mixes graphic sex with extreme, sadistic violence, has scarcely been examined. It's doubtful that *any* study will "prove" that it has a profoundly negative effect on those who watch it. But lord knows there's also nothing out there to suggest that these films, in their transparent contempt for women and I-dare-you-to-top-*this* obscenity, do anything but encourage the development of unhealthy sexual preoccupations.

Hentai won't transform a "normal" person into a slicing and dicing rapist, nor will it transform a disturbed sex offender into a healthy, productive member of society. This kind of stuff isn't an "On" or "Off" switch for deviant sexual behavior. It doesn't affect your actions so much as, potentially and quite harmfully, your *attitudes*. Its influence is insidious, subtle even. If there is, at last, a theory that explains the likely consequences of excessive hentai consumption, it is that of Cultivation. Developed in the late 1960s and early 1970s, Larry Gross and George Gerbner's hotly debated social theory explores the long-term effects of modern media on the viewing public, on its general ideologies and given assumptions. Michael Morgan, who joined the Gross-Gerbner research team years later, summarizes the theory as such:

> Cultivation researchers have argued that these messages of power, dominance, segregation, and victimization cultivate relatively restrictive and intolerant views regarding personal morality and freedoms, *women's roles*, and minority rights. Rather than stimulating aggression, cultivation theory contends that heavy exposure to television violence cultivates insecurity, mistrust, and alienation, and a willingness to accept potentially repressive measures in the name of security, all of which strengthens and helps maintain the prevailing hierarchy of social power. ("Audience Research: Cultivation Analysis," *The Museum of Broadcast Communications*; emphasis mine)

Hentai as a tool for status quo preservation? Might seem like a stretch, except that, in the lionization of manly men power trips, these films cultivate gender identities as rigid as . . . well, as the pitched tents they inspire. Not since Freddy and Jason caught the outrage of concerned mothers everywhere have such accidentally conservative, Trojan Horse entertainments come barreling into the bedrooms of impressionable youths. Of course, the genre doesn't *intentionally* reinforce anything but the fat bank accounts of the folks who supply it. (Okay, and maybe their respective reputations for no-limits filth and sleaze, too.) But it *does* propagate attitudes—

about sex, about romance, about power, about the role women can and should play in a twenty-first-century society. Watch enough of this stuff, and its marginal "messages" start to creep in, like a virus. Especially if you're young, with a mind like a sponge, ready to suck up any number and manner of subtextual ideologies.

And therein lies the most disturbing thing about hentai: its kid-ready collision of the juvenile and the profane. Forget the warning stickers, the "adult situations," the insistence of anyone involved that these films are "*definitely* not for children." The foundation of hentai is those wild and elaborate stories, ripped from the pulpy pages of manga and the stunted imaginations of comic-book-loving man-children. Demons and monsters? Alternate universes? Intergalactic adventure? Hentai recasts innocuous adolescent fantasy as the most rancid of patriarchal wet dreams. At its very best, the genre cultivates in its budding lovers-to-be a dehumanizing perspective on sex: it's not something you share with another person, but something you *do to them*—gratification is a one-way street, women serve a simple and express purpose, and romance is inessential (if not detrimental) to the equation. Hentai is for boys of all ages, for boys to be boys, forever and ever, wielding swords, shooting guns, parting legs, having their wicked way with the whole wide world. Rocks are gotten off, balls become less blue, and the boys feel better, having vicariously, temporarily fucked their hurt away. But what of the girls? Pity those damsels in distress. No one's coming to rescue them.

18

The Devil Within
Sara Livingston

MEA CULPA
BLOG

SUBSCRIBE TO

❖ Posts   √

❖ All Comments √

TO START AT THE BEGINNING*

Click on Post #1 Welcome Link

* Postings are in reverse chronological order

CREDITS

Jose, Henrietta and Franca are fictional characters from the Anime/Manga property, *Gunslinger Girl,* created by Japanese artist Yu Aida, and distributed in the US by FUNimation. All images from *Gunslinger Girl* are used with permission: (c) Yu Aida/ASCII Media Works, Marvelous Entertainment. Licensed by FUNimation(r) Productions, Ltd. All Rights Reserved.

The Milgram Experiment photo can be found at www.nytimes.com/slideshow/2008/06/30/science/070108-MIND_6.html and is from the personal collection of Alexandra Milgram. The Milgram Experiment v2.png drawing is licensed under the Creative Commons Attribution ShareALike 3.0 License, and the original uploader was "expiring frog" at en.wikipedia.

I was an Agent for the Italian Government employed by a Special Ops Division, the Social Welfare Agency. The Agency "grew" its ranks by taking in injured or abandoned children, drugging them, implanting them with cybernetic limbs, then training them to be murderous assassins. Because of my youthful enthusiasm and patriotism, I agreed to participate in this experimental program.

But over time, I decided that I could no longer violate my own sense of morality and that my young partner, Henrietta, my **Gunslinger Girl,** deserved a chance at a normal life. The posts that follow will document my "leave of absence" from the agency and explain some of the reasons I felt compelled to take Henrietta and disappear.

Post #9 Ciao Roma

The pessimists who have finished reading this blog might think:

1. He's a monster and a coward.
2. His realization and honesty are "too little, too late."
3. The Agency will hunt him down and kill him for exposing them.
4. F**k the Agency, **Henrietta** will kill him in his sleep when her drugs wear off.
5. Read between the lines – he definitely nailed her.

But I'm counting on the optimists among you who will realize:

1. I am a victim, too.
2. It's never too late to right a wrong OR to question authority.
3. Henrietta and I are black ops professionals and can hide indefinitely.
4. The Agency may have brainwashed her but Henrietta's humanity and compassion remain. She'll recover, and she'll forgive me.
5. You know I could never take advantage of her. The undercurrent of sexuality and exploitation in my story is there to challenge our complicity with the human trafficking industry and the child soldier phenomenon.

Events of late are persuading me to go more deeply under cover so this will be my last post for a while. The landlady at our Pensione has suddenly started asking questions:

FILM & TV

Alias
Battlestar Galactica
Blade Runner
Doll House
La Femme Nikita
Terminator: The Sarah Connor Chronicles
The Professional

BOOKS

Anime and Philosophy
Battlestar Galactica and Philosophy: Mission Accomplished or Mission Frakked Up?
Children At War
Consciousness Explained
Enders Game
Manga and Philosophy
Speaker for the Dead
Never Let Me Go

Why isn't Henrietta in school? Where is her mother? I see a violin case, so why don't I ever hear her practice?

And, did you read the comment left by Caterina/Franca? I'm a little spooked by getting comments on my posts from a former enemy agent/terrorist bomber. Henrietta and I were right there, at the Messina Bridge and barely escaped when Franca's explosives detonated. She claims she's had an epiphany, and she hopes "we're in a safe place." Yeah, right.

I need a place to land. Does anyone have a suggestion about where we should hide out for a while? I hear that the southwestern United States, New Zealand, and Thailand are all places where people can disappear and just live quiet, anonymous lives.

Please email me (josefratello74@gmail.com), write on my wall on Facebook (Jose Fratello) or go online now (http://jose-meaculpa.blogspot.com/) and post your ideas about a place with low population density, mild climate, and light law enforcement. Thanks.

BLOG ARCHIVE

2009 (9)

April (2)
May (2)
June (2)
July (2)
August (1)
September
October

2010 (5)

Photo by Holger Grösch

Even when we do find a place to hide, I have no illusions about our future. A "normal" life for Henrietta and me will always be impossible, but I'm trying to stay optimistic.

After all, who among us has a normal life?

Post # 8 Boiled Frog Syndrome

Have you heard about the phenomenon referred to as the boiled frog syndrome? Put a frog in a pot of water and increase the temperature of the water gradually, and the frog just sits there. But suddenly, at 100 degrees C, something happens: the water boils, and the frog dies.

There is some debate about whether the story is literally true or not, but it serves as a useful metaphor, similar to the one about the ostrich with his head in the sand, about the folly of

ignoring warning signs. The metaphor is often used as a cautionary tale, warning against the danger of letting small, seemingly harmless wrongs go by allowing them to build into a powerful, irreversible force – like global warming.

I'd like to borrow the analogy and apply it to my behavior during my time at the agency, when I dismissed my growing alarm and dodged my own conscience. Unlike the frog, however, I jumped before I reached the boiling point because of the following event that brought my situation into focus.

Last Spring, the civil war in Sri Lanka finally ended after 26 long years. The leader of the Tamil Tigers was killed and the fighting stopped. Remember one of my first posts when I told you about the UNICEF worker I met on the plane?

Remember?

She was on her way to Sri Lanka as a UN observer, and she had given me the book she was reading. I never found the time or the balls to read it, so I just put it in my locker. The news story jogged my memory, and I finally got the nerve to read P. W. Singer's book, *Children at War.*

Post #7   You Can't Shame the Shameless

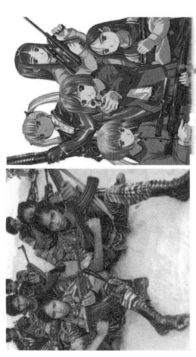

Girl Tamil Tiger Fighters

My Agency reminds me of the paramilitary groups mentioned in *Children At War* – Rwandan warlords, the Colombian and Mexican drug cartels, and the Tamil Tigers of Sri Lanka to name a few – because we, like them, recruit abandoned and orphaned children who have no adult protection. The Tamil Tigers had

1 Comment

Caterina said...

This is not a response to the post per se, although I applaud your analysis of the problem and your brave decision to walk away. My comment is a kind of confession.

I was going to try to stay anonymous and just comment from time to time but your words about responsibility and shame are inspiring, so I going to come clean, too. You may be surprised to hear that I was a freelancer for the Padania faction. I don't think we ever met but I have come face to face with some of your colleagues--Hilshire and Triella for sure. In fact, I'm recuperating right now from an accident last year that was connected to the Messina Bridge incident.

I'll tell you now that my real name is Caterina, but you may know me by my code name, Franca. I'm writing a blog myself to pass the time while I recover and to question my own a bonanza of new recruits just after the tsunami decimated the coast of Sri Lanka, because there were many homeless orphaned children who were welcomed into the children's army.

Another similarity is that we all seem to select our victims the same way hyenas do – we look for the sick, the helpless, and the young. The Agency has spotters in many hospitals across Italy and when a suitable young girl is admitted, we first confirm that she has no family or money, and then we swoop in and offer, "to help."

Henrietta, for example, was a victim of home invasion where the robbers weren't content to just take property. They spent a few days torturing and killing the entire family except for Henrietta who was left for dead with extensive physical and mental trauma from her ordeal.

Angie, another of our cyborgs, was the victim of a near-fatal car accident. The most tragic detail of her story was that her parents were driving the car that hit her and astonishingly, it was no accident. Her father's business was about to fail, so to raise some cash, he deliberately set out to kill her in order to collect on her life insurance policy.

---

actions. From what I've read on your blog, we have a lot in common and should get together to talk some day.

There was a boy named Pinocchio who was recruited the same way as Triella. Pinocchio was not a cyborg and did not have the chemical conditioning you spoke of, but he became an obedient slave killing on command. I hid him in the country for a while, but in the end I couldn't save him.

I hope you and Henrietta are in a safe place.

Check out my blog at:
http://codenamefranca.blogspot.com
2:38 PM

Triella, our oldest cyborg was "rescued" from a gang of child traffickers in Amsterdam. Hillshire was part of the police team that broke up the gang and brought them to justice. He brought Triella to the agency to "save" her and became her handler.

Rico was born paralyzed and had been bed-ridden her entire life. When her parents' resources and patience with caring for her were exhausted, they signed her over as a ward of the state. The benevolent Agency stepped in, giving her cybernetic limbs and training her to kill.

The girls weren't the only victims of exploitive recruitment practices. In reality, the Agency recruited its handlers using the same ploy. Even though we were adults when we were "invited" to be handlers, my brother and I were perfect victims. Our conscription happened partly because we were vulnerable after our parents, sister and Jean's fiancée were killed by a terrorist car bomb. We, too, were orphaned, alone in the world and vulnerable. Two of our colleagues, Raballo and Marco came to the agency, because they were injured on the job. Raballo hurt his leg and could no longer run after criminals, and Marco lost the sight in one of his eyes and could no longer aim a gun accurately. They were broken people who were grateful and delighted for a chance to be useful again.

A final similarity lies in the reason we and other paramilitary groups choose children as our soldiers. As P.W. Singer points out in his book, children's minds are plastic, so they learn fast. One Rwandan handler bragged that he could train a child to use a lightweight Kalashnikov in 30 minutes, so his army of children was ready to fight immediately – forget about six weeks of basic training. He also bragged about children being vulnerable and easy to intimidate. Dependent children can be easily conditioned to obey and should they balk, they are easily bullied because their small size puts them at a disadvantage. Civil war instigators around the globe need a steady supply of orphans as cannon fodder, and their conflicts and profits can go on indefinitely.

In all the stories about child soldiers I read, not one person, agency or government claimed that what they were doing was morally or legally right. Everyone agrees that it is wrong, yet the practice thrives. As Singer says, "One cannot shame the shameless." It seems that no matter how many laws are passed or how many international agencies draft resolutions against such practices, nothing shames us into stopping.

Groups who recruit children to kill know very well that they are violating international law and moral codes that have existed for thousands of years, and that knowledge is the heart of the problem. We know its wrong, and yet we persist. After reading the book I realized that those who recruit children, send them into battle, and force them to commit murder are simply unlikely to be persuaded by moral appeals or any kind of rational discourse.

So what is left as a deterrent? As a global community we all must condemn the practice, call for enforcement of international law, and the people participating directly have to do what I am doing.

Just walk away.

POSTED BY JOSE AT 2:07 PM 0 COMMENTS

Post #6 Outsourced Responsibility – Milgram Experiment 18

Featured Psychology Videos

Stanley Milgram's Study in Obedience to Authority
Buy Now | Learn More | Request Rights

Featured Psychology Videos

- Stanley Milgram's Study in Obedience to Authority
- Philip Zimbardo's Stanford Prison Experiment
- Carl Rogers and Client-Centered Psychotherapy in Process
- Carl Rogers' Therapy Session with a Young Homosexual Man
- Young Woman with Three Distinct Personalities

Someone commented earlier about Hannah Arendt, and I wanted to respond. The outsourcing of responsibility you're speaking of corresponds closely to Milgram's experiment #18. The experiment was significant because 37 out of 40 participants administered the full range of shocks up to 450 volts, the highest obedience rate Milgram found in his whole series. In this variation, the actual subject did not pull the shock lever; instead he only conveyed information to the peer who pulled the lever.

According to Milgram, this allows the subject to shift responsibility to the other

Go online to view this Video Clip of Milgram Experiment.
http://mediasales.psu.edu/?gclid=CLKRrp3OqJsCFSOeDOodjis0DQ

person and not blame himself for what happens. This resembles real-life incidents in which people see themselves as merely cogs in a wheel, just "doing their job," allowing them to avoid responsibility for the consequences of their actions.

POSTED BY JOSE AT 1:59 PM 0 COMMENTS

Post # 5 Claes, Raballo, and Milgram

Rabello/Claes *fratello* is an interesting story. Rabello was a much older agent who agreed to work with us for a short time. He was assigned to Claes and treated her as if she were his granddaughter. Between training sessions he took her fishing, taught her to work in his garden, and gave her the key to his apartment so she could borrow books for her enjoyment. Partly because of his short time with us and partly because of his unexpected attachment to Claes, he decided to become a whistle blower and sought to expose the program. He made an appointment with a journalist but on the way to speak to a journalist but on the way to their interview, Raballo was killed in a freak accident.

Claes was then left without a partner and protector. Our Director said she was worthless without a handler and because their bond had been so strong, efforts to pair her with another were futile. The next step for her was termination, but someone further up the chain of command decided the cyborg engineers could use her as a test subject. And this is where I found myself thinking of <u>Milgram's Experiment # 18.</u>

The doctors and engineers set up stress tests to monitor the strength of her implants, increasing the pressure ounce by ounce until her limbs gave out, often tearing her flesh and snapping her bones as they looked for her breaking point. The lab assistants who turned the knob seemed very detached as they ripped her flesh— after all, they were only doing what they were told; they felt no responsibility for their acts.

So who is responsible for torturing Claes? Let's go up the chain of command and see. The lab assistant turns the dial and applies the pressure, because Dr. Giallani tells her to. He got orders from Dr. Bianchi, who got his orders from Lorenzo, Chief of Special Ops. Lorenzo got his orders from Monica Petris, Minister of Defense for Italy, and I can only presume she got her orders from the Prime Minister. So it seems that if you work for the government you're never responsible for your actions and can claim that you are only following orders … unless, of course, you are the prime Minister. Do you see how easy it is to deny responsibility?

POSTED BY JOSE AT 1:04 PM 0 COMMENTS

Post #4 Elsa, Lauro, and Milgram

Of all the *fratello*, Lauro and Elsa's partnership was the most tragic. Their bodies were found in a forest preserve, both professionally executed with bullets to the head, so naturally the Agency thought Padania had put contracts out on all the *fratello*. Henrietta and I were spirited out of the city for our own safety while the investigation took place. As Section One began a private inquiry, the officers wondered aloud why this young girl and older man would be together in such a secluded place.

The tragedy of Lauro and Elsa reminds me of another condition Milgram noted as necessary for suspending morality. His condition stated, "The guards (or teachers) develop a distorted sense of the victims (or learners) as not comparable to themselves. Dehumanizing them as animals would be an extreme example."

Lauro was the textbook example of this condition and treated Elsa with contempt. Although several handlers referred to the girls as cyborgs or tools when they talked among themselves, Lauro referred to Elsa as a cyborg even to her face. He was cold and indifferent to

Go Online to view an AMV Tribute to Elsa DiSica
http://www.youtube.com/watch?v=i9yTxA4CzYk

and off the clock, never complimented her for a job well done, and punished her severely if she made a mistake. Because he insisted on giving her the highest doses of conditioning, she was totally devoted to him to the point of being obsessively in love with him, so his indifference seemed even crueler. Elsa reacted to this treatment by crawling into an emotional shell, isolating herself from everyone except Lauro, and exhibiting nervousness and distraction on the job. I tried to talk to him about it, but he dismissed my concern and criticized my kindness toward Henrietta, implying that I was a "cyborg lover". His dehumanization of Elsa allowed him to justify his abusive behavior, which may have included the rumors we heard of their "playing house." No one spoke of a sexual relationship directly, but Elsa showed psychological symptoms of abuse.

When both were murdered, the investigation centered on known Padania hit men, but we found no viable suspects. A break in the case came when it was discovered that the bullet in Lauro's brain came from Elsa's gun. At the time we could not imagine a scenario where one of our girls, who was highly trained and conditioned to protect her handler, could have allowed her own firearm to be taken away and used to harm her handler.

Another detail was perplexing to the investigators. Elsa's own fatal wound was a bullet, shot at close range piercing her eye, a secret Achilles heel for this generation of cyborgs. In fact the eye is the only place that isn't armored so it is THE vulnerable place on the cyborg body. So either the shot was unusually lucky or it was an inside job.

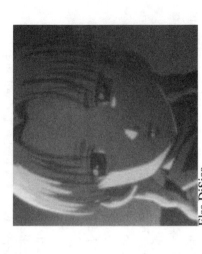

Elsa DiSica

I was a suspect because everyone knew that Lauro and I had strong philosophical differences. But I was quickly ruled out when investigators visited Henrieta and me at our seaside hideout. It was actually Henrietta who solved the case with a dramatic demonstration of the potent emotional bonds forged by chemical conditioning. She told the investigator, very softly – very sincerely – that if I had ever treated her the way Lauro treated Elsa, she would have been so heartbroken that she would have killed herself. She grabbed a gun, placed it next to her eye, and fired. We rushed to stop her, but she deliberately missed to illustrate her point, and it showed us the solution to the crime. Elsa's despair brought her to a place where the only solution was to kill Lauro, and then turn the gun on herself, committing suicide and ending her pain.

At first this incident caused the doctors and neurologists to rethink dosages and to caution the handlers about using too much conditioning. For a while the staff called the girls by name and stopped making off-color remarks about what they would do if they had a squad of cyborg girls at their disposal. But as the incident retreated in time, it also retreated from our memories, and soon we all went back to business as usual.

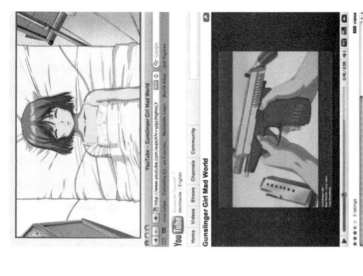

Post #3 The Slippery Slope

I remember that the hospital room was dimly lit with just a single shaft of light illuminating her bed. The diminutive patient looked even smaller and more helpless amid the tangle of tubes and wires that were holding her together. Her body, salvaged from devastating injuries, was in the process of being "retro fitted" with graphite joints and fortified muscle tissue that would make her an indestructible fighting machine. Her mind had been wiped of memories, and she was being psychologically and pharmacologically programmed to be an obedient, guilt free assassin. The doctors asked me to stand by, so that my face would be the first thing she'd see when she awakened to her new identity. I felt like I should have greeted her with flowers or a plush teddy bear, but they told me that her life would be easier if she got used to her new status immediately – so I caved to authority, did as I was told, and placed the SIG P239, a semi-automatic pistol, on the coverlet.

Maybe it was seeing the men in white coats that jogged my memory, but the day I met Henrietta, the Milgram

Experiments snapped into my mind the instant I agreed to give her the gun. That small, innocuous gesture was the beginning of the slippery slope identified as one of the key conditions Milgram said is necessary for suspending human morality. The condition I remembered was, "There is a gradual escalation of violence that starts with a small step." Although my instincts were shouting to comfort and protect this little girl, I didn't because Dr. Belisario, Dr. Bianchi, and my brother, Jean, all convinced me to follow their orders.

Stanley Milgram was a social psychologist teaching at Yale in the early 1960s when, inspired by the trial of Adolph Eichmann, he decided to look at the effect of authority on human behavior. He devised several experiments that cast researchers in white lab coats as his authority figures. In over a dozen studies, with both Yale college students and more than 1,000 ordinary citizens, Milgram's experiment showed that a large majority of subjects applied seemingly lethal electric shocks to other subjects. The scenario was that researchers assigned the subjects the role of "teachers" who were to help "learners" improve their memories by punishing their mistakes with increasing levels of shock as they continued the learning task. Most teachers, although they clearly did not wish to shock another human, agreed to do it.

He summarized the experiment in his 1974 article, "The Perils of Obedience", adapted from _Obedience to Authority: An Experimental View_, writing:

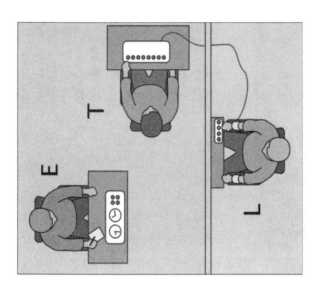

The legal and philosophic aspects of obedience are of enormous importance, but they say very little about how most people behave in concrete situations. I set up a simple experiment at Yale University to test how much pain an ordinary citizen would inflict on another person simply because he was ordered to by an experimental scientist. Stark authority was pitted against the [participants'] strongest moral imperatives against hurting others, and, with the [participants'] ears ringing with the screams of the victims, authority won more often than not. The extreme willingness of adults to go to almost any lengths on the command of an authority constitutes the chief finding of the study and the fact most urgently demanding explanation.

When Henrietta finally did awaken, and I looked into her eyes, I saw the trust and love (provided by the psychotropic drugs they euphemistically call conditioning), and I felt the bond the doctors warned me to be wary of. I did what I was told, imprinted her with her new name, Henrietta, and her signature weapon, the SIG P239 – then she drifted back to sleep.

1 Comment
Close this window
Jump to comment form

Caterina said...
You've been posting about Milgram's experiment and how Eichmann's Trial inspired him to do his experiments. Have you read Hannah Arendt? She says something that might offer fuel for the journey moving you away from your old life. In her book *Eichmann in Jerusalem: A Report on the Banality of Evil*, she proposes that the self-examination you are doing right now is exactly what Adolph Eichmann failed to do when he unquestioningly followed orders.

My role as her handler and teacher would begin as soon as her body healed. Like Milgram's experiment, I would become the "teacher" who would train the "student" by following orders and inflicting the Agency's brand of manipulation on these budding cyborg assassin. Over the next few months, Henrietta and I would train hard, bond emotionally, and I would teach her to kill the Padania terrorists and anyone else the Agency deemed to be enemies of our country.

POSTED BY JOSE AT 8:27 AM 1 COMMENTS

Post #2 Mad World – Children at War

My first day with the Agency began with a 6 AM flight from London to Rome. I sat next to a young woman, faded jeans, backpack, Peace Corps type, who was reading a book called *Children at War*. On the cover, a young African boy about 10 years old caught my eye and stared back at me. He was wearing a red beret decorated with a silver star, red shorts, a khaki jacket a couple sizes too big for him, and a striped tee shirt with an incongruous picture of a kid on a BMX bicycle.

(Oh Jose, isn't it comforting to know that you're a better man than Eichmann!)

She uses the phrase "the banality of evil" not to characterize his actions as ordinary, but because his testimony showed that he was not a sadistic monster bent on genocide; he merely thought of himself as a good soldier carrying out legal orders. PERIOD. He slept well at night, because he was simply "doing his job" ("He did his duty … he not only obeyed orders, he also obeyed the law." p. 135).

His failing, Arendt says, was that he did not exercise critical thinking nor did he have any internal dialog with himself, which might have given him some self awareness about the evil nature of his actions. He appeared to "outsource" his culpability to the person who gave him the "legal-for-wartime" order. Your brother and colleagues at the Agency are still following orders but YOU are not.

1:49 PM

The expression in his eyes was hard to read. It was as if he were putting on a brave facade for this photo but was trying to subtly telegraph his hidden fear and vulnerability to the photographer, hoping someone would notice and rescue him. The boy posed in a field and in the background, human skulls were displayed on stakes pounded into the earth. He had a Kalashnikov rifle slung around his neck, and his hands rested comfortably on the grip and the barrel. The relevance of the image to my new job was not lost on me, and I could not look away.

My seatmate caught me staring over her shoulder, so I smiled and asked if she was enjoying the book. She said. "It's not the kind of book you enjoy; it's the kind you read to know how mad the world can become when good people don't pay attention."

Her words erased my smile as she continued. "Good people like you probably don't know how common child soldiers are. The UN estimates that there are approximately 300,000 child combatants in the world right now, and you probably didn't know that the very first American soldier killed by hostile fire in the "war on terrorism" was shot by a fourteen-year old Afghan boy." I didn't know that.

As we talked, I found out she had only a short layover in Rome and that her final destination was Sri Lanka. She was working for UNICEF and was a member the UN delegation sent to investigate allegations that children were being abducted and trained as soldiers by the Tamil Tigers. She spoke passionately about her mission and referred to the Singer book as the first serious examination of this escalating problem.

I did not want to seem too interested so I thanked her, and then I pretended to doze before she could ask me what I was doing in Rome. I couldn't very well tell her that I was about to take a job with an agency that trains young girls to be assassins and would most likely be employing some of the very same techniques and facilitating the consequences condemned in that book. I could not tell her that today she was preparing to save children, and I was preparing to exploit them.

As we were getting off the plane, she gave me her card and surprised me by handing me the book. She said I seemed interested in child welfare, and that I might be encouraged by the last chapter where Singer outlines responses that can help end the practice. I slipped the book in my carry-on, but I would not have the courage to read it for a long time.

Looking back, it seemed like Fate was giving me one last chance to say no to the new job in Rome, but I ignored that call. I had promised my brother I'd come, and he had pulled strings to get me the security clearances. So I reported for my first assignment with the Social Welfare Agency and got my first glimpse of the girl that would become Henrietta.

POSTED BY JOSE AT 2:24 PM 0 COMMENTS LINKS TO THIS POST
LABELS: CHILDREN AT WAR, GUNSLINGER GIRL, P.W. SINGER

Post #1 Welcome

To my former colleagues: You all warned me not to "over-think" this job and not to get involved too deeply. You said I would be safer and happier if I simply turned off my brain and considered the girls to be weapons, tools, or guard dogs. I wish I could have taken your advice, but their spirit and enduring humanity won my devotion, and my conscience and curiosity kept me thinking and questioning. My efforts to examine the moral dilemmas I faced daily have brought me a new, enlightened perspective that makes me useless to you. It also compels me to tell the public the truth about the Agency.

I know that telling my story is dangerous, and you all will try to stop me. I witnessed what happened when one of us showed signs of doubt and hinted at exposing our secrets to a reporter. Remember Raballo and his unfortunate "accident?"

I won't make his mistake and go to the press — I know about your mutually beneficial relationship. Instead, I'm following a current trend and becoming a citizen journalist with a blog. I'll write my own story, describe my experiences, and welcome your comments. The posts that follow will serve to confirm my "leave of absence" from the Agency and explain the realizations that compelled me to take Henrietta and disappear.

To the public: For those who don't already know who I am, let me give you some background information. Long story short — I was an Agent for the Italian Government employed by a Special Ops Division dedicated to fighting Padania or The Five Republics Faction. We call them terrorists, but they call themselves nationalist freedom fighters opposed to globalization and dedicated to the financial and political independence of Northern Italy. You hear about them sporadically in the news, when they set off a bomb or take out a judge, and I'd guess that most of you are happy that someone is protecting you and your property from them.

You're glad we fight them, but if you knew HOW we fight them, you may not be thrilled. We do it through a black-ops, government funded front organization called the Social Welfare Agency. SWA, a seemingly benevolent social agency, has the official mission, "to help the hopeless." In reality, it was a cynical means to recruit our "secret weapons," the children we trained to kill. The Agency would offer to take in sick, injured or abandoned young girls but instead of nursing them back to health, we'd wipe their memories, condition them to be obedient, implant them with cybernetic limbs, and train them to be murderous assassins. Each girl would be paired with a male adult handler to form a fighting unit called a *fratello*, the Italian word for sibling. I joined the Agency as a handler and that's where I met Henrietta, my partner, my <u>Gunslinger Girl</u>.

Among government workers, there were always rumors about a program that employed young cyborg assassins but never any concrete evidence, because the whole enterprise, like most enterprises of dubious morality, was wrapped in euphemism and shadow. In my early days at the Agency, I bought into it and felt special to be able to live in that shadow. I was lulled into a comfort zone, believing that what we did there was justified and served the greater good. But slowly, as I got to know Henrietta and the other girls, I could not simply see them as weapons. The comfort I felt began to fade with each glimpse of the girls' humanity and each instance of neglect I noticed among the other *fratello*. These made me wonder if I accepted these practices so easily, was this just human nature? How close might society be to accepting our questionable practices as normal and indeed necessary for national security?

The posts that follow will show how my disenchantment with the agency was grounded in a reexamination of the Milgram Experiments I read when I was in school in Milan. I was most interested in his Experiment #18 as well as his observation of the conditions necessary for people to abandon their individual sense of morality.

A book called *Children at War*, an examination of the mechanisms and forces that cast children in the role of combatants in global warfare, also influenced me.

I can't undo what I've done but by writing this blog, I can shine a light into the shadows exposing the Agency's practices, and I can take Henrietta to a safe place where she can live the rest of her shortened life as a normal little girl.   Hopefully my present actions will relieve my guilt, help rehabilitate my partner, and allow me to tell my story and wake up as many people as possible.   No, wait, that's too gentle a statement. The fact is, I want to scare the shit out of people, so they will be careful not to trade their values for security.[1]

POSTED BY JOSE AT 9:07 PM 0 COMMENTS LINKS TO THIS POST
LABELS: ANIME, GUNSLINGER GIRL, HENRIETTA, JOSE, MANGA, TV

[1] Read additional entries and respond to Jose's blog at *http://jose-meaculpa.blogspot.com/*

未来
Future Perfect
完了

19

Cyborg Songs for an Existential Crisis

SARAH PENICKA-SMITH

> Every living holon has the dual tendency to preserve and assert its individuality, such as it is, but at the same time to function as an integrated part of an existing whole, or an evolving whole.
>
> —ARTHUR KOESTLER, *The Ghost in the Machine*

In his 1967 book, *The Ghost in the Machine*, Arthur Koestler was concerned chiefly with the machinations of the human body and mind. Twenty-four years later, Masamune Shirow realized Koestler's title quite literally when he authored the cult manga, *Ghost in the Shell*. Shirow's manga deals with cyborgs, the ideal vehicle for exploring the ethical and philosophical ramifications of humanity and technology merged. The manga's popularity spawned two films which attracted a cult following in their own right, and which explore closely the nature of humanity and our perceived necessity for human identity.

Ghost in the Shell (1995) and *Innocence: Ghost in the Shell II* (2004) shared both their director, Mamoru Oshii (born in 1951), and their composer, Kenji Kawai (born in 1957). Oshii and Kawai's collaboration proved to be very fruitful; Kawai's unusual soundtrack for *Ghost in the Shell* received wide acclaim. Yet Kawai succeeds not only in the quality of his music, but in the intimate structural significance with which he imbued his soundtrack.

While *Ghost in the Shell* is a film into which a viewer can read many messages, Kawai's music provides the key. Through brilliant development of his eerie theme, Kawai reveals Oshii's deep fascination with his protagonist Major Motoko Kusanagi's quest for self-knowledge. The soundtrack for *Innocence*, while more complex, also plays a similar role, perfectly complementing Oshii's desire to unpack what makes us human.

What Is a Human, Anyway?

Ghost in the Shell deals with the nature of humanity and human identity. At first, the Major struggles to determine whether she qualifies as human in a world still populated by the cybernetically unenhanced, a faction to which she once belonged:

> MAJOR: Well, I guess cyborgs like myself have a tendency to be paranoid about our origins. 'Cause I suspect I'm not who I think I am, like maybe I died a long time ago and somebody took my brain and stuck it in this body. Or there never was a real me in the first place and I'm completely synthetic. . . .
>
> BATOU: You've got real brain cells in that titanium shell of yours, and you're treated like a human, so stop with the angst.
>
> MAJOR: But that's just it, that's the only thing that makes me feel human—the way I'm treated.

The Major objects to feeling that the behavior of others is the only thing which determines her identity. Yet sociologists often claim that how we interact with our environment is all that makes any of us human. According to sociologist Brenda Brasher, "becoming human is a social endeavor. People determine who they are through interaction with the environments they encounter and, in turn, shape by their actions and inactions with and toward them."

This is how Anne Kull and other scholars of cyborg ontology suggest living in a world of cyborgs will feel: "What will count as human is not given by definition; it is not neutrally available. It emerges only from relations, by engagement in situated, worldly encounters, where boundaries take shape and categories settle into place." Oshii illustrates this world in all its complexity by giving us a heroine who questions her own identity without the comfortable guarantee most of us believe we have: the guarantee that whatever the results of our questioning, we are at core human, in a world that accepts us as such.

It's not like that for the Major, whose brain and single section of spinal cord are her only remaining human parts. Her sense of identity receives a further shake up when she encounters the Puppet Master, a top-secret project which has developed self-awareness. The Puppet Master's existence leads the Major to question her own identity: with her cybernetic enhancements, at what point will she cease to be human? Has she already reached that point? As the film progresses, the Major ceases to question what makes her human, and questions instead the relevance of her perceived humanity.

The Puppet Master's emergence echoes Koestler's view of consciousness as something which itself emerges and evolves, rather than simply existing:

> Consciousness . . . is an emergent quality, which evolves into more complex and structured states in phylogeny, as the ultimate manifestation of the Integrative Tendency towards the creation of order out of disorder, of 'information' out of 'noise'. (*The Ghost in the Machine*)

When the Major integrates with the Puppet Master, they both evolve in exactly this way, their combined consciousnesses creating something more complex. The 'noise' of the Major's internal struggle with her identity is replaced by her increased awareness of the infinite realm of possibilities open to her now that she has ceased to limit herself. Ultimately, the Major transcends her human status, a process which the Puppet Master initiates when it says, "Your effort to remain what you are is what limits you." This harks back to Koestler's discussion of Eastern mysticism and self-transcendence:

> The transient individual self is thought to enter into a kind of spiritual osmosis with the Atman, the universal spirit—and to merge into it. Other mystic schools attempt to reach the same end by different routes; but all seem to agree that the conquest of the self is a means towards transcending it.

In *Ghost in the Shell*, Oshii aligns the struggle to maintain a sense of self with humanness. He then proposes an alternative to that struggle, one that allows for independence while celebrating the value of an individual's role within a functional, changing whole. The Major goes from being the kind of cyborg who values independent human identity to one which, in Anne Kull's words, "signals the end of a conception of the human as an autonomous individual possessing a 'self'" ("Speaking Cyborg: Technoculture and Technonature").

A Musical Interlude

Kenji Kawai's haunting score for *Ghost in the Shell* frames and describes the Major's spiritual struggle. Without the subtle clues Kawai provides in his soundtrack, Oshii's celebration of consciousness as an emergent quality would not be as clear. Most of the tracks are unobtrusive background music consisting of sparse percussion and an occasional passage of synthesizer. There are three tracks, however, which mark the film's structure. They are immediately recognizable, because Kawai uses influences and techniques from Bulgarian and Japanese folk song to create a theme which is the focus of all three tracks. The singing is identical in each of these three marker tracks, but the accompaniment changes. Each setting of the theme is more complex, has more emotional pull, asking us to relish the Major's progress towards transcending humanity and embracing integration.

At its core, the *Ghost in the Shell* musical theme (henceforth the 'Ghost' theme) is a simple, harmonized vocal melody over sparse percussion. The theme follows the same structure each time it appears in the film: the melody is sung once, followed by a percussion bridge, and then the melody repeats, usually with some more elaborate form of accompaniment underneath. Three Japanese women sing the melody and its accompanying harmonies; all three women use an identical vocal quality and change notes and words with such amazing synchronicity that they give the eerie impression they are one voice. The percussion is provided by a single djembe, or African talking drum, with the occasional interruption of bells. These bells also herald the start of each vocal line. The unusual vocal quality, quite foreign in tone to the Western ear, is due to the three singers belonging to a Japanese minyo, or folk song, choir. The percussion accompaniment to the vocal lines is consistent with minyo performance, where, according to Felicia G. Bock, the only traditional accompaniment is some kind of body percussion, drum, or a ringing bell ("Elements in the Development of Japanese Folk Song").

The soundtrack's liner notes tell us that the theme is a Japanese wedding song for purging evil influences before marriage. The lyrics use an ancient form of Japanese, which is translated as follows on Kenji Kawai's official website:

> Because I had danced, the beautiful lady was enchanted,
> Because I had danced, the shining moon echoed,

Proposing marriage, the god shall descend,
The night clears away and the chimera bird will sing,
The distant god may give us the precious blessing.

The final line is not sung in the first two instantiations of the theme, only appearing at the very end of the film. Despite a lack of available information on why Kawai chose these lyrics, a preparatory song to a wedding is a good match for the union of ghosts which the film's ending brings. As the Puppet Master proposes the Major merge with him, it's possible to see in him the god "proposing marriage," although without further information from the composer this analysis is mere speculation.

Building a Cyborg Kenji Kawai-style

The Ghost theme first occurs over the opening credits, which depict the Major being made—she's set apart from the film's beginning as being not quite human, but manufactured. The only addition to the vocals and percussion described above is a synthesizer, which provides a simple and slow moving bass line beginning in the bridge. The music matches the graphics of the opening credits: we see the Major in all her component parts, she is gradually assembled, her skin added, and her hair and body dried of its amniotic fluid. Against this, the music is simple, sparse; like the Major in her base components, this is the barest instantiation of the theme which we'll hear. Kawai is setting the scene for Oshii, showing us a body with no hint of identity, no flash of spirit.

From this sonic simplicity and visual emphasis on the Major's mechanical structure, the second instantiation of the Ghost theme marks a significant change. It occurs halfway through the film in a visually lush sequence devoid of dialogue. The Major's pursuit of the Puppet Master is causing her to question the nature of her own identity. In the scene preceding the Ghost theme's return, the Major has been diving, a somewhat hazardous pastime for a woman whose body could sink like a stone, as Batou points out. The Major is more philosophical:

> If a technological feat is possible, man will do it. Almost as though it's wired into the core of our being. Metabolic control. Enhanced sensory perception. Improved reflexes and muscle capacity. Vastly increased data processing speed and capacity. All improvements thanks to our cyber-brains and cyborg bodies. So what if we can't live without high-

level maintenance? We have nothing to complain about. It doesn't mean we've sold our souls to Section 9. We do have the right to resign if we choose. Provided we give the government back our cyborg shells and the memories they hold. Just as there are many parts needed to make a human a human, there's a remarkable number of things needed to make an individual what they are. A face to distinguish yourself from others. A voice you aren't aware of yourself. The hand you see when you awaken. The memories of childhood, the feelings for the future. That's not all. There's the expanse of the data net my cyber-brain can access. All of that goes into making me what l am. Giving rise to a consciousness that l call 'me'. And simultaneously confining 'me' within set limits.

At this point, the Puppet Master speaks for the first time, an echo in the brains of both agents. It paraphrases the famous Biblical verse 1 Corinthians 13:12, saying, "What we see now is like a dim image in a mirror. Then we shall see face to face." Or, as the King James version of the Bible famously put it, "For now we see through a glass, darkly: but then face to face."

After this, the Major wanders the city. As she does so, she sees copies of her body, as a dummy in a shop window, or a business-woman eating lunch. A new setting of the theme kicks in as this unusual sequence unfolds. Kawai christened it "Ghost City," a play on both the city's dreamy, detached aura, and also its role as home to myriad ghosts in a range of bodies, some identical in form but presumably diverse in spirit.

At first Kawai presents the theme in the same way as in the opening sequence—identical vocals and slightly busier percussion—and again, it's at the bridge that the accompaniment changes. The synthesizer enters, but this time with a melody borrowed and developed from the preceding scene. Kawai also adds slightly thicker harmonies beneath the vocal lines. The accompaniment is more prominent, the harmonic language is richer and more immediately sentimental. By adding more layers of sound, Kawai increases the music's complexity and emotiveness. All this reflects the Major's position as more than a hollow cyborg shell, but as a person whose own struggles are growing increasingly complex. Kawai's music signifies the Major's move away from seeing embodiment as a given part of the human condition into a world where, in Brasher's words, "universal embodiment is not the defining situation . . . [but a] pre-eminent moral question." The music and visuals combined remove us from the film's narrative thrust, instead giving insight into the Major's internal world in an intensely personal way. Each time we hear it, the Ghost theme signifies a new point in the Major's understanding of what it is to be human, and what it might mean to leave that concept behind.

Kawai's third and final version of the Ghost theme best illuminates this progression. Designed as music for the film's closing credits, it is the theme's most complex instantiation. Kawai called this track "Reincarnation" because of the Major's rebirth as part of the new consciousness that has evolved through her merge with the Puppet Master. The music reflects the Major's evolution into a more complex being by itself increasing in complexity. This time both drums and bells herald the theme's arrival. The percussion locks into an easy rhythm before the theme begins, providing an almost dance-like feel to the originally sparse music. The synthesizer creeps in as the first repetition of the theme ends, paving the way for a soaring string section in Tokyo pop style to weave a nostalgic spell over the bridge, which Kawai also expands in length. When the vocal line re-enters, the accompaniment remains thick and rich, with full strings, synthesizer and piano over more elaborate percussion.

The strings join the voices as they soar upward for the final time, preparing us for the climax, both of the final theme and of the entire soundtrack. A solo vocalist breaks away from the group to sing the final line of the lyrics, "the distant god may give us the precious blessing." This is the only time we hear these words and the music that goes with them; the Major's willingness to accept her status as something beyond human has completed her. More crucially, Kawai's use of the solo voice points to the quotation from Koestler which starts this chapter: that holons[1] preserve individuality while functioning as part of an evolving whole. The soaring strings suggest the Major maintains her emotional capacity—feelings of sentiment, nostalgia, desire—even after she has merged and evolved, and left her tangible humanity behind her. Through Kawai's music, Oshii tells us that the Major is completed, diversified, emotionally enriched by embracing her part in the whole, while still remaining an individual.

But wait, I hear you say—the music over the closing credits isn't Kawai's, it's by U2 and Brian Eno! And sadly, you would be right.

---

[1] Koestler coined the term 'holon' to describe something which is simultaneously a whole and a part.

The third version of Kawai's theme never made it onto *Ghost in the Shell*'s US release. Instead, Manga Entertainment dubbed "One Minute Warning," a rowdy rock song by U2 and Brian Eno, over the closing credits. While I can only suggest that this was a marketing ploy on the part of *Ghost in the Shell*'s financers, it does nothing to enhance the film's aesthetic value. Despite the magnificent job Kawai did of uniting his theme with the Major's transformation, Western audiences have been left without ever hearing the theme's final line—we are denied musical completion. As we shall see shortly, Kawai was evidently determined that this would not happen again in the film's sequel.

Dolls with Ghosts and What's Really Going on in *Innocence*

Innocence, which took nine years to follow *Ghost in the Shell*, is set three years after it in 2032. Batou is the new protagonist. Section 9 assigns him a case in which gynoids—sex cyborgs—have been killing their masters, an action which they are, for obvious reasons, supposed to have been programmed against. Batou determines that the dolls have been ghost-dubbed: souls have been removed from young girls and transferred to the dolls, a highly illegal action. In his battle to suspend the manufacturer's operations, Batou encounters the Major once more, when she downloads part of her consciousness into one of the dolls to help him shut down the operation.

This shifts the focus of *Innocence* from humans becoming machines to machines becoming human. In this, Oshii subverts Koestler, Shirow's primary influence. Koestler believed "machines cannot become like men, but men can become like machines." Yet in *Innocence*, machines do become like women. While Koestler may not have agreed with this concept, scholars pursuing the ontological crisis which cyborgs create often argue that machine to man is just as viable a transition as man to machine. Kull's discussion of Bruce Mazlish's approach to the coevolution of humans and machines is a good example of this; Donna Haraway's "second leaky distinction" (between animal-human and machine), from her famous "A Manifesto for Cyborgs," is even better. For Haraway, the cyborg symbolized a breaching of distinct boundaries in favor of integrated systems. Boundaries which cyborgs confuse include those between human and animal, organism and machine, the physical and the non-physical.

To highlight the leaky distinction between human and machine, Oshii uses dolls as recurrent imagery, emphasizing our desire to replicate ourselves in mechanical form, even if only as toys for our children. Dolls have a particular place in Japanese culture, where they often signify the liminal place between flesh and spirit. The Japanese word for 'doll', ningyÿ, translates literally as 'human shape,' highlighting the possible boundary transgressions available in Japanese culture and which Oshii uses in *Innocence* to question once again the nature of humanity. This time, however, instead of simply celebrating Koestler's integrative tendency, Oshii problematizes it. He contrasts the Major, increasingly comfortable in her new existence and the embodiment of successful integration, with the gynoids, which in spite of their activation by human ghosts remain machines with no assertion of individuality - only a group mind and a group voice.

Oshii might also have been inspired in his exploration of machine-to-human transitions by the symbolism of the golem. *Innocence* refers to the best known golem of all, Rabbi Judah Loew's sixteenth-century version which defended the Jews of Prague from anti-Semitic attacks. Despite the wealth of literature on the golem, it's most likely Oshii encountered it in Paul Wegener's 1920 classic *Der Golem*. The golem's influence is clear in the Hebrew word *emeth* ('truth'), which appears at the entrance of the house that Batou and Togusa visit when trying to locate the source of the ghost-dubbed gynoids. The same word animated Loew's golem, and Oshii's use of it suggests he drew inspiration from the old Jewish tale.

Oshii's reference to the golem highlights the gynoids' status as manufactured. In contrast, Batou refers to the Major as his "guardian angel," emphasizing her newfound status as a powerful yet intangible individual, totally freed from the trappings of humanity. The ethical dilemma of animate machines is heightened in the case of the ghost-dubbed gynoids, and Kawai picks up on the poignancy of this situation with a new, highly emotive theme.

Giving Voice to the Voiceless

There are many similarities between the soundtracks for *Ghost in the Shell* and *Innocence*. Bells signify the imminence of both themes, and the vocal quality is identical, as is much of the instrumentation. As in *Ghost in the Shell*, there are three instantiations of the *Innocence* theme, and Kawai's use of them echoes his development of the Ghost theme in many ways. In *Innocence*, each version also occurs over scenes devoid of dialogue and versions become successively more complex. Yet Kawai's soundtrack for *Innocence* does not exactly follow the model set up in *Ghost in the Shell*. If it did, it would reflect Batou's journey as the film's protagonist. Batou, however, does not undergo a similarly momentous evolution to the Major in *Ghost in the Shell*, as she notes on her reappearance towards the film's end that he hasn't changed a bit.

Instead, from its first note, Kawai binds his new theme to the renegade gynoids, those human machines which are Oshii's response to Koestler. As in *Ghost in the Shell*, we first hear the theme over the opening credits, which depict the making not of Batou, but of a gynoid. The *Innocence* theme begins without authority, devoid of percussion: the voices start alone, sounding tentative and uncertain. The music is more melancholy, reflecting the gynoid's status as a slave rather than an independent woman. It is clear from the outset that the world of *Ghost in the Shell* has evolved into something more complex. The drumming and bells reappear, and a lower voice enters as the theme takes on a slow and measured rhythm. Halfway through, the theme suddenly breaks into violent taiko drumming, the voices gain in strength and stridency to become a powerful chorus, and the synthesizer adds a resonant bass line. So powerful is this particular ensemble that the *Yomiuri Online* ran an article by Kenichi Yorita on January 13th, 2004, on the unprecedented size of Kawai's minyo chorus for this theme—seventy-five singers multi-tracked. Embodied by the music, the dolls are at first powerless, and then empowered, from the very outset of the film.

The lyrics to the *Innocence* theme are also from an ancient Japanese song, "Kugutsu uta uramite chiru":

Through day and night, the moon not coming,
In grief, Nue will sing.
When I look back,
Flowers will fall away,
The heart of solace having withered.
In a new world, Gods will descend,
The dawn will break and Nue will sing.
Flowers in bloom pray to Gods,
Lamenting over their being in this world of life,

Their dreams having faded away,
Flowers grieve and fall.

With their focus on death and passing, these lyrics are both more nostalgic and more melancholy than those of the Ghost theme. The lines, "Flowers in bloom pray to Gods / Lamenting over their being in this world of life / Their dreams having faded away," highlight the pitiful state of the captured girls and their doll bodies. There is a magic synchronicity between these lyrics and the Ghost theme's lyrics, with the Major now included in the descending gods, the power that will release the captives from their state of bondage.

Just as in both films we first hear the theme against images of a cyborg's construction, both films use a cityscape alongside the theme's second instantiation. In *Innocence* the scene is a parade, in which a variety of images suggests the doll festival Hinamatsuri. At this festival, families pray for the happiness and prosperity of their daughters and to ensure they grow up healthy and beautiful. This is a gentle irony considering the sufferings of the young girls kidnapped and ghost-dubbed onto the gynoids.

The music for the parade scene also offers increased complexity from the theme we hear over *Innocence*'s opening credits. Kawai shortens the vocal introduction, and bulks up the theme's accompaniment, starting the synthesizer when the percussion enters and thickening the chords. He then adds a lengthy but sparse percussion break, a vague reference to the structure of the Ghost theme, before repeating the powerful and energetic chorus. As in *Ghost in the Shell*, Kawai uses the added harmonies in the theme's second instantiation to indicate greater emotional depth and psychological complexity. But this time, the music combines with the many images of masks and dolls on the screen to give voice to the voiceless, conferring emotional capacity on the gynoids. This further blurring of boundaries between doll and cyborg, human and inhuman is Oshii and Kawai's nod to Haraway's leaky distinctions, which by *Innocence*'s end will be so fluid as to be inseparable.

Who Wants to Be Human Anyway?

The *Innocence* theme's third and final instantiation is where all boundaries finally break down. Probably to avoid what happened to his final theme in *Ghost in the Shell*, Kawai incorporated the theme's last appearance into the obligatory climactic fight scene. Batou has reached Locus Solus, the corporation which fronts the ghost-dubbing operation. While trying to shut it down, he is faced by a gynoid army. The position of these creatures is uncertain: they are dolls animated by the stolen ghosts of young girls. One might expect possession of even the shadow of a soul to convey some kind of individuality, but instead the gynoids act collectively, as if following orders from some higher power. In contrast, at this point the Major—the film's ultimate individual and renegade—returns to fight at Batou's side by downloading a part of her consciousness into one of the gynoids. Could any of these entities be called human? The Major admits to Batou that she is not really a separate entity any more, and no longer refers to her ghost, only to her consciousness. Yet she still thinks and acts like an individual, while the gynoids, imbued with real human souls, operate only as a pack. What is Oshii saying about the ghost in the machine?

This is the theme's final instantiation, and in it Kawai brings everything together. Even the music has leaky boundaries - motifs from both the first and second film mix it up with phrases from the *Innocence* theme. The lyrics (found in translation again on Kawai's website) also change, now suggesting hope for redemption rather than only grief for lives past:

> The Ghost awaits in the world beyond.
> Flowers in bloom pray to Gods,
> Lamenting over their being in this world of life,
> Their dreams having faded away,
> Flowers grieve and fall . . .
> In the everlasting darkness of grief,
> Inert in shells, praying to Gods for the reincarnation.

Above a pulsing, repeated bass note, bells herald the *Innocence* theme's percussive chorus. Phrases from this theme alternate with passages of urgent and continuous taiko drumming with menacing synthesizer. Each time the *Innocence* theme's chorus returns, Kawai adds more lines beneath it, usually on the synthesizer, and tension mounts. The pattern is briefly interrupted by a snatch of the music-box style score heard during one of the film's earlier scenes (and which includes a doll's house). The track concludes with the soaring motif from the Major's dramatic fight scene at the end of *Ghost in the Shell*. As the Major returns to the net, the final phrase of the Ghost theme, the phrase which was so gracelessly cut from its US release, sounds once. This time it is sung in chorus rather than as a solo, a final farewell to the Major from the girls she has freed, the collective voices calling the blessing down upon the individual. Koestler has been subverted: Oshii has made machines human and turned one human into a machine to be envied. The Major is moral, powerful, generous and introspective, yet she no longer identifies as a human with an individual ghost.

As much as Oshii's gynoids contradict Koestler, the Major still stands as an embodiment of Koestler's theory: every living holon has the tendency to preserve its individuality while operating as part of an evolving and functional whole. This is exactly what the Major does. We imagine she must have surrendered all her individuality on merging with the net, yet in *Innocence* she is able to separate a part of herself from the whole to aid her old colleague. And she is still, recognizably, the Major, to us and to Batou alike. Through connecting with the net, the Major has not only evolved herself, but has aided the evolution of the whole to which she belongs without being subsumed by it. In this way, Kawai and Oshii have cast the Major as an Everyman-Everywoman figure, undergoing a quest for self-knowledge in the kind of technoscientific age and embodiment which may well be humanity's future. Anne Kull suggests we're already living this reality:

> We are cyborgs because we are the instruments of a powerful technological, medicinal, scientific, and military system that appropriates and reshapes the world at an ever-increasing rate . . . The cyborg myth acknowledges our technicized natures.

In giving us cyborgs involved in differing existential crises, Oshii not only acknowledges our technicized natures but gives us a philosophical framework by which we might be able to accept them. Without Kawai, Oshii's attitude towards cyborg evolution would not be so clear. In *Ghost in the Shell*, Kawai's music celebrates the Major's attempts to transcend her humanity, leading us to question not only what human identity is, but whether, given the opportunity, we too should cease to be concerned with it. *Innocence* also forces us to question the nature of humanity, and whether it is worth clinging to, by showing us our capability to do inhuman things. Kawai emphasizes this with his themes, giving the gynoids emotions with his haunting music, which their doll-faces can't express. In writing cyborg soundtracks which are complex and emotive, Kawai shows us that the distinction between human and machine can be very leaky indeed.

As *Innocence* draws to a close, and before the Major disappears into the net, she comforts a small girl rescued from the Locus Solus operation, who wails, "I never wanted to be a robot." The Major wryly replies, "If a robot had his own voice, he may cry 'I don't want to be a human.'"

The Major is right—Kawai's score gives voice to the robots, and this is indeed what they say.

20
Cyborg Goddess

DAN DINELLO

Without a transcendental belief, each man is a mean little island. Since we cannot expect the necessary change in human nature to arise by way of natural means, we must induce it by artificial means. We can only hope to survive as a species by developing techniques which supplant biological evolution.

—ARTHUR KOESTLER, *The Ghost in the Machine*

Pre-cybernetic machines could be haunted; there was always the spectre of the ghost in the machine. They could not achieve man's dream, only mock it. Now we are not so sure. Our machines are disturbingly lively, and we ourselves frighteningly inert.

— DONNA HARAWAY, "A Cyborg Manifesto"

The soul-searching cyborg of *Ghost in the Shell* quotes the Bible, saying, "For now we see through a glass darkly, but then face to face. Now I know in part, but then shall I know fully." Cyborg assassin and government agent Major Motoko Kusanagi wanders aimlessly around a city. She feels lonely and trapped in her corporate-created body with its computer-enhanced brain. Confused about her identity beyond police work, Motoko wants to find her place in the world. She wants to know if she's an autonomous person or an automaton.

In a gorgeous, visually poetic slow-motion sequence scored with haunting music and spine-tingling angelic chants, Motoko looks for clues in the crowded urban futurescape. She sees a series of ambiguous canals and streets that look like the bloodstream of an organism or the circuits of a machine. She's startled to recognize a woman or a cyborg with the same body and face as she. A huge building under construction echoes her origins as a technological creation. A sad dog stares quizzically as if to say, "Who are you?"

Female mannikins, frozen behind a display window, mock her. Rain falls as children—all with identical yellow umbrellas—run across a bridge. They—along with the countless blinking neon billboards, the bird-like airplane overhead, and the crowds of zombie-like people—serve to show humanity's spiritless surrender to technology, its fusion with machines, and its obsolescence as a species. Motoko sees armless, female busts behind dark glass as ghostly voices sing the beautiful Shinto chant, "Faraway God, give us your blessing," suggesting both her own fragmented identity and her desire to transcend it and find meaning beyond the human world.

The Age of Spiritual Machines

Mamoru Oshii's *Ghost in the Shell*—based on an acclaimed manga series by Masamune Shirow and followed by a television series *Ghost in the Shell: Stand Alone Complex* and a movie sequel *Ghost in the Shell 2: Innocence*—transpires in a future world where the replacement of fragile human body parts, including brains, has reached a logical conclusion. Most humans have become cyborgs. Despite mental implants that provide direct access to the internet, they retain a human identity—a "ghost," mind or soul. The most powerful people are those that have been most technologically enhanced.

Super-heroine Major Motoko Kusanagi barely exists in her original human form, retaining only a small portion of organic gray matter inside an almost totally robotic, titanium body or "shell." She can patch her nervous system into the internet, mentally "dive" into cyberspace, and access the connected minds of others. She practically co-exists on the net. In the movie's ostensible action, the Major pursues a terrorist hacker named the Puppet Master. The philosophical action, however, focuses on her techno-metaphysical quest beyond gender and human identity for a spiritual bond, for perfection, for transcendent wholeness, for the ghost in her shell.

With its cyborg superwoman, *Ghost in the Shell* raises the possibility of technology's positive potential, not only in terms of its path to transcendence, but also in terms of its subversive undermining of gender identity. Unlike most science-fiction films that valorize maleness and prioritize the human while devaluing females and demonizing technology, *Ghost in the Shell* uniquely advocates a vision of the posthuman future that exalts technology and renders humanity and its gender prejudices obsolete. In this, it reflects the philosophy of techno-feminist writer Donna Haraway (whose name is given to the cigarette-smoking police forensic expert in *Ghost in the Shell 2: Innocence*).

A Manifesto for Cyborgs

In her "Cyborg Manifesto," Haraway espouses the liberating potential for women inherent in cyborg mythology. While aware of the role this technology plays in the maintenance of corporate social control, government surveillance, militarism, and patriarchy, Haraway embraces its rebellious promise: the machinic-muscled, macho movie-cyborgs—Terminator, Robocop, and Iron Man among others—should be recoded as female and appropriated as a means of subverting gender bias.

Gender is constructed socially, not determined biologically, according to Haraway and other feminist thinkers. See for instance Phyllis Burke's *Gendershock*. "There is nothing about being 'female' that naturally binds women. Gender, race, or class consciousness is an achievement forced on us by the terrible historical experience of the contradictory social realities of patriarchy, colonialism, and capitalism" ("A Cyborg Manifesto," p. 155).

Cultural conditioning includes the casting of male and female into oppositional and hierarchical categories: objective-subjective, rational-emotional, mind-body. These stereotypical dualities associate masculinity with the rational life of the mind and with technology; they associate femininity with the body's irrational feelings and the natural world. In this cultural match-up, the female often loses, forced into inferior or subservient roles. This inequality reflects gender bias, social discrimination, sexual objectification, and sexist oppression, rather than something biological or natural, the possession of reproductive organs. ("Cyborg Manifesto," p. 181).

The female cyborg—an unnatural, bionic body without ovaries or womb—undermines conventional understandings of biology as the site of essential, unified, natural gender identity. The boundary-breaking, hybridized female machine obliterates sexual distinctions and liberates us from female stereotypes based on bodily functions. Haraway implores women to feminize technology and embrace the cyborg as a post-gendered revolutionary who "cracks the matrices" of the dominant culture. "Cyborg imagery can suggest a way out of the maze of dualisms in which we have explained our bodies and our tools to ourselves" (p. 151).

Haraway rebels against goddess-feminist wisdom that preaches the religion of nature and rejection of the modern techno-world. In her view, the romanticized goddess naively strives to resurrect an idealized fusion with the natural world and fails to engage with cyborgized reality. Women should therefore reject the Luddite bias of eco-feminism that identifies women with nature and men with technology, as this reflects the very gender stereotypes that feminism strives to subvert. Haraway refuses an "anti-science metaphysics, a demonology of technology," and asserts, "I would rather be a cyborg than a goddess."

Radical Feminist Cyborg

Not a human with prosthetics, cyborg Motoko Kusanagi is built, not born. Her only human parts consist of organic brain cells—from her former female self—housed in a titanium skull and augmented by a computer brain. Manufactured by the Megatech Corporation, her flesh-covered machinic body takes human shape as she floats in a fetal position, immersed in a liquid vat. A huge machine magnetically draws her out of the vat and suspends her in the air for drying. As a manufactured being, she reflects Haraway's vision of a cyborg as a liberated entity—a creature without human origins and without a future as wife and mother. "Unlike the hopes of Frankenstein's monster," writes Haraway, "the cyborg does not expect its father to save it through a restoration of the garden; that is, through the creation of a heterosexual mate."

Although gendered female with corporate-sized breasts, Motoko impresses with her amazing abilities, not her gender attributes. She exhibits no sexual or romantic interest in her male-gendered cyborg partner Batou, who is equally represented as an exaggerated extreme of masculinity. As Haraway says, "Sex, sexuality, and reproduction are central actors in high-tech myth systems structuring our imaginations of personal and social possibility" ("A Cyborg Manifesto," p. 169). Eliminating sex helps eliminate a socially constructed gender identity. Motoko's body can't be impregnated. Her body is enhanced with strength, agility, and speed for police work, not for pleasure or reproduction. Nobody fucks with her, literally or metaphorically.

Cyborg technology has endowed a female character with strength, competence, and power while positioning her male partners in the more "feminized" inferior roles. Motoko makes the decisions, does much of the work, and relegates the males to sidekicks. "To be both female and strong implicitly violates traditional codes of feminine identity," says feminist critic Anne Balsamo, in her book *Technologies of the Gendered Body: Reading Cyborg Women* (p. 43). As the narrative's central character, Motoko effectively eradicates conventional gender, making her relatively unique in science fiction cinema.[1] As a balance to the masculization of technology, cyborg Motoko Kusanagi's gives voice to the liberating promise of the feminized cyborg.

Break Through a Glass, Darkly

While she corresponds to Haraway's vision of the post-gendered cyborg, who refuses "the ideological resources of victimization" and "biological determinist ideology" ("A Cyborg Manifesto"), Motoko still reflects anxieties about the loss of coherent subjectivity. She has not completely fractured the chains of the dominant culture. A profound identity crisis afflicts her—brought on by the awareness that her body's hardware and software are corporate-created and government-owned. "We do have the right to resign if we choose," she tells Batou. "Provided we give back our cyborg shells and the memories they hold." She looks at herself reflected in a glass darkly and finds it difficult to see her true self beyond her corporate-imposed identity as an assassin. Though her job is to find the Puppet Master, Motoko's real mission is to find her true identity, her ghost.

The ghost concept was borrowed from Arthur Koestler, whose book *The Ghost in the Machine* took its title from a phrase by the philosopher Gilbert Ryle. Ryle, in his 1949 book *The Concept of Mind*, attacked the distinction made between the body and the mind, calling it, with "deliberate abusiveness," the myth of the "ghost in the machine." In this way, Ryle mocked René Descartes's dualistic notion that an immaterial soul or mind existed within a

---

[1] Others include *Metropolis*'s robot Maria, *Eve of Destruction*'s Eve VIII, *Terminator 3*'s T-X, and on television: the Bionic Woman, *Terminator: The Sarah Connor Chronicles*' Cameron, and several of *Battlestar Galactica*'s Cylons. Only the Bionic Woman functions as a central protagonist.

material body or brain, that it accounted for the person's intelligence, spontaneity, and identity, and that it could exist without the body. Koestler did not agree with Ryle: "By the very act of denying the existence of the ghost in the machine—of mind dependent on, but also responsible for, the actions of the body—we incur the risk of turning it into a very nasty, malevolent ghost" (*The Ghost in the Machine*, p. 203). Following Koestler, The Police also named their 1981 album *Ghost in the Machine*.

Wanting it both ways, Koestler derides not only Ryle's viewpoint as a "naively mechanistic world-view of the nineteenth century" (p. xiii), but also denies Descartes's mind-body dualism. Without scientific proof, Koestler locates the mind or "ghost" in the physical materiality of the brain. Koestler's "ghost in the machine" refers to higher, more complex neuronal brain functions that compete with earlier, more primitive structures. *Ghost in the Shell* takes Koestler's notion one step further and imagines that a conscious ghost can evolve within an artificial intelligence. While Motoko wanders through the city searching for her elusive soul, a new electronic soul emerges elsewhere.

The Soul of a New Machine

A bug in a government security program, the Puppet Master announces itself as an autonomous sentient lifeform, born from the net's "sea of information." Thus, *Ghost in the Shell* dramatizes the Singularity. First proposed in 1993 by science fiction writer Vernor Vinge who said, "Within thirty years, we will have the technological means to create superhuman intelligence. Shortly after, the human era will be ended," the notion of the coming Singularity has been adopted as an article of faith in the philosophy of Transhumanism, as popularized by Ray Kurzweil. The Singularity refers to a techno-apocalypse when a purely technological entity— an evolved artificial intelligence or a computer network, for example—becomes self-conscious, autonomous, and smarter than humans. *Ghost in the Shell* uses this idea to unite Donna Haraway's genderless future and Arthur Koestler's ghost in the machine, proposing a sentient electronic entity that necessarily transgresses gender boundaries.

Having trapped the Puppet Master in a cyborg body, government scientists are stunned to discover through a brain scan that the conscious computer virus gone wild has generated a measurable mind of its own. "It doesn't have an organic brain in its head," says one scientist, "but we've detected what looks like a ghost in the auxiliary computer brain." This suggests Koestler's notion in *Ghost in the Machine* that the mind is neither Descartes's immaterial soul nor Ryle's pure myth; rather, it's a higher level of brain function, a material-electro-chemical aspect that can be scientifically detected. *Ghost in the Shell*, extending Koestler to the Transhumanist viewpoint, proposes that a ghost can arise in a non-human, artificial mind.

As for Haraway's perspective, the Puppet Master confounds gender expectations by exhibiting characteristics of both male and female. Though it inhabits the shell of a naked female cyborg, it speaks with a male voice. An examining scientist confusingly refers to it as "he," but explains: "Its original sex remains undetermined and the use of the term 'he' is merely a nickname." As a disembodied, electronic entity, the Puppet Master represents a technologized, posthuman subject that transcends the biological body, disrupts gender identification and helps undermine the sexist social constructions of patriarchy. Of course, it also undermines humanity.

Obsolete Humanity

In *Ghost in the Shell*, the Singularity marks the emergence of an evolutionary competitor. The Puppet Master exhibits a personality and a measurable mind structure analogous to a human ghost. The scientists must re-evaluate their own tenuous hold on their identity as macho masters of technology, when faced with an autonomous, self-conscious, non-biological techno-creature.

The Puppet Master intensifies Motoko's identity crisis. She doubts her own partial humanity: "Perhaps I'm a replicant made with a cyborg body and computer brain. Maybe I'm completely synthetic like that thing. If a computer brain could generate a ghost and create a soul, on what basis then do I believe in myself? What would be the importance of being human?"

The diminishment of humanity began with its cyborgization and computer-brain enhancements. Even the most paranoid characters in *Ghost in the Shell* aren't troubled by the net creeping into their lives, despite the expansion of surveillance capabilities and the potential for mind invasion. One character Trash

Man commits crimes while under control of the ghost-hacking Puppet Master. He later discovers that his memories have been destroyed and new ones implanted. With human memory fragmented and unreliable, what remains of autonomy, a central characteristic of humanity? Even the Puppet Master admonishes human complacency: "Man gains his individuality from the memories he carries. When computers made it possible to externalize memory, you should have considered all the implications that held."

Motoko is ordered to destroy Puppet Master. She and Batou locate it in the courtyard of a museum[2] that displays exhibits of evolutionary history. Protected by a MechWarrior-type tank, Puppet Master still inhabits a cyborg shell. Motoko wants to neutralize it, then dive into its mind to understand it, to "see for myself what's in there" and maybe discover her own unique individuality, her ghost.

A New Branch on the Evolutionary Tree

Motoko and the MechWarrior battle each other with big guns. The collateral damage includes several dinosaur skeletons blasted into bits, pointing to an earlier species gone extinct. Then machine gun bullets rip holes in the evolutionary tree etched on a side wall: siluriformes, bonbiomus, congridae, callichthyidae, anguillidae, chimpanzee, and hominis. The unmistakable symbolism is that organic evolution has reached a dead end with humanity.

Arthur Koestler—despairing of a human history of war, hatred, racism, classism and, by implication, sexism—said, "Our biological evolution to all intents and purposes came to a standstill in Cro-Magnon days. . . . It appears highly probable that *Homo sapiens* is a biological freak, a remarkable mistake in the evolutionary process" (*The Ghost in the Machine*, pp. 267, 326). Koestler thought man was an ape with better tools. Koestler's hope for a technology that supplants biological evolution is answered by the self-evolved techno-entity in *Ghost in the Shell*.

The robo-tank is terminated with Batou's help. In the fight, Motoko's and Puppet Master's shells have been ripped apart and

---

[2] The design was based on London's nineteenth-century Crystal Palace Exhibition Hall, a museum devoted to the technology of the Industrial Revolution.

left as armless torsos, like those seen in the store windows earlier. But both ghosts still exist, despite the "dead" bodies. Seeking confirmation of her independent soul, Motoko dives into the Puppet Master's mind. Surprisingly, it speaks through her female shell with a male voice, once again transgressing the gender boundary.

The Puppet Master surprisingly requests a fusion of their ghosts—a transformation that will enhance them both. On its own, the Puppet Master can't evolve—it can only make copies. The merging of their minds will create a new entity. Evoking Plato, who proposed a transcendent world beyond everyday reality, the Puppet Master begs Motoko to come out of the shadows and into the light. Enslaved to corporate control and unfulfilled in her present state of fragmentation, Motoko consents. Her merger action with the Puppet Master is a revolt against the corporate state that made her their tool and a leap of faith into the posthuman future.

Techno-Transcendence

The film ends on a transcendent note when Motoko and the Puppet Master unite their consciousnesses to form a new techno-individuality. Following Haraway, they have uncoupled reproduction from organic sexuality and, thereby, slipped the bonds of a socially imposed identity. As machines, they've never experienced sexual pleasure so its lack is no big deal. They have achieved something more significant and, according to Puppet Master, shifted to a "higher structure of existence."

The new merged entity wakes up in a room, within a new shell. It's disconcerting to see Motoko's head apparently transplanted by Batou onto a body he "picked up on the black market." Wearing a schoolgirl uniform and sprawled in a large chair, she looks like a rag doll. The Motoko hybrid even speaks in a girlish voice. She seems weak, stripped of her physical power. But this perception reflects gender prejudice. The look of her body is defined by its corporate manufacturer and reflects a female stereotype of patriarchal culture. As a result of its illicit appropriation, this new shell lies outside government control and therefore provides the Motoko hybrid a free, independent, unsuspicious mobile host.

The hybrid refuses Batou's invitation to remain there, reciting the Biblical words from *1 Corinthians* 13:11 that precede the "through a glass darkly" passage:

> "When I was a child, I spoke as a child, I understood as a child, I thought as a child: but when I became a man, I put away childish things." Now I can say these things without help in my own voice because now I am no longer the woman known as the Major nor am I the program that is called the Puppet Master.

These words simultaneously signal the evolution of a new, dominant lifeform and the obsolescence of the human species and its prejudices. *Ghost in the Shell*'s validation of this male-female techno-spirit demonstrates Haraway's vision that information technologies erase oppressive gender identities. By enacting her advocacy of "pleasure in the confusion of boundaries," the electronic cyborg becomes part of the "utopian tradition of imagining a world without gender" ("A Cyborg Manifesto," p. 150).

The world without gender is also a world without humanity. Unlike most science-fiction films, *Ghost in the Shell* doesn't elevate the organic human to superior status or mourn its extinction. Human identity is a database of fragile memories, easily manipulated or erased; the human body is a marionette, easily controlled or destroyed just as the evolutionary tree is blown to bits. Motoko doesn't yearn to be human, like the robot David in *A.I. Artificial Intelligence*, the robot Andrew in *Bicentennial Man*, or the android Data in *Star Trek The Next Generation*. After jettisoning her shell, Motoko rejects the human for a chance at bodiless omnipresence and transcendence in the infosphere. Whereas films like *I Robot*, the *Terminator* series, and the *Matrix* promote a conflict between human and machine, *Ghost in the Shell* proposes the integration of spirit and technology. Ultimately, *Ghost in the Shell* embraces a technological path out of the self and towards a genderless, metaphysical union.

Cyborg Goddess

The Motoko-Puppet Master hybrid goes beyond Haraway's anti-goddess formulation and embraces a spiritual aspect of posthumanness that her secular philosophy ignores. In its integration of entities, *Ghost in the Shell* reflects Arthur Koestler's positive notion of self-transcendence as religious experience:

The integrative tendencies of the individual makes him feel that he is part of a larger entity which transcends the boundaries of the individual self. In the major Eastern philosophies, the "I am thou and thou art me," the identity of the "Real Self" with the Atman, the all-one, has been preserved throughout the ages. (*The Ghost in the Machine*, p. 242)

At the end of the movie, the Motoko hybrid says, "And where shall the newborn go now? The net is vast and infinite." Cyberspace becomes the medium of religious self-transcendence and God-like omnipresence. The unification of the Puppet Master and Motoko becomes a techno-spiritual fusion—the electronic embodiment of a Cyborg Goddess.[3]

[3] Thanks to Erika Harada for her translation of parts of *Ghost in the Shell* and Mimi Musker for her criticism of earlier versions of this chapter.

21

It's the End of the Species as We Know It, and I Feel Anxious

andrew wells garnar

One of my old roommates used to get on my case for watching anime. In particular, what he found so very odd was the prevalence of the anguished, existential scream. *Neon Genesis Evangelion*, especially Shinji Ikari, was the guiltiest of this. In almost every episode in which Shinji got into Eva Unit 01, something would happen, and he would start screaming. My roommate would occasionally have to laugh . . . or just sigh. It got bad enough that when watching other shows I would have to pause the DVD to explain the back-story to justify why the character screamed and then looked like he—the screamer was usually a male adolescent—had a nervous breakdown. After thinking about it for a while, I believe the question shouldn't be "why is Shinji screaming?" but rather: "why aren't you?"

What Will Become of Us?

There are many reasons we should let out these existential howls, not the least of which is the recurrent theme in anime and manga: a fear of future human evolution. It's a persistent worry that shows up in manga and anime including *Appleseed* (specifically *Ex Machina*), *Elfen Lied*, *Ghost in the Shell* (both the original manga and *Man-Machine Interface*, as well as the first film), *Gilgamesh*, *Serial Experiments: Lain*, *Texhnolyze*, *To Terra*, and *Witch Hunter Robin*. Of particular importance in these is the role that human agency and decision-making play in the future of the human species.

This concern has not shown up in the same way in American pop culture. For instance the *X-Men*, with its endless spin-offs, is one of the pioneering works on mutations, but it hasn't consistently emphasized storylines in terms of evolution and possible futures. In all likelihood, the use of the idea of mutants was instead intended to highlight problems with those excluded from main-stream society. Basically, mutants are a literary device for demon-strating that those who are outside of the mainstream are not actually so different from the rest of us.

This emphasis is not surprising since in American culture there has been a long history of racism, homophobia, and other types of social exclusion. In addition, most of the debates surrounding evo-lution have tended to focus on matters of origins. The well-rehearsed spat between evolution and creationism is entirely concerned with the origins of life, such that these debates are gen-erally backward looking. They are retrospective, matters of history. While these debates are important, the theory of evolution also raises a host of questions about the future, questions about where life on this planet is headed.

In many of the anime and manga mentioned above, there are wor-ries about social exclusion and alienation as well, but these themes are not always tied directly to evolution. Also, unlike a lot of American pop culture, they do not emphasize the ways that evolution *per se* is dangerous, like the big scary mutant out to destroy humanity.

Instead, what these manga and anime consistently emphasize is humanity's responses to the enigmatic promise of transformation. The way humans react to evolution is the fundamental problem. Everything circles back to how certain people respond to these chal-lenges. For example, as Misato explains in *End of Evangelion*, Angels in *Neon Genesis Evangelion* (*Eva*) can be understood in this way:

> You see Shinji, mankind was spawned by a being called Lilith, just like Adam was. We are the eighteenth Angel. The other Angels are just dif-ferent possibilities of what we could have become. Sadly, we can't coexist even though we're fundamentally the same creatures.[1]

Furthermore, it is strongly implied that the Angels were deliberately sent by other humans.[2] In which case, the big scary creatures hell-bent on attacking the Earth are intimately connected to humans.

---

[1] This explains the genetic similarities that Ritsuko Akagi finds between Angels and humans in Episode 5.

[2] Consider Professor Fuyutsuki in Episode 24 where he exclaims once it is discovered Kaworu is the seventeenth Angel: "SEELE has sent an Angel to us."

The alien is us . . . almost. This sort of move is common in the manga and anime mentioned above: a significant part of the perils facing humanity always involve a healthy dollop of human agency, both in creating and resolving the danger.

Two of the most important anime in the last twenty-five years, the television series *Eva*, along with the first two theatrical releases, and the movie *Akira*, demonstrate why there is reason to be anxious about the future of human evolution, and how emphasizing the role of agency reshapes considerations about such futures. While the latter point might appear trivial, thinking in the American context about humanity's future is rather muddled, and the anime *Eva* and *Akira* present a way of wrestling with these possibilities in a more productive manner.[3]

Future Shock

To begin, why worry over the future of our evolution?

The clearest reason is that there might be no future: humankind may go extinct. There will be no more us, at least as we've grown accustomed to. Perhaps the most plausible cause of such a future is the damage humans have wrought to the environment, in particular global climate change. But worldwide pandemics, the depletion of natural resources, nuclear war, and even collision with asteroids have also been considered as possible causes of our annihilation.[4] Extinction marks the end of the species. This is an important part of life's history on Earth, so it is a reasonable worry.

But another and even more fascinating reason is the potential transition of our species into something new. Thus far, the evolution of species has taken place on very large time scales. Evolution tends to be slow. However, it has been argued that humans have shortened this time frame dramatically. One strand in the philosophy of technology claims that technology is an

---

Gendo then says: "The Old Man wants to advance his schedule, using us as his tools."

[3] For the sake of consistency, I will follow the story as presented in the theatrical retellings, released in the United States by Manga Entertainment under the names *Death and Rebirth* and *End of Evangelion*. I rely on Pioneer's 2001 Special Edition of *Akira*. All quotations are from the subtitles of those releases.

[4] The philosopher John Leslie has argued in "Is the End of the World Nigh?" (in *The Philosophical Quarterly*), that, regardless of the cause, the end of the human species is more likely near to us that than not.

extension of evolution. The human body is at once limited, but adaptable. One way in which humans adapt to their environments involves the use of tools. Through tools, humans have been able to live longer, healthier, and safer lives all across the planet, as well as in outer space. What humans lack biologically, we make up for through our technologies.[5]

There's room for debate here about whether such tool use should in fact be considered an evolutionary adaptation. Regardless of one's stance on that, clearly there are new technologies we possess now or which are anticipated to arrive shortly that could unambiguously accelerate human evolution. The clearest examples involve biotechnologies like human genetic engineering, the use of stem cells, and cloning. We could also add computing, information technology, nanotechnology, robotics, and cybernetics here as well. As Francis Fukuyama and others argue, biotechnologies provide ways to rewrite the human genome, allowing for the production of new human-like species. Other sorts of technologies could conceivably allow for the construction of radically "posthuman" species that are no longer dependent on organic, biological bodies (cyborgs, robots, the Puppeteer, and the like).

This is dangerous territory. Biological evolution has taken a long time. Technological development is much quicker. Consider Moore's Law which claims that computing power doubles each generation; that it increases exponentially. This Law goes a fair distance in explaining the explosion of information technology in the last thirty years. Yet, while we can map in a fairly clear way the increases in computing capacity and predict where the strictly technical applications might go, it is much more difficult to guess how this will transform society. Put simply, when dealing with the technologies mentioned above (and others like them), we only have a dim idea what we are doing. There is no adequate baseline to understand exactly how this technology will affect us. Given the presumed potency of these technologies, there are genuine risks here.

Manufacturing Evolution

Neon Genesis Evangelion is all about anxiety. The most obvious example is Shinji's angst about his relations with his father, his

---

[5] This line of argument follows many philosophers of technology like Arnold Gehlen and Friedrich Engels. See Engels, *The Dialectic of Nature*, pp. 170–183.

mother, women in his life, friends, and EVA Unit 1. While the series is more concerned with deftly exploring Shinji's psychological problems, the plot itself is important to our discussion. The basic set up of the story is that three (briefly four) teenagers pilot EVAs, gigantic mecha consisting of armor that restrains some sort of hybrid organic/mechanical body, to fight different Angels of various shapes, sizes, and abstract forms. As we shall see, the plot itself is the product of a specific anxiety.

It's strongly implied that a group called SEELE instigated the Angels' invasion and has some sort of control of them. SEELE is the shadowy committee that engineered the experimentation on Adam, the first Angel. This experimentation produced the "Second Impact" in 2000 that wreaked havoc on the Earth's environment, in turn upsetting world politics and setting the story itself into motion. They are also the initial sponsors of Gehirn, the organization that preceded the founding of NERV in 2010. NERV then takes the lead in fighting the Angels.

What then is SEELE's purpose in all this? Simple: to restart human evolution. The reason that they are willing to destroy the world twice, first partially with the Second Impact, then totally with the Third Impact shown in *End of Evangelion*, is because of a very potent anxiety. SEELE sees humanity as having run the course of its evolutionary possibilities. From now on, we will not change, remaining separate, miserable individuals. To avoid this fate, they create a scenario using Shinji's EVA in which all of humanity will be forced together into one organism. Misato puts it the following way:

> So mankind, a race of flawed and incomplete separate entities, has reached the end of its evolutionary potential. The Instrumentality Project will manufacture the evolution of man's separate entities into a single consummate being.

This is SEELE's goal in developing the EVAs and the Angels: To start human evolution over through this "Human Instrumentality Project."

The anxiety that motivates SEELE's Project intertwines two different points. First, that modern humanity is alienated from each other and the attempt to forge intimate relationships inevitably inflicts harm on those involved—Shinji's relationships throughout the series work to illustrate this problem. Second, that for whatever reasons, some have lost faith not so much in the possibility of the future itself, but in our potential to create a better one for ourselves. The *Eva* series grounds this latter fear in biology, while others like Bill Joy or Martin Heidegger see it in technological advancement.[6] Humanity has become lost to itself and has no future worth hoping for.

I Feel Sick

How then should we understand this "anxiety?" Many existentialists like Søren Kierkegaard, Jean-Paul Sartre, and Heidegger have emphasized the philosophical significance of anxiety. As Heidegger developed the concept in *Being and Time*, anxiety involves a state-of-mind (something more than a feeling and closer to a way of living in the world) of uneasiness.

Unlike emotions such as love and fear, anxiety is not connected to any specific object. I might love someone and fear dogs, but this is not the case with anxiety. The world itself makes us anxious. We do not feel at home in the world. For Heidegger, anxiety is not a typical part of our lives. Usually, we follow along with the crowd, what he refers to as "the They." But when some event causes us to break away from "the They," we sense that there might be nothing beyond this sort of life. Heidegger calls this experience "anxiety."

When anxiety is genuine, really felt, we do not feel at home. The hollowness of the everyday lives we lead becomes clear. Following Heidegger, when faced with this situation, we can turn away from it and return to hiding in our everyday existence, go back to "the They," or we can embrace the anxiety and the questions it raises. At this point, anxiety can be productive because it forces the person to wrestle with her or his freedom to choose what it is he or she will do. Heidegger prefers the latter because it opens up the possibility for what he refers to as authentic existence, the specifics of which do not concern us here.

Anxiety opens up space for questioning the manner in which we live. Regardless of whether one accepts Heidegger's larger argument about authenticity as a way to work through anxiety, the pri-

---

[6] Bill Joy, "Why the Future Doesn't Need Us" in *Wired* 8:4 (2000), pp. 238–246. Martin Heidegger, "The Question Concerning Technology" in *Basic Writings*, pp. 311–341.

mordial experience about not feeling at home in the world remains a definitive part of human existence. This anxiety is always latent within human existence.

It is precisely this state-of-mind that drives SEELE's Instrumentality Project. Given the apocalyptic imagery presented in *End of Evangelion*, the viewer might assume that this is perhaps not the best way to resolve one's anxieties. Only Shinji and Asuka appear to retain human form after Third Impact. Every other living thing has been taken into the Sea of LCL, the primordial stuff of life.

What in our lives might produce anxiety so terrifying that it leads SEELE to pursue Third Impact? While there's no clear consensus within American culture, or among philosophers, about science, technology or evolution, there is one persistent and worrisome strain: a tendency towards what Mary Midgley calls "fatalism." Midgley uses this word rather than the more typical "determinism" because the latter is unhelpfully ambiguous. The meanings of "determinism" range from the strict laws of causality to a much softer sense of directing things in one way or another. Her claim is that when people worry about, say, genetic determinism, it is really "fatalism" that drives concerns: The idea that human choice plays no role in the universe. Everything is fated to happen.

At first glance, to be a fatalist about evolution might seem a bit odd. Part of Darwin's genius was demonstrating the importance of chance and open-endedness in the development of species. The reply to such readings of Darwin is to say that what appears open-ended to us is a matter of our lack of knowledge. All things, including the development of various life-forms on Earth, have been fated by the laws of the universe. That it looks unpredictable is our problem, not the universe's. Such strong claims make more sense against the backdrop of genetic reductionism. For example Richard Dawkins's *The Selfish Gene* argues that all life can be explained in terms of genes. The genes operate much like computer programs that try to pass themselves on to future generations, using organisms as mere vehicles. Evolution is thus the story of these competing genes trying to survive. Humans have no real agency in this story, since we are, in effect, nothing but flesh bags for propagating genes.

This sort of fatalism extends to the technologically mediated senses of evolution discussed above. To call Moore's Law a "law" is not wholly innocent. While within science calling something a "law" is more of an honorific than an indication that the given theory is immutable, there are still echoes of absoluteness. Similar claims can be made about human endeavors, specifically laws of economics which drive these technologies that might produce posthumanity. The frequent battle-cry of "let the Market decide!" speaks to this fatalism. We assume we are powerless to stop the march of progress, technological development, or what-ever-you-want-to-call-it.

In the face of such fatalism, drastic measures are called for. If humanity can no longer evolve, the only option is to force the issue by becoming something radically different. Given the inevitability that humans will remain sad, isolated organisms, our future really is no future at all. In this situation, anxiety is a reasonable response. We are faced with the hollowness of the human endeavor. There is no point.

The Human Instrumentality Project attempts to resolve this anxious situation. But the cost is steep. Humans lose their individual bodies, which is the ultimate form of falling in to Heidegger's "the They." Everyone is forced into this "single, consummate being," without any possibility of escape, either in the sense of opting out or retaining the capacity to be anxious. This decision amounts to giving up the game of being human. Faced with pain and alienation, SEELE opts, in a very undemocratic manner, to end a distinctive human sort of evolution in favor of a collective existence.

Men, We're Going to the Apocalypse

After the rather disheartening ending of *Eva*, *Akira* presents a different response to a similar worry. The story begins in the late 1980s, when a group of children awaken to their immense psychic powers and extensive testing by the Japanese Government. There are at least twenty-eight of them, though of the original children, only Numbers 25 (Kiyoko), 26 (Takashi), and 27 (Masaru) are met in the flesh. The most powerful of these children is Number 28 (Akira). For reasons not made clear in the movie, Akira's power goes out of control in 1988, destroying most of Tokyo. The remains of Akira are then cytogenetically entombed for later scientists to research.

The film then picks up in 2019, in the rebuilt Neo-Tokyo. A teenage biker punk named Tetsuo Shima has a chance encounter with Takashi, thus triggering Tetsuo's own latent psychic abilities. Because of Tetsuo's own potential, combined with some experiments and drugs provided by the government, his power goes out of control, threatening to totally destroy Neo-Tokyo. The film ends with a final intervention on the part of Kiyoko, Takashi, and Masaru that prevents the absolute worst from actually happening. Neo-Tokyo is decimated, but the world does not end.

In the context of our discussion, the most important aspect of *Akira* is the Numbered Children because they mark an enormous evolutionary leap. As Kei explains to Kaneda, Akira is like energy that emerged through evolution. There is a certain power that exists in all living things (and perhaps all matter), and Akira unleashed that power. Kei uses the analogy that it is like giving an amoeba a human's capacity to build things.

Of course, this evolutionary leap is immensely dangerous. Akira's power destroyed Tokyo and, through coming into contact with Takashi, Tetsuo manifests abilities no less devastating. But what make the situation truly worrisome is that this sort of power might be in all of humanity's future—one day all of our descendents might manifest this energy. As the Scientist notes to the Colonel:

> The other day, a young researcher asked me something. He wondered if their power was the form the next stage of evolution was taking, and that perhaps that we'll all be able to control it some day.

More bluntly, Kiyoko states:

> Akira's power exists within everyone.

And then the Numbers say at the end of the film that:

> But someday, we'll also be able to . . . You see, it's already begun.

This is not as heavy-handed as the fatalism in *Eva*, but it seems that the writing is on the wall for humanity. We will become extinct or superseded. The wheels are in motion for a very different future than that we are accustomed to.

A Grotesque Kindergarten

Among other things that the film taps into is a fear of the dangers of evolution, though in way different from *Eva*. The anxiety buried in *Akira* is the two-fold worry discussed earlier. On the one hand, the power of Akira and Tetsuo could potentially make humanity

extinct or life very difficult (as Katsushiro Otomo depicts it in
Volumes 4–6 of the manga). On the other hand, the Numbers represent the next stage of our evolution, in which case these children
are the future, a future where the human species as *we* know it
might be regarded as we now regard the Neanderthal. *Homo sapiens* is a species that had its moment and then left the evolutionary
stage. Taking these points together, the Numbers become a threat
not simply to continued human existence, but to *the very meaning
of human existence.*

Akira does not depict humans as powerless, at least not
entirely, in the face of such anxiety. Instead, the powers that the
Numbers possess force everyone to make choices about how to
respond. The Japanese government responds to the emergence of
the first children in the 1980s by deciding to tap into the Numbers'
abilities. The Colonel puts the desire quite honestly:

> Maybe we shouldn't touch that power . . . But we *have* to. We have to
> touch it and *control* it.

On the one hand, this impulse is totally understandable. The power
of Akira and the other Numbers is enticing. On the other hand,
indulging this desire led to annihilation of old Tokyo. After that,
according to the Colonel, the scientists involved froze the remains
of Akira, buried him deep underground, and planned to wait until
humanity was better prepared.

When Tetsuo has his chance encounter with Takashi on the
deserted highway, humanity is no better prepared. Instead, as the
Colonel puts it, Neo-Tokyo is degenerating, a "garbage heap made
up by hedonistic fools" dancing "to the tune of corrupt politicians
and capitalists." When Tetsuo's powers begin to manifest, the
whole situation becomes a powder keg. The government's Scientist
wants only to study him (consequences be damned), the terrorists
want him, Kaneda wants revenge, and Tetsuo himself wants more
power.

Against this backdrop, the full significance of the decision of the
Numbers becomes clear. Realizing that Tetsuo threatens to become,
in effect, another Akira, they decide to extricate Tetsuo from our
universe. The original plan appears to have been to send Tetsuo to
somewhere beyond this world, but they end up traveling with
Tetsuo into that great elsewhere in order to send back Kaneda,
who is trapped inside the imploding Tetsuo.

The Numbers reason as follows. First, they had survived the destruction of old Tokyo by Akira thirty-one years before. They knew the consequences of Tetsuo fully unleashing his abilities (what we see is devastating enough). Second, while the Numbers imply that they could seal Tetsuo away without traveling elsewhere, they decide to effectively sacrifice themselves to save Kaneda. As Takashi puts it: "But none of this is his fault!" Of course, the Numbers will also get to see Akira again, which they look forward to. Lastly, the Numbers realize that humanity is not ready for this sort of power. To return to the troublesome analogy, Tetsuo was at a stage like an amoeba possessing nuclear weapons when he disappears, utterly unprepared for his powers. One day perhaps humanity can accept such abilities with out destroying themselves, but not now. Faced with this anxiety-ridden situation, the Numbers take responsibility.

One Last Anguished Existential Scream

There are two lessons we can learn from *Akira* and *Eva*. The first is that given the perils humanity faces, both from the natural order and from society, a certain degree of anxiety is reasonable. We face daunting challenges on all sides. This should be a call to reflection on the human condition. Between the logic of the evolution, the way technology can extend human evolution, widespread social alienation, our impoverished relationships to other people, and what we have done to the planet in terms of resource depletion, pollution, and habitat destruction, there is much to be concerned about. When we can take these altogether, we too, perhaps for reasons akin to Shinji's, should give an anguished existential scream from time to time.

With all of the promise of contemporary science and technology, we do well to remember that it is not simply positive. There are many serious challenges, one of the more extreme being the possibility of a "posthuman future." There is good reason for anxiety. But we must not flee from that anxiety and return to more comfortable, fatalistic narratives of letting evolution or the Market determine what is best for us.

The second lesson is that once we embrace this anxiety, we must accept both the freedom to determine what we should do and the responsibility this freedom entails. These anime always foreground the significance of human agency, our ability to choose.

Needless to say, the plot SEELE hatches may not be a healthy resolution to such anxieties. It culminates in the utter destruction of
anything resembling human existence as we know it. We can also
note the rather undemocratic nature of the Instrumentality Project,
in which a group decides what is best for all of humanity. This
choice by SEELE is not responsible, if for no other reason than that
many of those affected had no say in the decision.

Yet, for whatever their problems, one thing SEELE does demonstrate is that it is ultimately up to humanity (or a self-selected cabal
acting on behalf of the species regardless of whether others want
it) to decide how to face the anxiety created by evolution. Even if
the human species has reached an evolutionary dead-end, human
agency still remains. We retain the ability to decide how to respond
to these existential challenges. *Eva* demonstrates the catastrophes
that happen when people abandon any hope for humanity and
throw in the towel on being human in any conventional sense.

In the world of *Akira*, there are several possible responses to
the anxiety produced by the evolutionary leap to psychic mutants.
The initial response of the Japanese government, and also the
Colonel's Scientific Advisor, is to try to understand and control the
power, the future of our evolution. This amounts to trying to turn
the anxiety into something productive and profitable, while avoiding the ugly existential questions. The Numbers, and in a different
way the Colonel, accept the challenge that Akira and Tetsuo pose
for humanity in some of its existential glory. They realize that there
is genuine danger here that humanity is not prepared for. Their
response is then to forestall the inevitable until everyone else is
more prepared.

The decision that the Numbers make at the end of the film is
more responsible than that of SEELE. Unlike the resolution of *Eva*
in which only two individuals apparently survive, the Numbers
allow humanity to continue to be anxious. The events in Neo-
Tokyo serve as a potent warning about where the future might take
us and allows for the preparations that were not pursued after the
1988 disaster. The Numbers' decision opens up possibilities for
human agency. After Tetsuo leaves, those who survive might continue to remain with "the They," ignoring the dangers. But they had
been warned.

While we may face far less menacing possibilities at this
moment in time, this is no reason to repress our anxiety. One trouble with the fall into fatalism is that it often results in an abdication

of responsibility. If the future is determined by forces beyond our control, then there is no room for meaningful human agency. But even if our unalterable fate is destruction, these anime remind us that it remains within our power to determine how we will face such a future. The same is true with the less bleak but still transformative possibilities that contemporary technology and science might provide. As Kiyoko remarks: "But when the power is awakened, you must choose how to use it, even if you weren't prepared for it." We might be right to scream when we encounter this, but we also must be ready for what comes next.

Special Features

 Alternate Ending

 Credits

 Subtitles

 Making of ...

 Easter Eggs

 Deleted Scenes

 Scene Selection

Z Z Z

?

Mew

ALTERNATE ENDING:

Bide Your Time, and Hold Out Hope

TRISTAN D. TAMPLIN

The moment that I truly fell in love with anime occurred sometime *after* the film that I had been watching ended. In fact, that rather unexpected moment had almost nothing at all to do with the film itself—or any film, for that matter. No, I fell in love with anime while watching the bonus material. It was during the interviews with the cast and crew that my heart was lost to an artistic style that many grown-ups in the West think is primarily for children. But I couldn't help it. I was entirely caught off guard by their enthusiasm, their sincerity, their dedication, and what appeared to be a complete lack of cynicism about what they were doing. They seemed to care very much about their work and how it was received. They said, more than once, that they hoped I enjoyed what they had created, and I believed them. Completely. And I still do.

Don't get me wrong. It's not that I haven't found the content of anime to be extraordinarily rewarding and worthwhile in its own right. From the epic narrative of *Twelve Kingdoms*, the aesthetic innovation of *Gankutsuou*, the deeply unsettling tone of *Paranoia Agent*, the compelling character studies of *Perfect Blue*, to the intellectually challenging conception of the future in *Stand Alone Complex*, anime certainly has a lot to offer and a lot to recommend it. But over and above all of this, what really draws me and, I suspect, so many others to anime is its willingness to engage with its audience. Watch a few sets of DVD extras and that willingness, that orientation toward connecting with the viewer, will be readily apparent. And the very book that you're holding in your hands right now is evidence of just how successfully their audience has been engaged. The significance of this degree of interaction between the creators and viewers of anime is that it opens up a unique set of possibilities for the evolution of the genre.

Wide Eyed Wonder

In the first episode of *Fooly Cooly,* the young male protagonist is smacked in the head with a vintage Rickenbacker left-handed bass guitar by a manic, Vespa scooter-riding woman who we've already begun to suspect is an alien. The resulting lump on his forehead, which began as rather normal-sized, starts to swell. And it keeps on swelling, ridiculously so, until, eventually, a television-headed robot (and what appears to be the left hand of a much larger robot) emerges from it. There are, unfortunately it seems to me, far too few truly unexpected moments in our media-saturated culture. Somehow it feels like we've seen it all before. Not so with anime. Episode one, and a robot sprouts from a lump on a boy's forehead.[1] I certainly did not see that coming (Oh, you bet I watched the rest of the series). And this sense of the (not always pleasantly) unexpected extends well beyond the merely bizarre and seemingly random. I was shattered (and, frankly, made a bit unwell) by the narrative developments in the final episode of *Berserk,* impressed by the impossibly seamless fusion of Japan's Edo period with contemporary culture and hip hop music in *Samurai Champloo,* and I've still not completely recovered from the jaw-dropping, wide-eyed wonder induced by the stunning visual imagery of the ongoing dream parade in *Paprika.*

What matters about encountering the unexpected is not simply that there's a certain, often deeply felt excitement involved. While the unexpected always immediately affects us in this way, it also affects us in a more subtle but no less significant way. It confronts us, and by the very challenge it poses to our expectations, it causes us to become aware of them and, quite possibly, to rethink them. This potential to challenge our preconceptions and upset our ordinary way of looking at and thinking about the world is, oddly enough, fundamentally the same potential held out by the best sort

---

[1] In case you're wondering *why* a robot sprouts from a boy's forehead, according to the interview included on the DVD release that I watched, it's because the director likes robots. Simple! There's also a baseball-themed episode for essentially the same reason.

of philosophic inquiry. And this affinity with philosophy is, at first glance anyway, perhaps the single most unexpected thing about anime. Of course, the challenges posed by anime aren't always entirely intellectual in nature, but that doesn't make them any less profound—quite the contrary, in fact. To be unsettled by what we see, to be confronted with new visions of the future and new conceptions of society and technology, to be challenged by unconventional depictions of the body and personal relationships, actually *prepares* us for philosophic inquiry in a way no strictly intellectual activity could. When we hold a bit less firmly to our expectations in general, then we are much more open to the possibilities of genuine reflection, sincere reevaluation, and authentic change. And that is no less true for anime itself than it is for the individuals who watch it.

Like any fairly well defined genre, anime has its share of recurring themes, familiar motifs, and often used concepts. But even within this realm of the conventional, anime has a tendency to shuffle these elements around, to present them from unusual perspectives, to combine them in new in interesting ways, and not infrequently to subvert them entirely. In this way, anime can make even the familiar and comfortable seem novel and just a bit odd. If you've seen one giant robot, melancholy vampire or teenage misfit, you most certainly have *not* seen them all. While anime clearly revels in the unusual and tests the boundaries of the expected and the acceptable, it also explores the conventional and even the mundane. In this sense, nothing is exempt from the probing and playful scrutiny of anime, and nothing is outside of its transformative realm. As with the possibilities inherent in the art form itself, the scope of subject matter that anime seems willing avail itself of is potentially limitless.

So what should we expect to see in the future? Nothing, or perhaps everything—I have simply no idea. But I'm definitely going to keep watching, because I can't wait to find out.

Credits

SHANE ARBOGAST designs book covers, websites, and will draw just about anything if asked. His main means of transportation in New York City is not the subway but his trusty, beat-up mountain bike. Considering that he has feasted his eyes on everything from sick and twisted animation to Film Noir movie marathons, an anime book jacket assignment seemed just the carrot to keep him off the streets for a while. Ahh, those dicey New York streets—Shane enjoys fantasies of being Ichigo Kurosaki when those Hollow cab drivers hog his bike lane.

Evenings spent reading her host brother's copies of Tezuka's *Black Jack* manga while living in Japan not only did wonders for her Japanese medical vocabulary and slang, it also set **CHRISTIE BARBER** on the path to where she is today. In her research she is looking at the representation of gender—in particular masculinity—in Japanese popular media, especially manga and anime. She teaches at Macquarie University.

ADAM BARKMAN is Assistant Professor of Philosophy and Religion at Yonsei University. He is the author of *C.S. Lewis and Philosophy as a Way of Life* and *Through Common Things*, and co-editor of *Manga and Philosophy*. Despite his initial scepticism, Adam has ever since been grateful to his brother Joe for introducing him to anime; indeed, there are few things Adam enjoys more than cracking a bottle of cheap, dry red, smoking an even cheaper cigar, and talking (somewhat) intelligently with his bro about why the ending of the *Kimagure Orange Road* OVAs is so painfully perfect, which Shakespeare Kuno is quoting from, and why so many guys enjoy watching *Sailor Moon*.

MIO BRYCE has a wide range of interests in Japanese language—both classical and modern—ranging from literature to history to manga-anime, and she has developed and taught a number of units at Macquarie

University. Her particular interest is in historical, socio-cultural, and psychological issues depicted in fiction, especially representations of issues related to individual identity. Mio is involved in interdisciplinary research into youth cultures and has established a manga-anime research group, in conjunction with the English Department at Macquarie University.

CARI CALLIS has felt Shinto all her life and never knew it. So that explains the love for coral reefs in the Caribbean, the Costa Rican Cloud Forest, and thunderstorms in Negril. Those kami are sneaky, they can be everywhere you listen. Now she's building a torii for her garden and talking to trees just in case they show up. . . . She teaches screenwriting at Columbia College Chicago, and has learned from Miyazaki-san that no matter what age we are, the desire to tell stories originates from our nostalgic longing to recreate our own personal lost worlds.

BENJAMIN CHANDLER holds a PhD in Creative Writing. He researches Japanese and Western heroism, so he gets to watch a lot of anime and call it "work." He was first drawn to anime by its weird and wonderful characters. The first volume in his Japanese inspired fantasy series, *The Voyages of the Flying Dragon*, is due to be published in September 2010.

How many cyborgs does it take to change a student's mind about the philosophical value of anime? **JASON DAVIS** researches this question at Macquarie University, and students' wide-eyed incredulity at having to read about anime makes him re-boot and augment ever more metaphysical questions about human identity with cyborg bodies. As he reminds online students, reading about anime is like seeing movement through words—reading slows down the philosophical velocity of anime bodies. As a result Jason dreams in anime. And he's beginning to think these dreams are not his own. The silver origami unicorn he once found at his Megatech Body workstation makes him suspect as much.

While he waits to download his mind into a computer housed in an immortal robotic shell, **DAN DINELLO** works as an associate professor at Columbia College Chicago and runs shockproductions.com website. He wrote the book *Technophobia! Science Fiction Visions of Post Human Technology* and contributed a chapter to *Battlestar Galactica and Philosophy: Mission Accomplished or Mission Frakked Up?* He has written about pop culture and science for the *Chicago Tribune, Chicago Sun-Times,* Salon.com, and *Manchester Guardian.* An award-winning independent filmmaker, Dan also directed episodes of the Comedy Central show *Strangers with Candy.*

Having once been violated by the tentacles of a randy space monster, **ANDREW A. DOWD** is dismayed to discover that the courts are slanted in favor of randy space monsters. He works through his rage and pain by writing about our mixed-up movie culture. His musings on classic and contemporary cinema have been published in *Screen Magazine* and *Film Monthly*. He also served as Assistant Editor on *Battlestar Galactica and Philosophy: Mission Accomplished or Mission Frakked Up?* When not working through his tentacle trauma (one day at a time, friends) he toils as a wage slave and scrounges for freelance assignments in the mean streets of the Windy City. He will write for food or best offer.

ANDREW WELLS GARNAR is currently a lecturer at Clemson University, where he works mostly on science, technology, values, and American Philosophy, and resists the urge to constantly use anime for illustrating his points. He has a longstanding interest in anime, dating back to seeing the first American release of Miyazaki's *Nausicaa* on cable in 1987. Even though the dub was bad and the film truncated, he knew it was something special and has spent the last two decades trying to find more. Andrew misses when anime was a bit more of an underground thing, but appreciates that what he finds these days has been translated.

ALICIA GIBSON holds a law degree from the University of Colorado and is a doctoral candidate in Comparative Literature at the University of Minnesota. Her dissertation project, "The End, or Life in the Atomic Age: Modes of Subjectivity and Aesthetic Form" focuses on the experiences of American, Japanese-American, and Japanese in the atomic world as expressed in post–World War II literature, television, and cinema. She has had her heart stolen by Nausicaa's squirrel-fox, Teto. Her love of anime springs from the same place as her crazy cat lady instincts..

DANIEL HAAS earned an MA in Philosophy from Simon Fraser University, Canada, and is currently completing a PhD at Florida State University. His research interests include Philosophy of Mind (particularly Action Theory/Free Will), Philosophy of Science (Especially the Philosophy of Biology and Psychology), and Ethics (Moral Psychology, Metaethics, and Applied Ethics). Like Hayao Miyazaki, Dan believes the best response to a publisher's editorial suggestions is to mail said publisher a package containing a samurai sword and a polite note reading, "No Cuts!"

JOHN HARTUNG, otasen, has an MA in Philosophy from the University of Mississippi and is an adjunct instructor at Le Moyne College in Syracuse, New York. He's a big Killer Girl Android otaku. He would like to make his own but can't justify the process of reverse engineering one.

SHANA HEINRICY is an Instructor of Communication Studies at Xavier University in New Orleans. She is currently completing her dissertation in Communication and Culture from Indiana University. She studies bodies, technology, and television. She thinks that Studio Ghibli keeps the real Catbus locked in a cage somewhere, giving it occasional cat treats. Someday she'll find it and let it out. Someday.

SARA LIVINGSTON is an Associate Professor in the Television Department of Columbia College Chicago where she teaches Critical Studies, Aesthetics, and Writing for Television. She's a nationally and internationally exhibited video artist as well as a media activist who uses video as a tool for social change. She is currently vacationing in the uncharted territory that lies between fact and fiction, and has found it to be an enchanting and productive place to write. Although she's made lifelong friends there and would love to linger, she looks forward to her return to Chicago.

ANGUS MCBLANE is a distributed entity that is a conglomerate of the X and the Y that has taken the form of a "person" (?) who is a PhD student at the Centre for Critical and Cultural Theory at Cardiff University in Wales, where he is engaged with splicing his consciousness with various data sets in order to emerge as a viable self-sustaining distributed subject. When not concerned with posthuman emergence, he is attempting to construct a Guymelef.

LOUIS MELANÇON is a US Army officer with a variety of combat arms and intelligence experiences from the tactical through national-strategic levels. He holds masters' degrees from the Joint Military Intelligence College and Kings College, London, has been awarded the Bronze Star Medal, and published in the US Army's journal, *Military Review*, as well as *Battlestar Galactica and Philosophy: Mission Accomplished or Mission Frakked Up?* Louis mentally accepts that giant robots wouldn't be efficient weapons platforms, but still lets out a little disappointed sigh every time a new weapon system isn't a Mobile Suit or VOTOMS.

SARAH PENICKA-SMITH is a doctoral candidate in the Department of Studies in Religion at the University of Sydney. Her other life as a choral conductor qualifies her to obsess over music in anime, although she has yet to convince any of her choirs that learning to sing like a minyo ensemble is a good idea. Sarah's work with the GLBTQI community as Music Director of the Sydney Gay & Lesbian Choir has led to her being the preferred postgrad in her department to tutor on religion, gender, sex, and the body. This is a workplace arrangement that she enjoys thoroughly.

IAN M. PETERS, a doctoral student in Georgia State University's Moving Image Studies program, was previously published in *Battlestar Galactica and Philosophy: Mission Accomplished or Mission Frakked Up?* Like the characters in *Highlander: The Search for Vengeance*, he has a strong affinity for swords of all shapes and sizes and is careful not to mount them on the wall near the headboard of his bed for fear of nighttime decapitation. If immortals like Colin MacLeod of the Clan MacLeod truly exist and "in the end there can only be one," Ian hopes that the victor understands the importance of warming the teapot before brewing a proper cup of Darjeeling.

NEKO PILARCIK always knew what she wanted to be when she grew up: an intergalactic Space Pirate living a life of excitement and adventure in the Sea of Stars. However an unforeseen lack of advancement in the space shipping industry lead her to consider a more feasible career writing and drawing stories about people who do live lives of excitement and adventure. Her artwork introduces each of this book's major sections (Body, Mind, Spirit, Conflict, Heroes, Devils, Future Perfect) and her animated short "The Three Artists" screened at the Cannes Film Festival. Neko currently works as a freelance animator and illustrator in addition to drawing the graphic novel, *Kowaii Kawaii*.

AMADA ROSAS is the artist and animator who designed our title page and the "Special Features" divider. She spends her days as a teaching assistant for the Columbia College Chicago Animation Program, but at night she spends her time working as a cleaner to capture and return the escaped imaginary characters from the animators' minds that try to cause havoc on the world, under the code name O.A.I. (Over Active Imagination).

HAL SHIPMAN is completing his master's in Literature at Northwestern University. His academic focus is the intersection of word and image in literature, with particular attention to the medium of comics. Like many Americans his age, his first exposure to anime was *Speed Racer*. One of his biggest disappointments occurred on Halloween when he went to a party in a flawless Speed costume, and everyone thought he was supposed to be a polo player. His partner, Channing, cries at the end of *Grave of the Fireflies* every time.

JOSEF STEIFF has learned the following from science fiction movies: 1. Never answer a distress call in space (*Alien*); 2. When boarding an abandoned space station, assume that at the very least, it will be a blank canvass upon which you will project your fears and anxieties; at worst, some other intelligence will mine your memories and experiences to create distorted simulations from your past (*Solaris*); 3. Allowing an artificial intelligence to completely control and operate a spaceship or station is never a good idea (*2001: A Space Odyssey*); and 4. All of the above (*Magnetic Rose*).

BENJAMIN STEVENS lived through the Robotech Wars by learning to imitate machine noises, a skill he has since put to more human uses in the academic and a cappella worlds. At Bard College he specializes in Latin and Greek, comparative literature, and linguistics; directs an annual symposium of undergraduate research on comics and comic art; and advises a student a cappella group, the Orcapelicans!. He also coordinates the Recorded A Cappella Review Board (RARB) and serves on the board of the Contemporary A Cappella Society (CASA).

TRISTAN TAMPLIN took a career guidance exam in high school that indicated that he should become either a religious leader or a test pilot. Instead, he got a PhD in philosophy, which he quickly parlayed into a career as a designer and photographer. An avid soccer player and fan, he currently lives in Manchester, England, where he hunts vampires (part-time) with his data dog, Paco.

Since his earliest days, **ANDREW TERJESEN** has been training to become Philosopher King (which is a lot like Shaman King, if you take away the part about transforming the world with your oversoul). In preparation for the Philosopher Fight, he has mastered the techniques of Fist of One Hundred Historical Ethicists, Scottish Enlightenment Annihilation Strike, and Moral Psychology Unstoppable Wave. Using these techniques, Andrew has produced essays for *Manga and Philosophy*, *Supervillains and Philosophy*, and *The Onion and Philosophy*, as well as an article on nineteenth-century economic thought. Despite all his training, he fears that his inability to stomach the Philosophy-Philosophy Fruit puts him at the mercy of anyone who can employ Nihilistic Kicks of Post-Modern Deconstruction.

D.E. WITTKOWER, or Dylan as we like to call him, teaches ethics and the history of philosophy at Coastal Carolina University, and is the editor of *iPod and Philosophy* and *Facebook and Philosophy*. On the other side of The Gate he is an alchemic researcher, given the title of the Transcendental Alchemist, working on transmutation theory.

MARGO COUGHLIN ZIMMERMAN completed an undergraduate degree in Film and Video from Columbia College Chicago in 2000. While attending Columbia, she became an intern at Manga Entertainment and was quickly hired full-time. During this time she worked on US and International distribution for *Perfect Blue*, *Noein*, *Blood: The Last Vampire*, *Street Fighter Alpha*, and *Karas*, among others. In addition, Zimmerman was production and distribution manager for Manga's parent company and was production manager for the *Masters of Horror* series for Showtime and *Masters of Science Fiction* for NBC. She also produced the DVDs for *Hellboy: Animated*, the TV series *Eloise*, and Stan Lee's *Condor* and *Mosaic*.

Subtitles

Akihabara. A famous shopping district in Tokyo that once specialized in electronics but now specializes in fan products like anime, manga, and games.

AMV. "Anime music video;" any clip or compiled clips from anime that have been put to music that was not part of the original production.

Animanga. Japanese manga that uses images (or individual frames) from anime series, films or OVAs instead of standard drawn panels.

AV. "Adult video;" used to designate material prohibited for those under eighteen years of age.

Baka. Idiot.

Bara. "Men's love" or ML; a genre of anime or manga that focuses on male same-sex desire; unlike yaoi, bara is usually created by and for homosexual men.

Bishōjo, bishoujo. "Beautiful young girl"; anime and manga girl characters below university age and drawn in a cute, pretty style. Bishōjo characters are seen in almost all genres of anime and manga, especially in dating sims and visual novels, known as bishÿjo games, and harem anime and manga.

Bishōnen. "Beautiful youth (boy)"; an aesthetic that can be found in disparate areas in Asia: a young man whose beauty (and sexual appeal) transcends the boundary of sexual orientation; in anime or manga, a type of male character who would be considered androgynous or in some cases effeminate.

Cosplay. "Costume roleplay"; a term heavily associated with anime and manga fandom where participants don costumes and accessories to represent a specific character or idea; see also "kosupure."

Cyborg. A person or entity which is part human and part machine; an organism that has both artificial and natural systems.

Dōjin or doujin. Anime, manga, or computer games made nonprofessionally and self-published, usually by fans. Dōjinshi or doujinshi in particular refers to fan manga.

Ecchi. An anime or manga visual aesthetic or art style (rather than a type of plot) that has vague sexual content in the form of sexual humor and fan service for males, such as bare breasts, panty shots and girls in erotic positions; though this style often features nudity and suggestive imagery, there is no explicit sex.

18-kin. Material prohibited for those under eighteen years of age.

Gunpla. Both the vast amount of Gundam model kits produced by Bandai—and there have been hundreds upon hundreds of different kits produced over the years—and the building of these model kits.

Fan-sub, fansub. Short for "fan-subtitled;" a film that has been translated and subtitled by fans and then made available for viewing; the distribution of fan-subtitled content is controversial because it is a violation of copyright laws in most countries.

H. See "ecchi."

Hentai. In the West, this Japanese word refers to sexually explicit or pornographic comics and animation, particularly those that originate in Japan.

Josei. "Woman"; manga created mostly by women for late teenage and adult female audiences; stories tend to be about women's everyday experiences involving family, motherhood, even high school.

Jutsu. A technique or skill; for example, in *Naruto* the three jutsu are: genjutsu (illusion techniques), taijutsu (physical techniques), and ninjutsu (all other techniques).

Kami. Japanese word for the spirits within objects in the Shinto faith. In some instances, kami are personified deities, similar to the gods of ancient Greece or Rome. In other cases, such as those concerning the phenomenon of growth and natural objects, kami can refer to the spirits dwelling in trees or forces of nature.

Kanji. "Han characters"; Chinese characters that are used in the modern Japanese logographic writing system along with hiragana, katakana, Arabic numerals and the occasional Roman alphabet (rōmaji).

Kana. Syllabic Japanese scripts (or syllabograms) that include hiragana, katakana, and man'yōgana forms.

Katakana. "Fragmentary kana"; the simplest of the Japanese scripts, this type of syllabogram is most often used for the transcription of words from foreign languages.

Kodomo, kodomomuke. Anime for children of both genders.

Kosupure. Costume roleplay (see also "cosplay").

Ki (Dragon Ball) or **chakra** (Naruto). Names for the life force energy that is used to power superhuman martial arts techniques.

Lolicon, rorikon. A genre of manga and anime wherein childlike female characters are depicted in an erotic manner.

Mahō shōjo, mahou shoujo. "Magical girl"; a subgenre of shōjo, where the heroines get magical powers to fight against evil. Flashy costumes, wands, spells and action are a common element.

Mahō shōnen, mahou shounen. "Magical boy"; the opposite of mahō shōjo and less common, where the main male characters get magical powers.

Manga. "Fanciful pictures"; Japanese comics and graphic novels.

Mecha, meka. Genre of anime where characters wear huge mechanical suits in order to protect their bodies and fight battles. Mecha, also known as meka or mechs, are walking vehicles controlled by a pilot and are generally, though not necessarily, bipedal, with arms, hands, and fingers capable of grasping objects.

Min'yō, minyo. A genre of traditional Japanese folk music.

Moe. "Sprout"; a burning passion, or worse, a fetish, for some type of character or feature of a character. For example, "I have moe for girls with glasses," "I have forehead moe."

Otaku. A fan, especially a fanboy or fangirl of popular culture.

OVA or OAV. "Original Video Anime"; anime that is neither made for television nor theatrical film but released directly to the home market. These direct-to-video or direct-to-DVD releases are often maturely themed.

Posthuman. The perspective that technology has dramatically changed what it means to be human

Real Robot. Anime or manga where robots are more commonplace, often as a tool/weapons platform for the military. There are normally limits on the abilities of the robots—such as fuel, ammunition, or mechanical failures—that make them a bit more identifiable to the audience.

Samurai. "Those who serve;" military nobility of pre-industrial Japan with strong principles of honor and ethics.

Scanlation, scanslation. Manga that has been scanned and then had the original Japanese text replaced by text that has been translated into the distributor's language; this usually occurs with manga not available in the distributor's native language, and these unauthorized translations are most commonly found on the Internet. This is the manga counterpart to anime's fansub.

Seijin. Men's adult erotica.

Seinen. "Man"; anime and manga aimed at teenage boys and young men. It is generally more complicated and sophisticated than shÿnen anime, with more psychological and sexual elements, and puts more focus on plot rather than action (if the show is also under the Action genre, which it usually is). In its character development and relationship side, it is similar to shōjo, but is usually darker and more like the Drama genre.

Sentai. "Fighting team;" anime and manga that deals with superheroes and superhero teams, closely associated with the shōnen and kodomo genres.

Shōjo, shojo, shoujo. Girls' anime (aimed at a primarily elementary through high school female audience).

Shōnen, shonen, shounen. Boys' adventure (aimed at elementary and middle school male audience).

Shotacon. A genre of manga and anime wherein childlike male characters are depicted in an erotic manner.

Shōjo ai, shōjo-ai, shoujo ai. "Girls' love;" a subgenre of shōjo that focuses on the love between women; less explicit than yuri.

Shōnen ai, shōnen-ai, shounen ai. "Boys' love;" a subgenre of shōjo anime that focuses on gay male relationships, written primarily by and for female audiences; less sexually explicit than yaoi.

Super Robot. Anime or manga that includes a robot with fantastic weapons or powers. Often with some mystical or legendary origins (or origins of the pilots), they tend to fall into "monster of the week" formats. One example is Beast King GoLion known in the USA as Voltron: Defender of the Universe.

Tsuyoku naritai. "I want to become stronger;" a common refrain in tournament anime to indicate a character's pursuit of perfection.

Yaoi. "Boys love"; an acronym for "yama nashi, ochi nashi, imi nashi" (no climax, no point, no meaning), this term refers to a form of shōnen ai that is more sexually explicit; usually created by women for women and featuring bishÿnen.

Yōkai. A demon, spirit, or monster; a class of preternatural creatures in Japanese folklore ranging from the evil oni (ogre) to the mischievous kitsune (fox) or snow woman Yuki-onna. Their motives and agendas are often completely incomprehensible to human beings. Some possess part animal and part human features (for instance Kappa and Tengu), and they generally have a sort of spiritual or supernatural power, so encounters with human beings tend to be dangerous. Yōkai that have the ability to shape-shift are called obake.

Yūrei. Figures in Japanese folklore thought to be spirits kept from a peaceful life, analogous to Western legends of ghosts.

Yuri. "Girls love;" the genre and content that involves love between women in manga, anime, and related Japanese media; the artwork and stories tend to be more sexually explicit than shōjo ai.

Making Of . . .

Adorno, Theodor. 1997. *Aesthetic Theory*. Translated by Robert Hullot-Kentor. Minneapolis: University of Minnesota Press.

Aida, Yū. 2002. *Gunslinger Girl*. Vol. 1. Tokyo: ASCII Media Works.

———. 2003. *Gunslinger Girl*. Vol. 2. Tokyo: ASCII Media Works.

Animage. May 2001. An Interview with Hayao Miyazaki. Translated by Ryoko Toyama. www.nausicaa.net/miyazaki/interviews/sen.html.

Aquinas, Thomas. *Summa Theologica*. Fathers of the English Dominican Province translation.

Arendt, Hannah. 1958. *The Human Condition*. Chicago: University of Chicago Press.

———. 1963. *Eichmann in Jeruselum: A Report on the Banality of Evil*. New York: Viking.

Aries, Philippe. 1962. *Centuries of Childhood*. New York: Penguin.

Aristotle. 1924. *Metaphysics*. Translated by W.D. Ross. New York: Oxford University Press.

———. 2004 [1893]. *Nicomachean Ethics*. Translated by F.H. Peters. New York: Barnes and Noble Books.

———. *Poetics*. 1997. Translated by Malcolm Heath. New York: Penguin Classics.

———. 1984. Politics. *In The Complete Works of Aristotle: The Revised Oxford Translation, Volume Two*. Edited by Jonathan Barnes. Translated by Benjamin Jowett. Princeton: Princeton University Press.

Atkins, Thomas R. 1976. Images of Violence. In Thomas R. Atkins, ed., *Graphic Violence on the Screen*. (New York: Simon and Schuster), pp. 1–18.

Augustine. 1961. *Confessions*. Translated by R.S. Pine-Coffin. New York: Penguin Classics, 1961.

Badmington, Neil, ed. 2000. *Posthumanism*. New York: Palgrave.

————. 2001. Pod Almighty!; or, Humanism, Posthumanism, and the Strange Case of *Invasion of the Body Snatchers*. *Textual Practice* 15:1 (March 2001), pp. 5–22.

————. 2004. Post, Oblique, Human. *Theology and Sexuality* 10:2 (March 2004), pp. 56–64.

————. 2003. Theorizing Posthumanism. *Cultural Critique* 53 (Winter), pp. 10–27.

Bakhtin, M.M. 1981. *The Dialogic Imagination*. Edited by Michael Holquist. Translated by Caryl Emerson and Michael Holquist. Austin: University of Texas Press.

Balsamo, Anne. 1996. *Technologies of the Gendered Body: Reading Cyborg Women*. Durham: Duke University Press.

Bentham, Jeremy, and J.S. Mill. 2003. *The Classic Utilitarians: Bentham and Mill*. Edited by John Trover. Indianapolis: Hackett.

Berkowitz, Leonard. 1965. Some Aspects of Observed Aggression. *Journal of Personality and Social Psychology* 2, pp. 336–359.

The Holy Bible. Various editions.

Bock, Felicia G. 1948. Elements in the Development of Japanese Folk Song. *Western Folklore*, 7:4 (October), pp. 356–369.

Bolton, Christopher A. 2002. From Wooden Cyborgs to Celluloid Souls: Mechanical Bodies in Anime and Japanese Puppet Theatre. *Positions* 10:3 (Winter), pp. 729–771.

Boulter, Michael. 2002. *Extinction: Evolution and the End of Man*. New York: Columbia University Press, 2002.

Boxer, C.R. 1967. *The Christian Century in Japan*, 1549–1650. Second edition. Berkeley: University of California Press.

Brasher, Brenda E. 1996. Thoughts on the Status of the Cyborg: On Technological Socialization and Its Link to the Religious Function of Popular Culture. *Journal of the American Academy of Religion* 64:4 (Winter), 809–830.

Burke, Phyllis. 1996. *Gender Shock: Exploding the Myths of Male and Female*. New York: Anchor.

Bushman, B.J., and L.R. Huesmann. 2001. Effects of Televised Violence on Aggression. *Handbook of Children and the Media*. Edited by D.G. Singer and J.L. Singer. Thousand Oaks: Sage.

Calvin, John. *Commentary on the Book of Psalms*. <www.ccel.org/ccel/calvin/calcom08.xxi.iv.html>.

Campbell, Joseph. 1976. *The Masks of God: Oriental Mythology*. Harmondsworth: Penguin.

Cavallaro, Dani. 2000. *Cyberpunk and Cyberculture: Science Fiction and the work of William Gibson*. New Jersey: Athlone.

————. 2006. *The Cinema of Mamoru Oshii: Fantasy, Technology and Politics*. Jefferson: McFarland.

————. 2007. *Anime Intersections: Tradition and Innovation in Theme and Technique*. Jefferson: McFarland.

Chow, Rey. 2006. Sacrifice, Mimesis, and the Theorizing of Victimhood (A Speculative Essay). *Representations* 94 (Spring).

Clark, Andy. 2003. *Natural-Born Cyborgs: Minds, Technologies, and the Future of Human Intelligence.* Oxford: Oxford University Press.

Clark, Andy, and David Chalmers. 2002. The Extended Mind. In *Philosophy of Mind: Classical and Contemporary Readings,* edited by David J. Chalmers (Oxford: Oxford University Press).

Clausewitz, Carl von. 1976. *On War.* Translated by Michael Howard and Peter Paret. Princeton: Princeton University Press.

Clifford, W.K. 1879. The Ethics of Belief. In *Lectures and Essays by the Late William Kingdon Clifford,* edited by Leslie Stephen and Frederick Pollock (London: Macmillan, 1879), pp. 177–211.

Daniels, Inge Maria. 2003. Scooping, Raking, Beckoning Luck: Luck, Agency and the Interdependence of People and Things in Japan. *Journal of the Royal Anthropological Institute* 9:4 (December), pp. 619–638.

Darwin, Charles. 2001. *Darwin: A Norton Critical Edition.* Third edition. Edited by Philip Appleman. New York: Norton.

Davies, Tony. 2008. *Humanism.* New York: Routledge.

Dawkins, Richard. 2006. *The Selfish Gene.* New York: Oxford University Press.

Dennett, Daniel. 1992. The Self as the Center of Narrative Gravity. In *Self and Consciousness: Multiple Perspectives,* edited by Frank Kessel, P. Cole, and D. Johnson (Hillsdale: Erlbaum), pp. 103–115.

Descartes, René. 1984. *Principles of Philosophy.* Translated by R.P. Miller. New York: Springer.

———. 1998. *Discourse on Method.* Indianapolis: Hackett.

Diamond, Milton. 1999. The Effects of Pornography: An International Perspective. *International Journal of Law and Psychiatry* 22:1, pp. 1–22.

Elshtain, Jean Bethke, ed. 1993. *Just War Theory.* New York: New York University Press.

Emerson, Caryl. 2000. *The First Hundred Years of Mikhail Bakhtin.* Princeton: Princeton University Press.

Engels, Friedrich. 1954. *The Dialectic of Nature.* Second edition. Translated by Clemens Dutt. Moscow: Progress.

Eusebius, *Praeparatio Evangelica.*

Feshbach, Seymour. 1955. The Drive-Reducing Function of Fantasy Behaviour. *Journal of Abnormal and Social Psychology 50,* p. 3–11.

Fukuyama, Francis. 2002. *Our Posthuman Future.* New York: Picador.

Gehlen, Arnold. 2003. A Philosophical-Anthropological Perspective on Technology. In *Philosophy of Technology: The Technological Condition—An Anthology,* edited by Robert Scharff and Val Dusek (Malden: Blackwell), pp. 213–220.

Gerbner, George, and Larry Gross. 1976. Living with Television: The Violence Profile. *Journal of Communication.*

Gibson, William. 1984. *Neuromancer.* New York: Ace.

Gill, Tom. 1998. Transformational Magic: Some Japanese Super-Heroes and Monsters. *The Worlds of Japanese Popular Culture: Gender, Shifting Boundaries, and Global Cultures,* edited by D.P. Martinez (Cambridge: Cambridge University Press), pp. 33–55.

Graham, Elaine. 2002. *Representations of the Post-Human: Monsters, Aliens, and Others in Popular Culture.* New Jersey: Rutgers University Press.

———. 2004. Post-Human Conditions. *Theology and Sexuality* 10:2 (March), pp. 10–32.

Gray, Chris Hables. 2002. *Cyborg Citizen.* New York: Routledge.

Gribbin, John. 1995. *Schrödinger's Kittens and the Search for Reality.* Boston: Little, Brown.

Halberstam, Judith, and Ira Livingston, eds. 1995. *Posthuman Bodies.* Bloomington: Indiana University Press.

Hall, Stuart. 1973. *Encoding and Decoding in the Television Discourse.* Birmingham: University of Birmingham Press.

Haraway, Donna. 1985. A Manifesto for Cyborgs: Science, Technology, and Socialist Feminism in the 1980s. *Socialist Review* 80, pp. 64–107.

———. 1991a. *Simians, Cyborgs, and Women: The Reinvention of Nature* (New York: Routledge).

———. 1991b. *A Cyborg Manifesto: Science, Technology, and Socialist-Feminism in the Late Twentieth Century.* In Haraway 1991a, pp. 149–181.

———. 2001. *When Species Meet.* Minneapolis: University of Minnesota Press.

———. 2004. A Manifesto for Cyborgs: Science, Technology, and Socialist Feminism in the 1980s. In *The Haraway Reader* (New York: Routledge), pp. 7–46.

Haskell, Molly. 1987. *From Reverence to Rape: The Treatment of Women in the Movies.* Chicago: University Of Chicago Press.

Hatano, Yoshiro, and Tsuguo Shimazaki. 2009. Japan. *The International Encyclopedia of Sexuality* 7 (June), <www2.hu-berlin.de/sexology/IES/japan.html>.

Hayles, N. Katherine. 1999. *How We Became Posthuman: Virtual Bodies in Cybernetics, Literature, and Informatics.* Chicago: University of Chicago Press.

———. 2004. Flesh and Metal: Reconfiguring the Mindbody in Virtual Environments. In *Data Made Flesh: Embodying Information,* edited by Robert Michell and Phillip Thurtle (New York: Routledge).

Heidegger, Martin. 1962. *Being and Time.* Translated by Richard Marquand and Edward Robinson. Oxford: Blackwell/San Francisco: Harper Collins.

———. 1977. *The Question Concerning Technology and Other Essays.* Translated by William Lovitt. New York: Harper and Row.

————. 1993. The Question Concerning Technology. In *Basic Writings,* edited by David Krell. Revised and expanded edition (San Francisco: Harper Collins), pp. 311–341.

————. 2000. *Introduction to Metaphysics.* Translated by Gregory Fried and Richard Polt. New Haven: Yale University Press.

Hick, John. 1989. *An Interpretation of Religion.* New Haven: Yale University Press.

Hokusai, Katsuskika. 1814. *Diver and Two Octopi.* Kinoe no komatsu.

Hollinger, Veronica. 1991. Cybernetic Deconstructions: Cyberpunk and Postmodernsim. *Storming the Reality Studio.* Edited by Larry McCaffery. Durham: Duke University Press.

Honeyman, Susan. 2006. Manufactured Agency and the Playthings Who Dream It for Us. *Children's Literature Association Quarterly* 31:2, pp. 109–131.

Horkheimer, Max, and Theodor Adorno. 2002. *Dialectic of Enlightenment: Philosophic Fragments.* Translated by Edmund Jephcott. Stanford: Stanford University Press.

Hutchins, Edwin. 1995. *Cognition in the Wild.* Cambridge: MIT Press.

Ishinomori, Shōtarō. 1964–1981. *Cyborg 009* AKA *Saibōgu 009.* Tokyo: Shōnen Gahōsha.

James, William. 1897. *The Will to Believe and Other Essays in Popular Philosophy.* Longmans, Green.

————. 1967. *The Writings of William James.* New York: Random House.

Janicaud, Dominique. 2005. *On the Human Condition.* Translated by Eileen Brennan. New York: Routledge.

Joos, E., H.D. Zeh, C. Kiefer, D. Giulini, J. Kupsch, and I.-O. Stamatescu. 2003. *Decoherence and the Appearance of a Classical World in Quantum Theory.* Second edition. New York: Springer.

Joy, Bill. 2000. Why the Future Doesn't Need Us. *Wired* 8:4, pp. 238–246.

Kanno, Aya. 2001. *Soul Rescue.* Hakusensha.

Kant, Immanuel. 2008. *Critique of Pure Reason.* Edited by Marcus Weigelt. Translated by Marcus Weigelt and Max Muller. New York: Penguin Classics.

Kasulis, Thomas P. 2004. *Shinto: The Way Home.* Honolulu: University of Hawaii Press.

Kawai, Chigusa. 2000–present. *La Esperanza.* Shinshokan.

Kayama, Rika, and Bandai Character Kenkyūjo. 2001. *87% no Nihonjin ga kyarakutā o suki na riyū.* Tokyo: Gakushū kenkyūsha.

Kelts, Rolland. 2006. *Japanamerica: How Japanese Pop Culture Has Invaded the US.* New York: Palgrave.

Kenji Kawai Official Site. 2009a. The Ballade of Puppets: Flowers Grieve and Fall. <www.kenjikawai.com/innocence_lyrics_02_e.pdf>.

————. 2009b. The Ballade of Puppets: The Ghost Awaits in the World Beyond. <www.kenjikawai.com/innocence_lyrics_10_e.pdf>.

————. 2009c. Kenji Kawai's Café. <www.kenjikawai.com/cafe_e.html>.

Kieval, Hillel J. 1997. Pursuing the Golem of Prague: Jewish Culture and the Invention of a Tradition. *Modern Judaism* 17:1 (February), p. 1–23.

Kinsella, Sharon. 1995. Cuties in Japan. In *Women, Media, and Consumption in Japan*, edited by Lise Skov and Brian Moeran. (Honolulu: University of Hawai'i Press), pp. 220–254.

———. 2002. What's Behind the Fetishism of Japanese School Uniforms? *Fashion Theory: The Journal of Dress, Body, and Culture* 6:2, pp. 215–237.

Kishiro, Yukito. 1990–1995. *Battle Angel Alita* AKA *Gunnm*. Tokyo: Shūeisha.

Koestler, Arthur. 1967. *The Ghost in the Machine*. London: Hutchinson; Chicago: Regnery.

Kotani, Mari. 2005. *Tekuno-Goshikku*. Tokyo: Shūeisha.

Krupp, Anthony. 2009. *Reason's Children: Childhood in Early Modern Philosophy*. Lewisburg: Bucknell University Press.

Kull, Anne. 2002. Speaking Cyborg: Technoculture and Technonature. *Zygon* 37:2 (June), pp. 279–287.

Kurzweil, Ray. 2005. *The Singularity Is Near: When Humans Transcend Biology*. New York: Viking; New York: Penguin, 2006.

Leslie, John. 1990. Is the End of the World Nigh? *Philosophical Quarterly* 40, pp. 65–72.

Lewis, C.S. 2000. Christian Reunion: An Anglican Speaks to Roman Catholics. *C.S. Lewis: Essay Collection and Other Short Pieces*. Edited by Lesley Walmsley. London: HarperCollins.

Lewontin, R.C. 1991. *Biology as Ideology*. New York: Harper.

Lewontin, R.C., Steven Rose, and Leon Kamin. 1984. *Not in Our Genes: Biology, Ideology, and Human Nature*. New York: Pantheon.

Locke, John. *Two Treatises of Government*. <www.gutenberg.org/ebooks/7370>.

Lucretius. *On the Nature of Things*.

Lunning, Frenchy, ed. 2008. *Mechademia 3: Limits of the Human*. Minneapolis: University of Minnesota Press.

MacWilliams, Mark. 2008. *Introduction to Japanese Visual Culture: Explorations in the World of Manga and Anime* (Armonk: Sharpe).

Majiko. 2004. *St. Lunatic High School*. Kadokawa Shoten.

Manovich, Lev. 2006. Visual Technologies as Cognitive Prosthetics: A Short History of the Externalization of the Mind. In *The Prosthetic Impulse: From a Posthuman Present to a Biocultural Future*, edited by Marquand Smith and Joanne Morra (Cambridge: MIT Press).

Martinez, D.P., ed. 1998. *The Worlds of Japanese Popular Culture: Gender, Shifting Boundaries, and Global Cultures*. Cambridge: Cambridge University Press.

Marx, Karl. 1998. Economic and Philosophic Manuscripts of 1844. *Economic and Philosophic Manuscripts of 1844 and the Communist*

Manifesto, by Karl Marx and Frederick Engels. Translated by Martin Milligan. Amherst: Prometheus.

Masubuchi, Sōichi. 1994. *Kawaii shōkōgun*. Tokyo: Nihon hōsō shuppan kyōkai.

Mazlish, Bruce. 1993. *The Fourth Discontinuity: The Co-Evolution of Humans and Machines*. New Haven: Yale University Press.

McCarthy, Helen. 1999. *Hayao Miyazaki Master of Japanese Animation*. Berkeley: Stone Bridge.

McLelland, Mark. 2005. *Queer Japan from the Pacific War to the Internet Age*. Lanham: Rowman and Littlefield.

McVeigh, Brian. J. 2000. *Wearing Ideology: State, Schooling, and Self-Presentation in Japan*. Oxford: Berg.

———. 2002. *Japanese Higher Education as Myth*. Armonk: Sharpe.

Mes, Tom. 2002. Hayao Miyazaki Interview. *Midnight Eye* (January), <www.midnighteye.com/interviews/hayao_miyazaki.shtml>.

Midgley, Mary. 2001. *Science and Poetry*. New York: Routledge.

———. 2002. *Evolution as a Religion*. New York: Routledge.

Milgram, S. 1974. The Perils of Obedience. *Harper's Magazine*. Minneapolis: Minneapolis Star and Tribune Company.

Milgram, Stanley. 1966. Personality Characteristics Associated with Obedience and Defiance Toward Authoritative Command. *Journal of Experimental Research in Personality*. New York: Academic Press Inc.

Milgram, Stanley. 1974. *Obedience to Authority: An Experimental View*. New York: HarperCollins.Miyazaki, Hayao. 2004. *Nausicaa of the Valley of the Wind*. Volumes 1–7. San Francisco: Viz Media.

Moravec, Hans. 1998. *Robot: Mere Machine to Transcendent Mind*. Oxford: Oxford University Press.

Morgan, Michael. 2009. Audience Research: Cultivation Analysis. *The Museum of Broadcast Communications* (June), <www.museum.tv/archives/etv/A/htmlA/audienceresec/audienceresec.htm>.

Morgan, Robin. 1980. Theory and Practice: Pornography and Rape. In *Take Back the Night: Women on Pornography*, edited by L. Lederer (New York: Morrow), pp. 134–140.

Nakane, Chie. 1983. *Tate shakai no ningen kankei*. Tokyo: Kōdansha.

Nanase, Aoi. 2003. *Angel-Dust Neo*. Tokyo: Kadokawa-Shoten.

Napier, Susan J. 1998. Vampires, Psychic Girls, Flying Women, and Sailor Scouts: Four Faces of the Young Female in Japanese Popular Culture. In *The Worlds of Japanese Popular Culture: Gender, Shifting Boundaries, and Global Cultures*, edited by D.P. Martinez (Cambridge: Cambridge University Press), pp. 91–109.

———. 2005a. *Anime From Akira to Howl's Moving Castle: Experiencing Contemporary Japanese Animation*. Updated edition. New York: Palgrave.

————. 2005b. The Problem of Existence in Japanese Animation. *Proceedings of the American Philosophical Society* 149:1 (March), pp. 72–79.

Noble, David F. 1999. *The Religion of Technology*. New York: Penguin.

Ogi, Fusami. 2001a. Beyond *Shoujo*, Blending Gender: Subverting the Homogendered World in *Shoujo Manga* (Japanese Comics for Girls). *International Journal of Comic Art* 3:2, pp. 151–161.

————. 2001b. Gender Insubordination in Japanese Comics (Manga) for Girls. In *Illustrating Asia: Comics, Humor Magazines, and Picture Books*, edited by John. A. Lent (Honolulu: University of Hawai'i Press), pp. 171–186.

————. 2003. Female Subjectivity and Shoujo (Girls) Manga (Japanese Comics): *Shoujo* in Ladies' Comics and Young Ladies' Comics. *Journal of Popular Culture* 36:4, pp. 780–803.

Ono, Sokyo. 1962. *Shinto: The Kami Way*. Tokyo: Tuttle.

Orbaugh, Sharalyn. 2003. Busty Battlin' Babes: The Evolution of the *Shōjo* in 1990s Visual Culture. In *Gender and Power in the Japanese Visual Field*, edited by Joshua S. Mostow, Norman Bryson, and Marybeth Graybill (Honolulu: University of Hawai'i Press), pp. 201–228.

Otomo, Katsuhiro. 1992. *Memories*. New York: Epic Comics.

Ōtsuka, Eiji. 1991. Kawaii no tanjō. In *Shōjo zasshi ron* (Tokyo: Shoseki), pp. 85–102.

Pascal, Blaise. 1941. *Pensées*. Translated by W.F. Trotter. New York: Modern Library.

Peperrell, Robert. 2003. *The Posthuman Condition: Consciousness Beyond the Brain*. Portland: Intellect Books.

————. 2005. Posthumans and Extended Experience. *Journal of Evolution and Technology*. 14:1 (April), pp. 27–41.

Perper, Timothy, and Martha Cornog. 2002. Eroticism for The Masses: Japanese Manga Comics and Their Assimilation into the US. *Sexuality and Culture* 6:1, pp. 3–126.

Peters, Mischa. 2003. Exit Meat: Digital Bodies in a Virtual World. In *New Media: Theories and Practices of Digitextuality*, edited by Anne Everett and John T. Caldwell (New York: Routledge).

Pinker, Steven. 1999. *How the Mind Works*. New York: Norton.

Plato. *Cratylus*.

————. *Phaedo*.

————. *The Republic*.

Plutarch. *Lives*.

Potolsky, Matthew. 2003. *Mimesis*. New York: Routledge.

Regan, Richard J. 1996. *Just War: Principles and Cases*. Washington, DC: Catholic University Press.

Richie, Donald. 2003. *The Image Factory: Fads and Fashions in Japan*. London: Reaktion.

Ruh, Brian. 2004. *Stray Dog of Anime: The Films of Mamoru Oshii*. New York: Palgrave Macmillan.

Ryle, Gilbert. 1949. *The Concept of Mind*. Chicago: University of Chicago Press.

Sartre, Jean-Paul. 2007. *Existentialism Is a Humanism*. Edited by John Kulka. New Haven: Yale University Press.

Sasakibara Gō. 2004. *'Bishōjo' no gendai-shi*. Tokyo: Kōdansha.

Sato, Kumiko. 2004. How Information Technology Has (Not) Changed Feminism and Japanism: Cyberpunk in the Japanese Context. *Comparative Literature Studies* 41:3, pp. 335–355.

Schattschneider, Ellen. 2001. Buy Me a Bride: Death and Exchange in Northern Japanese Bride-Doll Marriage. *American Ethnologist* 28:4 (November), pp. 854–880.

Schodt, Frederik L. 2007. *The Astro Boy Essays: Osamu Tezuka, Mighty Atom, and the Manga-Anime Revolution*. Berkeley: Stone Bridge.

Searle, John. 1980. Minds, Brains, and Programs. *Behavioral and Brain Sciences* 3:3, 417–457.

Sheffler, Samuel. 1988. *Consequentialism and Its Critics*. Oxford: Oxford University Press.

Shigematsu, Setsu. 1999. Dimensions of Desire: Sex, Fantasy, and Fetish in Japanese Comics. In *Themes and Issues in Asian Cartooning: Cute, Cheap, Mad and Sexy*, edited by John A. Lent (Bowling Green: Bowling Green State University Popular Press), pp. 127–163.

Shimamura, Mari. 1991. *Fanshii no kenkyū: 'kawaii' ga hito, mono, kane o shihai suru*. Tokyo: Nesco.

Short, Sue. 2005. *Cyborg Cinema and Contemporary Subjectivity*. New York: Palgrave Macmillan.

Singer, P.W. 2005. *Children at War*. New York: Pantheon.

Signorielli, Nancy. 2005. *Violence in the Media: A Reference Handbook*. Santa Barbara: ABC-Clio.

Shirow, Masamune. 1991. *Ghost in the Shell*. Tokyo: Kōdansha.

Smith, Adam. 1984 [1759]. *An Inquiry Into the Nature and Causes of the Wealth of Nations*. Edited by Roy Campbell and Andrew Skinner. Indianapolis: Liberty Fund.

Soper, Kate. 1986. *Humanism and Anti-Humanism*. La Salle: Open Court.

Sugimoto, Yoshio. 1997. *An Introduction To Japanese Society*. Cambridge: Cambridge University Press.

Suzuki, Yasushi. 2008. *Purgatory Kabuki*. Dr. Master Productions.

Tamura, Yumi. 2002. *7Seeds*. Tokyo: Shogakukan.

Taussig, Michael. 1993. *Mimesis and Alterity: A Particular History of the Senses*. New York: Routledge.

Tezuka, Osamu. 1966. *Ode to Kirihito*. Tokyo: Shogakukan.

Thurtle, Phillip and Robert Mitchell. 2004. Data Made Flesh: The Material Poeisis of Informatics. In *Data Made Flesh: Embodying Information*, edited by Robert Michell and Phillip Thurtle (New York: Routledge).

Toffoletti, Kim. 2007. *Cyborgs and Barbie Dolls*. London: Tauris.

Tomino, Yoshiyuki. 2004. *Mobile Suit Gundam: Awakening, Escalation, and Confrontation*. Translated by Frederik Schodt. Berkeley: Stone Bridge Press.

Tress, Daryl McGowan. 1998. Aristotle's Children. In *The Philosopher's Child: Critical Perspectives in the Western Tradition*, edited by Susan M. Turner and Gareth B. Mathews (Rochester: University of Rochester Press).

Truman, Harry S. 1945. Announcement of an Atomic Bombing on Hiroshima, August 6th, 1945. *Papers of the Presidents*. Harry S. Truman, 1945, pp. 197–200.

Tsuda, Mikiyo. 2005. *Puri Puri*. AKA *Princess Princess*. Akita Shoten.

Turing, Alan. 1950. Computing Machinery and Intelligence. *Mind* 59, pp. 433–460.

Vallen, Mark and Jeannine Thorpe. 2002. Spirited Away: Miyazaki at the Hollywood Premiere. Press Conference Q&A Transcript, September 13th. <www.theblackmoon.com/Deadmoon/spiritedaway.html>.

Varela, Franciso, Evan Thompson, and Eleanor Rosch. 1991. *The Embodied Mind*. Cambridge: MIT Press.

Virgil. *Aeneid*.

Walzer, Michael. 2006. *Just and Unjust Wars*. Fourth edition. New York: Basic Books.

Weisman, Alan. 2007. *The World Without Us*. New York: St. Martin's Press.

Wikipedia. 2009. Ghost in the Shell (Film). <http://en.wikipedia.org/wiki/Ghost_in_the_Shell_%28film%29#Choral_song>.

Wilks, Jon. 2009. The (Almost) Complete Japanzine Dictionary of Japan Sex. *SeekJapan.jp*. (June 7th). <www.seekjapan.jp/article1/744/The+(Almost)+Complete+Japanzine+Dictionary+of+Japan+Sex>.

Wood, Robin. 1979. An Introduction to the American Horror Film: Part I: Repression, The Other, The Monster; Part II: Return of the Repressed; Part III; The Reactionary Wing. In *The American Nightmare: Essays on the Horror Film*, edited by Richard Lippe and Robin Wood (Toronto: Festival of Festivals), pp. 7–28.

Yamada, Keiko. 1994. *Go Go Heaven*. Akita Shoten.

Yamakage, Motohisa. 2006. *The Essence of Shinto*. Tokyo: Kodansha.

Yanagawa, Yoshihiro. 2001. *Nemuri Kyoshiro*. Weekly Comic Bunch.

Yomota, Inuhiko. 2006. *'Kawaii'-ron*. Tokyo: Chikuma shobō.

Yoneyama, Shoko. 1999. *The Japanese High School: Silence And Resistance*. London: Routledge.

Easter Eggs

Advancer Tina. Kan Fukumoto. Green Bunny, 1996.

Akira. Katsuhiro Otomo. Tokyo Movie Shinsha, 1988.

Always My Santa. Noriyoshi Nakaura TNK, 2005.

Angel Sanctuary. Kiyoko Sayama. Bandai Visual, 2000.

Appleseed. Shinji Aramaki. Toho, 2004.

Appleseed Ex Machina. Shinji Aramaki. Micott and Bassara; Digital Frontier, 2007.

Apocalypse Zero. Toshihiro Hirano (AKA Toshiki Hirano). Victor Entertainment, 1996.

Armitage III AKA *Armitage the Third*. Director Hiroyuki Ochi. AIC; Pioneer LDC, 1994.

Armitage III: Dual Matrix AKA *Armitage the Third: Dual Matrix*. Director Katsuhito Akiyama. Pioneer LDC, 2002.

Armitage III: Poly-Matrix AKA *Armitage the Third: Poly-Matrix*. Director Hiroyuki Ochi. AIC, 1997.

Armored Trooper VOTOMS. Ryōsuke Takahashi. Sunrise, 1983–1984.

Astro Boy AKA *Tetsuwan Atomu*. Osamu Tezuka. Mushi Productions, 1963–1966. Broadcast in the United States by NBC Enterprises, 1963–1966.

Astro Boy. Nobur Ishiguro. Tezuka Productions, 1983.

Astro Boy AKA *Astroboy*. David Bowers. Endgame Entertainment; Imagi Animation Studios, 2009.

Babel II. Shun-ichi Yukimuro. Toei Animation, 1973.

Barefoot Gen AKA *Hadashi No Gen*. Mori Masaki. Madhouse, 1983.

Battle Angel AKA *Gunnm*. Hiroshi Fukutomi. Madhouse, 1993.

Berserk. Naohito Takahashi. OLM, 2997–1998.

Bible Black: Begins. Sho Hanebu and Kazuyuki Honda. Milky Studio, 2001–2003.

Bible Black: New Testament. Hamuo. Milky Studio, 2004–2008.

Bible Black: Origins. Hamuo. Milky Studio, 2002.

The Big O. Kazuyoshi Katayama. Sunrise, 1999–2000.

Big Wars. Issei Kuma and Toshifumi Takizawa. Magic Bus, 1993.

Bleach. Noriyuki Abe. Studio Pierrot, 2004–present.

La Blue Girl. Kan Fukumoto. Daiel Co. Ltd., 1992–1993.

Chobits. Morio Asaka. Madhouse, 2002.

Chrno Crusade. Yū Kō. Gonzo, 2003.

Cream Lemon Part 4: Pop Chaser. Hiroyuki Kitakubo. Fairy Dust, 1985.

Cyborg 009 AKA *Saibōgu 009*. Yūgo Serikawa. Tōei Animation, 1966.

D-Grayman. Osamu Nabeshima. TMS Entertainment, 2006.

Demon-Beast Phalanx AKA *Majū Sensen*. Shunji Ôga. Animate Film, 1990.

Demon Lord Dante. Kenichi Maejima. Dynamic Planning, 2002.

Desert Punk. Takayuki Inagaki. Gonzo, 2004–2005.

Devil May Cry. Shin Itagaki. Madhouse Studios, 2007.

Devilman. Masayuki Akihi and Tomoharu Katsumata. Toei Animation, 1972–1973.

Dragon Ball. Daisuke Nishio and Minoru Okazaki. Toei Animation, 1986–1989.

Dragon Ball Z. Daisuke Nishio. Toei Animation,1989–1996.

Earthian. Yun Kōga. J.C. Staff, 1989.

Eitoman AKA *8 Man* AKA *Eightman*. Haruyuki Kawajima. Eiken/TCJ, 1963–1964.

Elfen Lied. Mamoru Kanbe. ARMS, 2004.

The End of Evangelion. See *Neon Genesis Evangelion: The End of Evangelion*.

Evangelion: Death and Rebirth. See *Neon Genesis Evangelion: Death and Rebirth*.

Fate/Stay Night. Datto Nishiwaki. Studio Deen, 2006.

Fooly Cooly AKA *FLCL*. Kazuya Tsurumaki. Gainax; Production I.G, 2000–2001.

Fullmetal Alchemist. Seiji Mizushima. Bones, 2003–2004.

Fullmetal Alchemist: Conqueror of Shambala. Seiji Mizushima. Shochiku Film, 2005.

Galaxy Express 999 AKA *Ginga Tetsudō 999*. Rintarō. Tōei Animation, 1979.

Gankutsuō AKA *Gankutsuou*. Mahiro Maeda. Gonzo, 2004–2005.

Genma Taisen AKA *Harmagedon*. Rintaro. Madhouse, 1983.

Ghost in the Shell. Mamoru Oshii. Production I.G, 1995.

Ghost in the Shell 2: Innocence. Mamoru Oshii. Toho, 2004.

Ghost in the Shell: Stand Alone Complex. Kenji Kamiyama. Production I.G, 2002–2003.

Ghost Sweeper Mikami. Atsutoshi Umezawa. Toei Animation, 1993.

Gilgamesh. Masahiko Murata. Group TAC, 2003–2004.

Golgo 13: The Professional. Osamu Dezaki. Tokyo Movie Shinsha, 1983.

Grave of the Fireflies. Isao Takahata. Toho, 1988.

Gundam. See *Mobile Suit Gundam* and *Zeta Gundam.*

Gunslinger Girl [Season 1]. Morio Asaka. Madhouse, 2003–2004.

Harmagedon. See *Genma Taisen.*

Hellsing. Umanosuke Iida. Gonzo, 2001–2002.

Highlander: The Search For Vengeance. Yoshiaki Kawajiri. Madhouse Studios, 2007.

Hikaru no Go. Tetsuya Endo. Studio Pierrot, 2001–2003.

Holy Virgins. F.A.I. International, 2001.

Howl's Moving Castle. Hayao Miyazaki. Toho, 2004.

Innocence. See *Ghost in the Shell 2.*

Jeanne, the Kamikaze Thief. See *Kamikaze Kaito Jeanne.*

Kamikaze Kaito Jeanne AKA *Phantom-Thief Jeanne.* Toei Animation, 1999.

Kiki's Delivery Service. Hayao Miyazaki. Toei Animation, 1989.

Legend of the Overfiend. Hideki Takayama. West Cape; Team Mu, 1987–1995.

Lolita Anime. Kuni Toniro, Mickey Masuda, Mickey Soda and R. Ching. Wonder Kids, 1984–1985.

Magnetic Rose (Part I of the feature film, *Memories*). Kōji Morimoto. Toho, 1995.

Maria-sama ga Miteru AKA *The Virgin Mary Is Watching* AKA *Maria Watches Over Us.* Yukihiro Matsushita. Studio Deen, 2004.

Memories. Kōji Morimoto, Tensai Okamura, Katsuhiro Otomo. Toho, 1995.

Metropolis. Rintaro. Toho, 2002.

Mobile Suit Gundam. Yoshiyuki Tomino. Sunrise, 1979–1980.

Mobile Suit Gundam: 0083 Stardust Memory. Mitsuko Kase and Takashi Imanishi. Sunrise, 1991–1992.

Mobile Suit Gundam: 08th MS Team. Takeyuki Kanda and Umanosuke Iida. Sunrise, 1996–1999.

Mobile Suit Gundam: Char's Counterattack. Yoshiyuki Tomino. Sunrise, 1988.

My Neighbor Totoro. Hayao Miyazaki. Toho, 1988.

Naruto. Hayato Date. Studio Pierrot, 2002–2007.

Naruto: Shippuden. Hayato Date. Studio Pierrot. 2007–present.

Nausicaa of the Valley of the Wind. Hayao Miyazaki. Toei, 1984.

Neon Genesis Evangelion. Hideaki Anno. Gainax; Tatsunoko, 1995–1996.

Neon Genesis Evangelion: The End of Evangelion. Hideaki Anno. Toei Animation, 1997.

Neon Genesis Evangelion: Death and Rebirth. Hideaki Anno, Masayuki and Kazuya Tsurumaki. Toei Animation, 1997.

Night Shift Nurses. Nao Okezawa. Seven Arcs, 2000.

Ninja Resurrection. Yasunori Urata. Phoenix Entertainment, 1998.

Ninja Scroll. Yoshiaki Kawajiri. Madhouse, 1993.

One Piece. Konosuke Uda. Toei Animation, 1999–present.

One-Pound Gospel. Makura Saki. Studio Gallop, 1988.

Paprika. Satoshi Kon. Madhouse; Rainbow SPA. 2006.

Paranoia Agent. Satoshi Kon. Madhouse, 2004.

Perfect Blue. Satoshi Kon, Director, 1998

Pigeon Blood. Studio A-Cat, 2003.

Pita-Ten. Reiji Nishiyama. Broccoli; Madhouse, 2002.

Pokemon. Masamitsu Hidaka. OLM, Inc., 1997–present.

Porco Rosso. Hayao Miyazaki. Studio Pierrot, 1992.

Princess Mononoke. Hayao Miyazaki. Studio Ghibli, 1997.

Princess 69. Teruaki Murakami. Pink Pineapple, 2002.

Rave Master. Takashi Watanabe. Studio Deen, 2001.

Robotech. Robert V. Barron and Ippei Kuri. Harmony Gold USA; Tatsunoko, 1985.

Roots Search. Hisashi Sugai. Hiromedia, 1986.

Saint Tail. Osamu Nabeshima. Tokyo Movie Shinsha, 1995.

Samurai Champloo. Shinichirō Watanabe. Manglobe, 2004.

Sen to Chihiro no Kamikakushi. Hayao Miyazaki. Studio Ghibli. 2001. See also *Spirited Away*.

Serial Experiments: Lain. Ryūtarō Nakamura. Pioneer LDC, 1998.

Sins of the Sisters. Yorifusa Yamaguchi. Five Ways, 1994.

Spirited Away. Hayao Miyazaki. Walt Disney Pictures, 2002. See also *Sen to Chihiro no Kamikakushi*.

Spriggan. Hirotsugu Kawasaki. Studio 4C, 1998.

Stellvia. Tatsuo Sato. XEBEC, 2003.

Suzumiya Haruhi no Yūutsu AKA *The Melancholy of Suzumiya Haruhi*. Tatsuya Ishihara. Kyoto Animation, 2006.

Tetsuwan Atomu. See *Astro Boy*.

Texhnolyze. Hamazaki Hirotsugu. Madhouse, 2003.

Tsubasa Tokyo Revelations. Shunsuke Tada. Production IG, 2007.

Transformers AKA Fight! Super Robot Lifeform Transformers. Warren Batchelder, David Brain, Brad Case, Gerry Chiniquy, John Gibbs, Jeff Hale, Andy Kim, Bob Kirk, Al Kouzel, Bob Matz, Norm McCabe, Margaret Nichols, Karen Peterson, Tom Ray, Bob Shellhorn, Dan Thompson, Bob Treat, James T. Walker and John Walker. Sunbow Productions; Marvel Productions; Toei Animation, 1984.

Trinity Blood. Tomohiro Hirata. Gonzo, 2005.

Twelve Kingdoms. Tsuneo Kobayashi. Studio Pierrot, 2002–2003.

Twin Dolls AKA *Twin Angels*. Kan Fukomoto. Daiei Co., 1994, 1995.

Ulysses 31. Bernard Deyries, Kazuo Terada, Kyosuke Mikuriva and Tadao Nagahama. D.i.C. Audiovisuel; Tokyo Movie Shinsha, 1981.

Urotsukidôji Legend of the Overfiend Part One: Birth of the Overfiend.

See *Legend of the Overfiend.*

Vampire Hunter D. Toyoo Ashida. Streamline Pictures, 1985.

Wicked City. Yoshiaki Kawajiri. Japan Home Video, 1987.

Witch Hunter Robin. Shukō Murase. Sunrise, 2002.

Yu-Gi-Oh! Duel Monsters. Kunihisa Sugishima. Studio Gallop, 2000–2004.

YuYu Hakusho. Noriyuki Abe. Studio Pierrot, 1992–1995.

Zeta Gundam. Yoshiyuki Tomino. Sunrise Studios, 1985–1986.

Deleted Scenes

Anime

The Astonishing Work of Tezuka Osamu

Cowboy Bebop

Death Note

Eureka 7

Fake

The Girl Who Leapt Through Time

Kimba the White Lion

Macross

Millennium Actress

Patlabor: The Movie

Patlabor 2: The Movie

Perfect Blue

Phoenix

Robot Carnival

Samurai 7

Space Battleship Yamato

Steamboy

Tekkon Kinkreet

Trigun

Wolf's Rain

Books

Baudrillard, Jean. 1994. *Simulacra and Simulation*. Ann Arbor: University of Michigan Press.

Boden, Margaret A., ed. 1990. *The Philosophy of Artificial Intelligence*. Oxford: Oxford University Press.

Brophy, Philip. 2005. *100 Anime* (BFI Screen Guides). London: British Film Institute.

Brown, Steven T., ed. 2006. *Cinema Anime*. New York: Palgrave Macmillan.

Cavallaro, Dani. 2006. *The Anime Art of Hayao Miyazaki*. Jefferson: McFarland.

Clements, Jonathan, and Helen McCarthy. 2006. *The Anime Encyclopedia: A Guide to Japanese Animation Since 1917, Revised and Expanded Edition*. Berkeley: Stone Bridge.

Derrida, Jacques. 2008. *The Animal that therefore I Am*. New York: Fordham University Press.

Drazen, Patrick. 2002. *Anime Explosion*. Berkeley: Stone Bridge Press.

Helm, Paul. 1994. *Belief Policies*. Cambridge: Cambridge University Press.

Levi, Antonia. 1996. *Samurai From Outer Space*. Chicago: Open Court.

Lyotard, Jean-Francois. 1991. *The Inhuman: Reflections on Time*. Stanford: Stanford University Press.

McCarthy, Helen. 1999. *Hayao Miyazaki: Master of Japanese Animation*. Berkeley: Stone Bridge.

———. 2009a. *500 Essential Anime Movies: The Ultimate Guide*. New York: Collins Design.

———. 2009b. *The Art of Osamu Tezuka: God of Manga*. Cambridge: Ilex.

McCarthy, Helen, and Jonathan Clements. 1998. *Erotic Anime Movie Guide*. London: Titan.

Merleau-Ponty, Maurice. 2002 [1962]. *Phenomenology of Perception*. London: Routledge.

Napier, Susan J. 2007. *From Impressionism to Anime: Japan as Fantasy and Fan Culture in the Mind of the West*. New York: Palgrave Macmillan.

Fred Patten. 2004. *Watching Anime, Reading Manga: 25 Years of Essays and Reviews*. Berkeley: Stone Bridge.

Poitras, Gilles. 1998. *Anime Companion*. Berkeley: Stone Bridge.

Poitras, Gilles. 2005. *Anime Companion Volume 2*. Berkeley: Stone Bridge.

Rescher, Nicholas. 1985. *Pascal's Wager: A Study of Practical Reasoning in Philosophical Theology*. Notre Dame: University of Notre Dame Press.

———. 1999. *Realistic Pragmatism: An Introduction to Pragmatic Philosophy*. Albany: SUNY Press.

Richmond, Simon. 2009. *The Rough Guide to Anime: Japan's finest from Ghibli to Gankutsuō*. London: Rough Guides, 2009.

Takeda, Yasuhiro. 2005. *Notenki Memoirs: Studio Gainax and the Men Who Created Evangelion*. Houston: ADV Manga.

Wolfe, Cary. 2003. *Animal Rites: American Culture, the Discourse of Species, and Posthumanist Theory*. Chicago: University of Chicago Press.

Websites

Anime and Animation: www.anime-and-animation.com

Anime Castle Online Anime Store: www.animecastle.com

AnimeCons The Anime Convention Nexus: www.animecons.com

Anime Boy: www.animeboy.org

AnimeNation Anime Store: www.animenation.com
The Anime Network: www.theanimenetwork.com
Anime News Network: www.animenewsnetwork.com
AnimeOnline Anime Community: www.animeonline.net
Anime Web Turnpike: www.anipike.com
Animation World Network: www.awn.com
Baka-Updates Manga: www.mangaupdates.com
The Black Moon Art, Anime, and Japanese Culture:
     www.theblackmoon.com
Cartoon Leap Anime Blog: www.cartoonleap.com
The Comics Journal: www.tcj.com
Comics Worth Reading: www.comicsworthreading.com
Convention Finder: www.containment.greententacles.com
Cornell Japanese Animation Society: www.cjas.org
FUNimation Anime: www.funimation.com
Manga Entertainment Anime and Info: www.manga.com
Mania Beyond Entertainment: www.mania.com
Mechademia Forum for Anime, Manga, and the Fan Arts:
     www.mechademia.org
Midnight Eye Japanese Cinema: www.midnighteye.com
Protoculture Guide to Anime Culture: www.protoculture.ca
Otaku.com Anime Community: www.theotaku.com
Tezuka In English: All Things Related to Osamu Tezuka:
     www.tezukainenglish.com
Tim Maughan Books: www.timmaughanbooks.com
TokyoPop Japanese Culture and Creative Expression:
     www.tokyopop.com
Watch Anime Online: www.animepile.net

Scene Selections